You Can't Take The Steam Out Of Me

By Colin Robins

Should there be a doubt as to the authenticity of the adage 'Once a footplateman always a footplateman' this picture will dismiss it.

Pictured on the platform above are ex-British Rail Yeovil Town footplateman. The 'reunion' was arranged courtesy of the Yeovil Junction Steam Centre on the 17th December 2009.

Many of us had not met for over 45 years and yet the cordiality was instant and sincere.

Colin Robins

FOREWORD

Having known Colin Robins only since 2008 - we first met at a Portsmouth Regional Groups meeting of the Mid-Hants Railway Preservation Society - it seems that we both had a lot in common... we were both certified 'Railway Nuts!' Whereas Colin spent a lifetime surrounded in the coal dust, grime and sweat on the footplate, I have spent my time portraying my train-spotting escapades via the publication of five railway books.

It was instantly recognised that when Colin asked me to write a 'Foreword' for this book, we would both be on the same track, and it has been a pleasure to share his memories and compare them to my experiences. What an incredible memory this ex-Yeovil engine shed man has brought to light, and as you read the contents of the nostalgic book you will find that 'no stone has been left un-turned' - you can almost smell the coal dust and oily rags as his many escapades unfold!

Colin can rightly be identified as a pure unadulterated Somerset chap, complete with that broad dialect and this will be uncovered as you turn the pages of this book. It has been a pleasure conversing with the author in the compilation of 'You Can't Take The Steam Out Of Me'. As I mentioned to Colin, to have your memories printed is a great honour, as future generations, not only relatives and friends, but those who frequent libraries and museums will be able to read and recreate what conditions were like working on the railway in the days of steam... lots of hard graft, dangers and unpredictable situations did happen - but in his words "it was a job of work that you enjoyed - all so very satisfying at the end of the day"

Michael G. Harvey

Cover illustrations:
4-6-2 MN Class 35028 *Clan Line* near Milborne Wick. 08.05.2010 - Roger Marsh Collection

Published in 2010

Published by Colin Robins
© Colin Robins 2010

CONTENTS

CHAPTER 1

'MY EARLY RAILWAY RECOLLECTIONS'

During a Railway Safety Lecture the question was posed "Colin, what influenced you into becoming a railwayman?" My reply was that I had always been interested in transportation by rail. The correct response however, after I had given the matter deeper consideration, was more profound and related to my unusual formative years.

At the tender age of four I found myself in the care of my father's parents at their home in Crewkerne Somerset. The (then Southern Railway) main line from Waterloo to Exeter was a short half a mile up the road.

I well recall waking during the night to the alarming commotion of engines struggling and at times driving wheels slipping in their endeavour to haul their full loads up the 1 in 80 bank and through the tunnel. I had no idea at that time as to what those "Devil in chains" sounds were. My young friends were equally puzzled.

My uncle George, a leading porter at Crewkerne Station lived next door, his wife (my father's sister) would take me on visits to the station. As I got older these trips would blossom into full eight hour shifts.

Alfie Riglar, my uncle's father was the crossing keeper at Crewkerne Gates. At times my young friends and I were the bane of his life, we would turn up with our home made go - carts and try to get Alf to open up for us, his reluctance was understandable as he had four heavy signals to pull plus the weighty gates to man - handle. Memories spring to mind of sitting at their table as a train, travelling at speed raced past the cottage. The shuddering vibrations would send the oil filled table lamp on a quick step across the table.

Plunger telephone as operated by Alfie, prior to his Sunday excursion - Photo M.G. Clement collection

Sunday evenings resulted in the longest period between trains. Alfie would bell Yeovil Junction and Honiton on the plunger operated phone, each location had its own code, to ascertain if there was any alteration to the booked service. Then, satisfied that there would be no slip up he would quick march to the Globe Inn at Misterton, down a couple of ciders and beat an even speedier, but probably, less direct retreat back to duty. His one big blot, to as far as his son could discern was a clear record of service book, occurred on his last day before retirement. He had a large vegetable and fruit garden at the rear of that long gone crossing cottage. Alf was hard at it when he heard a shout, poor man could have had a seizure, for there at the top of the vegetable patch was the fireman of the up Atlantic Coast Express, second in importance to the Devon Belle. Ain't you going to pull the signal off or are the bloody spuds of more importance"

This real life character had closed the gates to road traffic and failed to pull off his signals. Incredible but true!

I have a vivid picture in mind of a heavy freight moving so slowly on the severe up gradient between Hewish Crossing Signal Box and the bank summit. The guard, leaning over the veranda rail waving to this ten year old. There was in retrospect so many tugs and pulls of a railway culture.

SO TO MY OWN RAILWAY EMPLOYMENT AT CREWKERNE STATION AS A 15 YEAR OLD IN 1950

Young and carefree, my ambition to be a regular footballer was shot down in flames when I was told by the Station Master that I would be required for duty until 4pm every Saturday. Yes, a six day working week, mundane to say the least, whitening the platform edges, (a wartime measure that lingered) and cleaning just about everything. To the chagrin of the S.M. I was soon to find a niche to my liking - giving a hand in the goods yard. At first the boss man didn't object providing, I did my cleaning and attended all passenger traffic. Also the yard staff reported that I was a very able extra hand, but my main duties, that of keeping the station spick and span did start to wane, I used to get reprimanded, but I think it was a case of turning the blind eye.

Crewkerne was a very busy station with the freight yard filled to capacity. I was also given the daily task of stock taker. Every day by 10am rain or shine all types and numbers of wagons, whether they were full, empty or required for loading, even ropes and wagon sheets, would have to be collated on the stock returns and phoned through to Axminster.

I refer to humorous moments which made my day. Gems recalled include the very large mounted on metal advertising hoarding that went missing. The S.M. questioned me on its absence, I honestly didn't have a clue, all came to light however on the evening of the 1951 Crewkerne Carnival. Mounted on a local coal merchant's lorry was the Railway

Tavern tableaux, "Charlie Mops the man who invented Beer", depicted on the absent bill board. The perpetrator was my uncle's opposite shift partner in the booking office, Dave Pettitt. The S.M. who was to the front of the full house attendance at the procession had a very serious chat with young David. He told senior members of staff however, that he and his bride split their sides with laughter. Mr. Cobley later transferred to S.M. at Gillingham, the Dorset one. Dave became S.M. at a station in Surrey before returning with his family to his beloved Somerset. Dave, what a gifted man he was, when doing the ticket sales account he had the talent to

Crewkerne staff. (From L to R) George Riglar, Harry Peterson, S.M. C. Cobley and Ben Smaldon. 1952 - M. Clements collection

be able to add up the pounds shillings and pence as one as he quickly came from top to bottom of the accounts ledger. A wit and a half was my old mate.

Every morning Mr. Cobley went to town with the previous day receipts, obtaining his transport via the array of cycle's in the 'Secure' left luggage sector. In his wake, away went uncle in his horse racing, book keeper's guise on yet another hi-jacked cycle to the Queens Hotel. I was getting on with the cleaning, probably windows. Suddenly I was knocked over by the re-appearance of the Boss Man. How uncle and his self didn't collide I could not imagine "Colin where's George? I've got a flat tyre", then in an extremely serious vein, he had realised the booking office door was locked "Colin I'm asking you again where is he". "Sorry Mr. Cobley I don't know". I fearfully replied. "Right, I'll get to the bottom of this if it's the last thing I do". As he disappeared into George's den he sealed uncle's fate by stating the following little gem. "You won't be able to warn him as I will be watching you through the booking office window". I was well and truly trumped and the S.M. held all the aces. After an allotted time, and if things had not gone bananas, well before the return of his nibs. Uncle without a care in the world and as happy as a sand boy came breezing onto the stage, sorry, platform. I tried desperately to gesticulate but such was his relaxed state of mind my feeble nodding was pointless. I remember as if it was yesterday feeling the Station Masters steely gaze on me from behind that window. In marched the so unsuspecting leading porter, the roar that greeted him confirmed he had indeed walked into the lions den. I got in as close as possible, talk about being read the riot act, my close confederate was threatened with the sack, and instant dismissal all at the same time, even the station gossip, namely the signalman in his box at the Yeovil end of the platform heard the thunder clap. Eventually after the so stern S.M. had with another mount from the same stable, left again for the bank, a distinctly ashen faced uncle came out for fresh air, I could not believe his first words to me in his best Somerset. "Yer don't thee tell thee anty about this

mind" Good old uncle George he worked hard and played hard, bit of a rough character but with a heart of gold, dare I suggest, you may not find his like today, and the aftermath, things went quiet for a bit. I was given the job of getting to the Queens via a circular route to collect the bets. After a not so long period the trips to the Bank and Queens were back to normal, but George always made sure the bike on top and therefore the one the S.M. would take was in good nick, and as a back up he was a firm believer that lightening doesn't strike the same tyre twice.

I never won the best kept station award. My school mate Ron Poole the junior at Chard Junction (his father was the crossing keeper at Huish Gates, the crossing house was home) won that, to everyone apart from me, coveted gong. There was a down side to my best mates chosen station. The 'Wilts United Dairy Factory'. On occasions he had to deliver correspondence, after duty we would often cycle towards our homes together, he was very quiet one early evening and for good reason. He had been humiliated 'A prank to them' by some female workers after one such delivery. He had made up his mind that he was not going

4-6-0 H15 City breed E332 enters Crewkerne tunnel with an up Express on 2-8-1928 - M. Clements collection

to work the next day - I remember feeling down regards his problem. His Dad, a real gent, coaxed my friend into sensibility, we hardly met after National Service. I heard that he had found a niche on the Signal and Telegraph. Ron was a lovely caring person.

Embarrassed – my S.M. certainly was when uncle informed me that I was going to be instructed re: cleaning the ladies toilet. I was to plead ignorant to the facts, i.e. one container adorned with the inscription "soiled dressings". I did as urged. Soon after this humorous and knowing chat I was called into the office to find one hesitant spluttering S.M. explaining the facts of life to this dumb for the first time junior porter. Did uncle split his sides. This episode may seem a little cruel, even harsh, but fun was had at each others expense and seldom was annoyance shown. Mr. Cobley later heard via the grapevine (one signal box) of this little ruse and had a laugh with the perpetrator. I claimed and got half a crown pocket money out of the leading porter, although I expect it did the rounds at the Queen's Hotel.

A severe dressing down came about with a large insurance claim attached. An Exeter based relief porter and I unloaded a large consignment of paint destined for a local retailer, I was advised by the senior hand to stack a two wheeled barrow with what I argued should have been two barrow loads. In broad Devon brogue I was told, "Eel be arite me boey", and so with a well remembered cry of "Drive on Macbeth", myself between the shafts and himself behind we headed down the ramp for the sleeper crossing. Immediately my feet were off the ground as I exerted my colossal weight of nine stone on the front two legs of the now run away (bomb) barrel. Devonshire was to the rear fighting a losing battle attempting to deter the inevitable, as I got to the point where all three of us, the barrel, him and I should have turned to take us across the foot crossing towards the signal box, I put feet to the ground and jerked left. The whole contraption with me still between the shafts turned over. The Signalman reported that it was a miracle I was not seriously injured, which is more than I can say

for the load of expensive paint, all, as they say, burst asunder. No real blame was afforded to me but we never saw the relief porter again, which to me in my innocence was a shame as I considered him to be a good laugh, which was how I judged people, did I have some learning to do.

At that time the togetherness among the workforce of Shunters, Porters, Checkers, Goods shed staff, Lorry drivers, Platform staff and Signalmen at Crewkerne was tangible. There was sufficient goods traffic to keep a Chief clerk and three assistant's fully occupied. Pay day was Thursday, all including the retired staff whose pension incidentally was derisible, received their pennies through the booking office window. I used to be privy to such private matters through my association with all business involving that particular office. One railwayman who had retired as a signalman after 50 years service would receive less

4-6-0 N15 King Arthur class, passes Crewkerne with the up Atlantic Coast Express on 2-8-1928
- H.C. Casserley collection

4-4-0 L111 E154 Crewkerne tunnel with westbound freight on 2-8-1928
- H.C. Casserley collection

then five shillings (25p) a week. Contributing a sum to a pension scheme had never been adopted. Unlike the Post Office where my Postman guardian enjoyed a contributory pension that was mandatory.

I would offer a thoughtful assessment that as many as sixty staff including platelayers would call at the ticket office window. When one considers the population of the town in the early fifties would have been (educated guess) from three to four thousand, it is obvious that the Railway Industry filled an important and robust niche.

Another little occurrence comes to mind involving relief staff which could be coupled to the tipped over barrow episode – I got to know and feel comfortable with that grade. This at times had a down side as the following venture will expose. My young Lady friend and I were on the homeward leg of a trip to that most beautiful of seaside resorts, Lyme Regis. On the platform I asked a familiar relief porter if he could arrange a first class compartment for us. As soon as the resident Adams tank engine with its two ancient coaches came to a halt, he locked the requested door and told us to wait on the platform until the run round movement had been completed. This enabled the train to be pulled back

to the main line station of Axminster. We then entered our "personal" compartment. (I should have smelt a rat as this was just too easy). For so many who have not had the privilege to observe the severe curvatures, heavy gradients and spectacular Dorset and Devon views that short branch journey afforded, I can tell you, that after all these years admiring open English countryside, I have found no better. On arrival at Axminster our complacency was abruptly shattered. The considerate gesture evolved into a poisoned chalice, my kind friend had played a cruel trick on such an unsuspecting couple of innocents and had LOCKED the compartment door. Panic! The up stopper from Exeter to Salisbury was running in and we couldn't get out, the promise to get home on time plan was shot down in flames. We would get it in the neck. Suddenly a porter appeared from nowhere and unlocked the door, across the platform we scurried like the preverbal scalded cat and got aboard. We had been set up. Although in good fun and spirits we did not appreciate it at the time. That escapade certainly did the rounds. Uncle chivvied me when I next reported for duty as did Uncle Tom Cobley – S. M. Signalmen and all. It was a requirement of the grade of Junior Porter that they be in possession of a thick skin, if not one would not last the pace.

CHAPTER 2

MY TRANSFER TO THE MOTIVE POWER DEPARTMENT

During 1951 I submitted a request to my S.M. for a transfer to the Motive Power Department at Yeovil. This was granted with the proviso, that as it would not be immediate my seniority on the M.P. would commence from the date of application.

In October 1952 my request was at last granted. I had enjoyed companionship and the whole atmosphere of my period as Junior Porter. Realising I was accepted by men of such varying age groups had given me confidence. That confidence took a hard knock when contrary to the promise given me by my S.M. in the presence of the local N.U R. secretary, I found that my seniority would commence from the day of transfer.

Throughout my footplate career that lost year put me at a disadvantage when passing through the links which was structured by a strict seniority culture. I was now the junior cleaner at Yeovil Town Motive Power Department. After 2½ years of confidence building I was at a stroke on the bottom rung again. During that period of patiently waiting for my transfer many 15 year old cleaners had been taken on – all were now senior to me – can't remember feeling in any way dejected but I did harbour a grudge against persons of senior grade who had without a doubt duped me.

I was introduced to a pattern that would be part and parcel of my life for the next 45 years – Shift work, easy going to commence with, 8am-4pm days, 4pm-12pm late, and 12pm-8am nights.

There was an intense rivalry between shifts, (known as gangs) fostered for obvious reasons by the chargemen,

seniority filtered down from top to bottom of each gang and was strictly adhered to. When there was a position to be filled in the main line links for a fireman the senior cleaner would be up graded to fill that vacancy, indeed at times when additional services had to be covered the cleaning gangs would be greatly reduced. The same number of engines however was expected to be cleaned on each shift whether the gangs were depleted or not. A mixture of oil and paraffin was used, each Yeovil allocated engine was given a liberal coating and cleaned off with rough cloths known as rusties. It was dirty work in the extreme, structures above the driving wheels were soaked and later wiped off whilst standing and moving along the framing, one had to have a long reach indeed to manage the top of the boiler. There was no way could I at five foot six inches manage the feat. The way open to us shorties was to haul ourselves up on to the safety rail which ran from the smoke box along the boiler to the cab. In retrospect this was a decidedly dangerous manoeuvre, one slip from that height, even the thought of such a spill gives me the shudders. The reason there was, as far as I can recall, no such fall is down to the fact that all who took such a liberty recognised the precarious position they had placed them selves in and were therefore ultra careful.

There was many an opportunity for sky larking, I quickly learnt to keep an eye open for thrown cloths soaked in that repugnant mixture. There was a bond between us cleaners, however the senior hands, some of whom were ex - services, had left their youth behind and they would show anyone who pushed their luck what discipline was all about. Some situations they would put the very young cleaners through were too ridiculous for words, it is a wonder that serious injury was not caused.

On the night shift, the chargehand would visit each cleaned engine and run a white cloth along the outside motions, should that cloth have the slightest stain, he would insist all rods on that particular engine be cleaned again, heaven help the culprit responsible. Harsh regime? I do not think the discipline did us any harm at all, and compared with our National Service which we all had to endure it was as nought.

The base, in which we had a small locker provided was a communal concrete cabin, coaling and shed staff used the facilities for meals and ablutions. It was certainly no place for privacy or refinement, there was hot water a plenty supplied via an enormous iron kettle, (had a job lifting it when it was empty) this was used for washing and tea making – it seemed akin to a lunatic asylum at times, there could be a 60 year old, completely starkers pouring boiling water into the sink then handing the kettle for someone to refill from the same sink in which he was washing. Soapsuds, water, coal dust abound, and through an opening, where I am sure once had been a door, would be the young lads partaking of the contents of their lunch boxes prepared by unsuspecting mums, some of whom would faint at the sights their innocent young ones had, there was no option, to witness.

The cleaning duties had a two fold purpose, every item whether static or moving had to be cleaned, all apart from the obvious, i.e. firing irons etc. was a mystery, we were continually asking questions of the more experienced, this provoked healthy debate, in general all wished to learn as much as possible as in the back of our minds there lingered a certainty – that we would one day be using the items in focus with intent.

I was now earnestly involved in a position that was totally removed from my so relaxed singularly defined duties at Crewkerne. Here was a commitment to work as a team. I soon realised that the decision to transfer from the traffic grades was the best move I could have made. There was a dark cloud on the horizon however, that of two years National Service, I would be eighteen years of age in February 1953, then it would be a game of "When would my conscription date drop on the mat?" So as for each of our age group it was a case of putting that thought on the back burner. It is probably a correct assumption of others that westo's watch their wallets, I prefer to suggest that we are a little more sensible "screwed on" and don't waste what we've worked hard to accumulate. I had got used to a flat basic weekly rate of pay, now with rostered Sundays and enhanced remuneration for night work our little nest egg was looking decidedly healthy.

There was an accepted ethos that the railway rule book is studied, and the instructions concerning footplate staff be given special attention. Should further encouragement be required we had only to remind ourselves that the motive power inspector himself would be examining us as to our suitability to become "A passed cleaner able to act as fireman". Returning from a firing duty the cleaner in question would be quizzed incessantly as to how he got on. I paid attention with more then a little envy. The thought occurred, "If only I had started my career here on the Motive Power Department". That was not rational and I knew it. I had now arrived, end of self analyse.

David Pettit looking out of Hardington signal box in 1953, the box closed in 1959.
- M.G. Clements collection

CHAPTER 3

CLEANING GANG, ALL BUT INCINERATED

Other duties included the sand furnace, this was a device for drying wet sand so as the sand boxes on each steam engine could be replenished before its next duty, most engines had gravity fed sands operated by the fireman using a push pull lever on the footplate this enabled dry sand to be fed between the driving wheels and the rail to assist adhesion. (Bulleid pacific's had steam operated sands). The drier was 15-20 ft. in length x 5ft with sides to give it depth. A fire extended the full length under the dryer. There was a pit and firing door, coal was shovelled through and under the sand, great practice and fun was had. Should a shift let the fire out all hell broke loose and the firing squad was mustered – there was one infamous occasion when that did happen, which could have led to dire consequences. Our great friend and cleaner comedian one John Coombes felt responsible for the fire which to one and all was dead, everyone's mate would have none of this pessimism so preceded to the stores and returned to the scene with a full bucket of paraffin. With a cry of "out of the way boy" he let fly with the contents from the pit trying to reach all four corners of the sand furnace grate and slammed the door, wait – nothing happened, Coomber then made a near fatal mistake, he decided to open the door to have a little shuftie – Whoosh!! – The fire was not out after all – took every hair off our mate and singed the gang at the same time. The velocity was so great it aroused the rest of the depot. Seriously, how fortunate John and the gang was, not to sustain severe injury. The absurdity of youth, failure to see danger when it's staring you in the face. If my memory serves me right John had to go to hospital.

The junior on the 4pm–midnight late Sunday duty was allocated the task of oiling the inside motions of one of the two "M7" Drummond 0-4-4 tank engines allocated to Yeovil shed for branch duties to and from the Junction. (I'm sure on reflection this was an unofficial practice arranged to assist the booked preparation duty). On the Sunday in question I was that junior. The senior cleaner was a lad who favoured the practical joke. The "M7" tank had to be stopped on a pit in a position where the oiling points were accessible, even then one had to be a contortionist to lever the body up between the rods (straps) and big ends so as the corks could be removed and the topping up commence. With full feeder (oil can) having pushed myself up via the lip of the pit, I was perched behind the big ends with much apprehension, as any one in that position was fully aware that it would only take a slight movement of those motions to crush a person to pulp. John had scared me previously by shouting "Look out Colin there's one coming in on top" in sheer panic I had hit the pit bottom. This time however when he issued the same cry, I wasn't going to be deceived into taking avoiding action but carried on removing each cork in turn as I filled their reservoirs. With the completion of the task I climbed down, bent double to emerge and find a "King Arthur" 4-6-0 engine with its front end buffers only a yard away from the tiny "M7" branch tank. To say I was shocked would be an understatement. My mate the senior cleaner more than, recognised my fright and anger. Suffice to say he never played that trick again.

CHAPTER 4

WHAT HAVE I LET MYSELF IN FOR?

As I was senior in age I was given the opportunity of covering the position of boilersmiths mate. He unfortunately was not a well man. As this meant a full adult pay packet there was no way I was going to decline. I soon found that it entailed the most arduous, dangerous and unhealthy work imaginable. During strict periodic maintenance and exams the fire box of the engine had to be cleaned, this included the stays, even the fire bars were removed, the crust that is formed along the sides of the box between services could only be removed with hammer and chisel, in fact all traces of corrosion had to be cleaned off. In the present days environment the Health and Safety Executive would insist on a range of devices to protect against such severe dust, complete lack of pure air, damage to eyes and ears etc. There were no such aids. Just a cloth around the mouth and tied in a knot at the back of the neck. My first and lasting impression as I entered the first box through the fire hole door was self critical "Why on earth did I not find out before hand what the position entailed" Now I was up to my eyeballs in the proverbial. The boilersmith Frank Fields was a slight wizened individual nearing retirement, he showed no fear what so ever of heat and dust, before a fire box was any where near cool "Frankie boy" would be in there kneeling on a piece of damp sacking going about an inspection. He explained in about five minutes flat what was expected of me - a very intricate set of tools consisting of a blacksmiths hammer and chisel and the indispensable, wait for it, one stiff and one soft hand brush. All residues was to be dumped into the ash pan, looking back, I still feel nausea at the memory of finding it difficult to see and breath through that thick clinging dust. It was said that the grade of boilersmith had a higher rate of lung disease by far then any other. I would concur. There was also more then an element of danger, the engine involved would be immobilised with the obligatory "Not to be moved" board on the buffer beam, never the less when isolated in the box one felt the rumble and vibration of an engine on the adjoining track, one could be forgiven for feeling a shiver of apprehension which more then once caused me to hold my breath. Every extra shilling I earned as a mate to Frankie Fields was without question well deserved.

Another extra money earner was arranged by a fellow cleaner Terry Edwards, he would suggest to the Depot

Master that if he wanted a specific wagon of coal, sand or what ever unloaded, Robins and Edwards would be willing to do it, often it would be emptied before our eight hour shift was up, with a extra two hours pay in the coming wage packet.

My period as a cleaner was from my transfer date of October 1952 until my National Service commenced on 25th of June 1953 – so brief and yet so full of incident it seems incredible all was compacted in to those nine months. The British Rail Rule Book issue 1950 contained 239 rules, one had to have a good general knowledge of these regulations and their attendant appendices. Mutual Improvement Classes had been staged at the depot for as many years as anyone could remember, this was the norm at motive power depots throughout the system. It is amazing that there was no encouragement from management to attend, neither was this so important voluntary institution financed. At my depot the venue was spartan in the extreme, an unused and dilapidated room was put at our disposal. It did however contain an open range fire which was lit only for this single Sunday morning class. The 8am to 4pm cleaners were on the ball and excelled in this cause, best quality coal would be banked up and white hot by 10.30am. When not on that shift I would often cycle the ten miles from home such was my eagerness to attend.

Our tutors were indeed unsung heroes who did not seek plaudits, (not that they would have achieved any) but gave much free time to impart with professionalism and dedication, their expert knowledge to the betterment of others. The M.I. classes were as a group the only avenue that was open for us to learn. In the late fifties the situation was to change as instruction classes for fireman provided by British Rail were set up, with official instructors. We will touch on the continued Mutual Improvement Classes later. I was therefore prepared for the call to become a passed cleaner which would enable me to be booked out as a relief fireman should the need arise. The gentleman to examine me regarding my suitability to attain this lofty position was the motive power inspector. The redoubtable Mr Sam Smith. He was in essence from the true tradition of footplate inspectors, both feared and highly respected. Mr Smith (he was referred to as Sam) certainly had an aura about him. His attire was most imposing consisting of an ever present black homburg, dark suit and immaculate bow tie. Swarthy in stature and stern in countenance he was held in high esteem, indeed he only had to alight at Yeovil Junction and the bush telegraph would sound alarm bells, action stations would be sounded at the depot with cries of "Look out there's a Sam about" and I am not joking! I had been smug in the belief that my tutoring was sufficient to field any queries. So was there apprehension, you bet there was.

As I made my way from the cleaners cabin with the calls of "Sam will sort ee out" ringing in my ears, this seventeen year olds outward impression of confidence had inwardly evaporated. Across the lines by the water column to the office block with its adjacent Drivers and Fireman's cabin I ascend the stairs to the general office where chief clerk Reg Bartlett and his side kick Jack Kerswell hold residence.

When his nibs arrived I found him to be civility itself, having a few words with my governor and managing to bring me into the informal talk. Now down to business. I was asked if I regularly attended the mutual improvement classes after which it was into the rule book. On request I explained the duties of a fireman from meeting his driver. I had to name and describe the function of each item of essential footplate equipment, the twelve detonators in their metal case and accompanying two red flags provoked debate. Engine destination head code, white discs were used on the Southern, containers re oils and three paraffin head lamps, not forgetting the all important storm sheet. I remember stating that detonators are flat and round and about two inches across with a flexible strap attached to each side so as when the det is placed in position on the flat of the rail the two straps pass around the upper flange of the rail to make it secure, instructions for their use are contained in rules 55 to 60 of the 1950 Rule Book. I quote from rule 57 "detonators are used for the purpose of attracting attention of the trainmen" I was very cautious when handling the bangers for the instruction in rule 58 is still etched in my mind "detonators must be carefully handled as they are likely to explode if roughly treated". I forever made sure that they were not stored next to the hammer! I described the method used for getting an engine ready for service from the preparation of the fire, sand boxes, trimming the tender, couplings hung correctly to checking the ash pan and smoke box door. There was not a practical test. After fielding questions on the rules appertaining to the detention of trains on running lines, it was impressed on me how important it was that the fireman should listen intently to his driver's instructions and carry them out implicitly. After which seemed to me hours, but I expect was closer to forty minutes I was told, "Well done young man" you have passed. With words of encouragement and good advice from the Inspector imbedded in my mind I took my leave from the top office and floated down the stairs as if on air.

As soon as I came down to earth I contacted Reg and Jack to thank them for relaxing me. Clerks such as these two individuals were indispensable but probably not unique, their workload in retrospect appears awesome, they had to cater for the needs of a workforce of close to one hundred men operating such diverse activities as charge men, fitters, boilersmiths, coaling, washing out engines, shedmen, storemen, labours, and footplate staff, plus their holidays and sickness cover. The rosters to work the diagramed duties afforded to the depot were numbered and shared into links or sets at the discretion of the local trade union departmental committee. The more sociable signing on times and work of higher quality was more often then not collated into the link containing the senior men. Discretions, disciplinary, individual and personal requests, grievances, hours and over time worked each day, allocation of uniforms and protective clothing, ordering of all materials from a cloth for cleaning to a clinker shovel, the list I could make endless, all had to be dealt with through this two man office, bear in mind also that this was way before that present day instant at the touch recall information machine the computer, (bless it) no wonder the shelves in that office were full to bursting with books and regulatory matter. Clerical grades everywhere must have operated a superb filing and reference system.

The shed master was usually recruited from the head fitter's grade and had a remit to make sure his keep was run in a most disciplined, correct and efficient manner. The grade was held in high esteem by the footplate staff as they were fully aware of their mechanical prowess and excellent knowledge of rules and regulations. I resumed with my cleaning duties and occasional spells in the confines of the black, sorry, grey hole, namely the firebox until along came a certain day and when I hit the jack pot.

CHAPTER 5

AT LONG LAST, MY FIRST FIRING DUTY

I was required for a firing turn, "Great". My driver was one George Vickory. Unknown to George he was regarded by all my immediate colleagues and most certainly many others as a hero, he would not have wished this patronage as he was and is of a quiet and unassuming nature, nevertheless this was only seven years after the war, George along with many of his railway colleagues had volunteered for the services. He had served for many missions as a Lancaster Bomber Rear Gunner. Incidentally if we had been able to look into that crystal ball and move forward twelve years we would find George playing a significant card in the hand I held which was to enable me to gain promotion to a driver's position at Portsmouth.

A change over engine was required at Templecombe. What a snip of a turn for a first timer, always was a believer in beginners luck. Once upon the footplate of one of Yeovil's own 'U' class engines No 31791, I was full of my own importance.

On so many occasions when the gang was not cleaning I would take the opportunity to shout up to the fireman who was squaring (disposing) up or getting one ready (preparing) "Any chance to come up mate?" they could not say any other then, seeing these were the guys who planted the idea of moving to the motive power in the first place. "Come on up then Crewkerne".

Getting our engine ready after all the coaxing came as second nature. In fact I prepared the engine in the exact manner that was described to Inspector 'Sam' on my pass to be a fireman examination. After inspecting the fusible lead "boiler safety" plugs, tube plate and brick arch, in goes the baffle plate. Lifting the long clinker shovel from the tender I lever the fire across and make it up from just under the door slopping towards the front of the box. Engine sands checked. Etc. Lit tail lamp on the smoke box end and in no time at all, my driver is back on board having completed his oiling and supervising me as the on the footplate lubricator is replenished. Chuffed with what I've done and certain that I have impressed my mate I am as pleased as "Larry". Driver tests the brake, tender brake off and we drop back and take water, I tidy the tender and then as suggested follow him for my first "Official visit" to the much revered sanctuary of the drivers cabin, alias mess room.

On board after the cuppa - a touch on the whistle, off comes the tender brake, a lift of the regulator and 2-6-0 No 31791 moves forward out of the depot. We stop, the driver is peering along the tender in order to observe the ground signal, off it comes, now in reverse the regulator is eased off its face and we are away, the sticks 'signals' are in our favour as we canter through the Town platforms under Newton Road Bridge and out towards Yeovil Junction. To the left we liaise with the Western Region main line.

Little did I realise at this early stage in my footplate career that there was intense rivalry between the opposing Western and Southern Regions. I would note that if a chance arose to show superiority, that chance was seldom neglected.

All signals are in our favour as we pass the wartime installed South Junction signal box. With reverser and regulator set we are using as little steam as possible. Approaching the Yeovil Junction home signal gantry, I am informed that the left hand signal which is off will take us on to the down local platform line. We pass "A" box to our left, continuing we cross the up local, up fast, and down fast lines, that first time experience of the unique sound and vibration of steel wheels carrying an immense body of metal across so many interchanges and flanges of track gave me a thrill, and I was only on a light engine.

I would never in my wildest of dreams imagine that the day would dawn when I would be hitting extensive crossovers at very fast speeds, indeed it is solely a footplate (Front end) sensation reserved exclusively for that grade of railwaymen.

Now along the down platform with its impressive red brick waiting rooms, toilet, storage and office facilities. The down local starter signal is off, we follow through and come to rest over a ground signal, it clears and we reverse into the down bay siding. I jump off and pull the obvious set of points that will take us onto the turn table. As the engine passes I show as much professionalism as I can muster by jumping on to a moving vehicle. (Expertise acquired disobeying the S.M. in Crewkerne yard).

Engine balanced, I am given instructions on how to turn engine's of various tonnage without breaking into a sweat. The engine is secured with cylinder steam release cocks open. The vacuum pipes on engine and table are connected, the driver then opens his vacuum brake ejectors which in turn provide the table mechanism with power. He now joins me on the control panel. I move the control lever and "hay presto" we have action, around we go. Nothing to it until we have to marry the table set of rails with the set on terra firma, after a couple of misses, much to my driver's mirth I get them joined up and locked.

Back on board we put the storm sheet in place for the tender first leg to Templecombe. I now make up the fire and soak the tender, place the main line head code on the tender and tail lamp on the smoke box end. I have adjusted the fireman's best friend (The blower control wheel) so as smoke and fumes do not blow back onto the footplate from the open firebox door. I will much later learn that the title "Best Friend" alludes to the boost the fire receives when the control handle is moved. The further it is turned the greater the velocity of steam that passes through the smoke box therefore increasing or decreasing the vacuum, as nature abhors a vacuum the firebox gasses would be drawn through the boiler tubes as opposed to moving back through the firebox door. In other words, if you can't get the ******* to steam whack on the BLOWER! Down Bay ground signal off, we move to a position over the controlling points from the down to up (Salisbury) lines. An up fast belts by at what seems to me an incredible speed. I watch as it hurry's through the Junction from my side of the cab. From "B" box the station and its four tracks curve to the right, the built in cant accentuates the impression that a train is dangerously tilting, all was a terrific plus to my unaccustomed eye as the 4-6-0 "Merchant Navy" class and its twelve coaches wound away from view. I was probably dreaming "What an act to follow". We follow, tender first on the up through road. As the storm sheet impedes the Drivers view he came over to my side to check that the starter signal is off. We pass the Junction "A" signal box. The up advance signal is checked by my driver as the line continues its curve to the right. My mate has a few words with me regards procedure when a signal is first sighted from the fireman's side. I appreciated his situation, here he had a lad on his first trip, he did not wish for him to think his competence was in question, so what better way then to have a quiet confidence building talk.

I was to recall this reasoning in years to come when I would many times be in his exact situation. From that day I would make a point of shouting loud and clear "OK." The starter, advance, distant or whatever the signal portrayed. We are now on track for Sherborne, I am over George's side of the footplate and he is explaining the features of the road (track) and line side from the enginemen's view point. The danger of sharp coal splinters blowing back from the tender and the resultant damage to the footplate crews eyesight was to my knowledge never assessed, I can recall just one solitary Driver that sported eye protectors and he was a Yeovil man, yet another reminder that Health and Safety certainly sat on the tail lamp. We clank along at probably 30 mph.

The Sherborne distant (warning) signal is at caution, the breath of regulator is closed, as we drift under the A352 Dorchester road bridge towards the home signal, as this is my first footplate sighting of the area I am made aware of the details regarding up sidings and goods yard. I remember having to tame my eagerness which was persuading me to take in both sides of the engine at the same time, (in other words I wished to be an earlier version of Marty Feldman) as far as I could discern there was not a unfilled wagon slot in the goods yard such at that time was the involvement of using rail to move the Country's merchandise. As the home signal is clear my mate gently lifts the regulator, we go through the station, the starter is off, we continue over the road crossing and sight the cleared advance signal. I am surprised by the imposing height of the signal box, which was then sighted off the down road. Sat on the fireman's tip up seat taking in the scene my focus is suddenly riveted by an imposing ancient building situated on high ground

off the down road. I shout a query to George who informs me that I am gazing at Sherborne Castle. Crossing the footplate I am informed that should we have had a heavy freight or passenger train on the end of the screw coupling I would have been bending the back, as from Sherborne the gradient rises continually at 1 in 80 for over two miles. I am advised to relax and enjoy it as next time I come this way there may not be time to look over the side.

The distant signal for (the closed in 1965) Milborne Port is off. As we approach the home signal and station we are on a near level gradient. Throughout this short journey I have been having expert appraisal regarding gradients, area's of interest, bridges and the like, the significance of markers that footplatemen identify as triggers so as in poor visibility they will instinctively recognise where they are in proximity to a signal are made known to me.

In retrospect I honestly marvel at the uncanny skills of top link men in their late fifties up to retirement at 65. At major main line depots their link structure would include the tightly timed early morning paper trains. Please try to visualise their working environment. Coal dust at times abound. Blinding light every time his mate thrusts his right foot down on the fire door control peddle, exhaust steam spewing down and along the boiler casing. At times his view is all but obliterated. The deafening and harsh, only heard on the footplate, metallic cacophony. These men had without a doubt nerves of steel, at an exact spot they would slam down the regulator, open the blower to lift the smoke drift to clear their view, spot their quarry (signal, stick, board and other ******* names when it's at caution). If green, then lift the regulator to the roof with both hands, the right hand then jabs across shutting off the blower control, all this in one automatic movement. Another wonder of mine since we are on the subject, is how when this top of the pops high adrenalin position abruptly reached its conclusion, did the body and nerve system cope. There was never a niche for a winding down period, last day on the job would in all probability be one as described, next day kaput, end of story etc.

Sorry for that run up a short siding. (Deviation). We are now on the last leg of the trip, we breast a short incline and the gradient falls away I'm told at 1 in 100 into Templecombe. My first sighting of this major transfer yard is the long shunting siding (neck) situated directly down the bank from the up main line, to say this unaccustomed eye was impressed would have been a under statement, as the home, (controlling the entrance to the station) signal is at danger our progress is minimal which gives me ample time to take in as much as is possible, little did I realise that this yard and its staff would in the future become as familiar to me as my own home depot. I remember been hypnotised by its so unexpected size, as the signal came off I moved over to my side of the cab I found there was also a large down side yard. In fact just to wet the appetite, in that self same down yard I was to play a part in a true cavalier scene which was both mind boggling and side splitting, but on the down side the sequence of events could well have led to the demise of the then 24 year old Colin in the most bizarre of fashions, but that in my best Somerset, "Me mates" is for the future.

Now, stood over the controlling ground signal, which will take us into the up yard our observation is to the fore which makes a welcome change. "Dummy (ground signal) off mate" I am pleased that my word is accepted, this seemingly small gesture gave me pleasure and confidence. As we move slowly down the yard I whack the injector on and build up the fire under the door, if my relief requires steam all he has to do is push the fire to the front of the fire box. I cleared this strategy with my driver and I do believe he was impressed, or did I perceive a twinkle in the eye.

We stop opposite the top yard shunters cabin. After tidying up the footplate I screw "hand brake" her down. The foreman informs us of the position of our return change over engine. My mate reasoned that we should not hang about as the sooner we got back to our home depot the more likely we were to get an early finish. This initial visit impressed on me the utmost importance of keeping one's mind fully alert to the danger that constant and unexpected shunt movements present. I was to witness the awful outcome of slips in concentration regards personal safety on the railway, and I will tell you something - they STAY with you.

We made it to the engine observing that the correct head code had been put in place and checking that the lit tail lamp was displayed on the tender, put our kit in the lockers, saw we had adequate steam and that the boiler gauge glass level was satisfactory. My mate shot away to coax the signalmen into letting us have the road for a quick get away. I got the old girl ready for the 'Engine First' return trip to our depot.

The news from the box was that we would get away after the next down service. "Keep your eye on the ground signal Colin". It comes off, "OK Mate". Our Maunsell "U" class moves to position itself over yet another controlling ground signal. The down service pulls out. I observe it climbing away up the bank. With an "OK mate" we go ahead over the cross over points and onto the down main. I'm looking ahead, this is more like the real thing. I am told that the service we're following is a semi fast so we will keep as tight to it as possible. The advance signal clears. The regulator is given a more aggressive lift, the cut off via the reverser is adjusted as we go from a trot to a decided canter, myself feeling confident decide to fire up, my driver however surveys the depth of fire and tells me that we have ample to see us to the depot where I have to clean the fire.

We top the 1 in 100 out of Templecombe. As we pick up speed we catch the Milborne Port distant signal at caution, the vacuum brake handle is applied and almost immediately blown off (lifted) as the distant is cleared. Under the A30 bridge and we're shut off and coasting down the 1 in 80 with, as I expected a touch of vacuum brake applied, we swing through a cutting and onto a straight. Sherborne distant is sighted at caution, the home, starter and advance signals are cleared on approach. There is four level miles from Sherborne to Yeovil Junction. As we gobble up those miles it proves to me that when travelling at speed on a light engine it feels more secure to vacate the seat and stand balanced with each hand holding on to a fixture.

Yeovil Junction distant is at caution. The down main home signal and after a cautious approach through the station the down main starter clears. We have now returned to our start line on the dummy beside Yeovil Junction "B" box, our lucky streak persists as it is pulled off. No sheet to protect us and we definitely weren't going to hang about to erect one as the priority is an early finish, over the crossover onto the up slow, I have the injector on, we stop on the up platform and I race to change the head code and replace the tail lamp from tender to smoke box end. George is playing the pep pipe over the tender in order to keep any dust down. Further down the line of my Railway career I would describe such interaction between footplate crews as team work at its best.

I'm back on the footplate, the gantry sited up local to branch starter comes off as does the advance, the regulator is opened. My driver remarks that if you show a hand that conveys an intention that you will act swiftly then very often the reaction will be in like vein. Another gem for the memory box.

We run along the double tracked branch, to the left the railway bank drops steeply to the course of the River Yeo, we continue through South Junction, traverse to the left and the Yeovil Town home signal is sighted in the clear position, touch of whistle to remind the unwary near the foot crossing and we're under the Newton Road Bridge onto home territory, along the platform, starter off, looking to the right I acknowledge the signalman's wave and we're over the depot entrance controlling signal, again no wait, it's off and in we go, mission accomplished. I was much impressed by this rapid return but would learn that it was far removed from the normal, as at that time rail was the major player in the transport league therefore corridors across busy junctions were continually restricted by main line services and cross junction shunts. It is now a case of back to basics, the road (points) is set and after replenishing the tender we are stood screwed down on the disposal pit. First the smoke box. I grab spanner, hammer, in case the spanner requires persuasion, and the brush, throw them into the bucket, drop the shovel onto the deck then, (like a complete idiot) jump from footplate to the deck. Race to the smoke box end and deposit the tools onto the framing. The news from the foreman is that once we have squared up we can make our way, great! I know the working timetable like the back of my hand and realise that if I get a move on I would be able to catch a branch out to the junction that connects with the down stopping service to my home town.

My driver tells me to get a move on with the smoke box as he would give me a start on the fire. "Cheers mate". Up on the front end I hear the rush of exhaust steam as the blower is given a twist, it's good that I have the hammer as my wrists are not strong enough to move the nuts on the smoke box door, a belt from hammer to spanner wins the argument, the door is pulled open, and I'm into it, shovelling the fine ash onto the ground, door closed and lugs tightened, ash on front end cleaned off, tail lamp removed and the fireman for the day is footplate bound. Taking the kit aboard my driver tells me he has put the fire up one side of the box and lifted the clinker from the fire bars. I thank him for his patience in assisting me on my first firing turn. With "It was no problem" he is away. I would certainly have to pull out all the stops to enable me to get my train home. My determination won the day, by the time both sides of the fire had been cleaned and banked up one side, the long handled pricker and clinker shovel heaved back onto the tender, plus raking through the ash pan I was running short of two equally important commodities, namely time and breath. I pull the damper levers open, grab my personal kit and jump yet again unwisely to the deck, then away over the sleeper foot crossing to make

the desired branch in the nick of time.

In fact I had not been in any way shape or form clever, for in racing I had completely disregarded the golden rule that adds strength to the adage "More hurry less speed". Footplate work is by its nature extremely dangerous and to throw caution to the wind is courting serious injury to say the least. To be honest as I thought on my way home of how reckless I had been in my quest, I vowed to be more responsible in the future.

CHAPTER 6

FRUSTRATIONS - THROUGH LOSS OF OPPORTUNITIES

Now approaching my all important eighteenth year I was to rue the effect of the deception which lost me eighteen months seniority, the enjoyment and feeling of carrying out a task of importance on that one firing turn left me yearning for more. I was however thwarted literally at every turn. (Pun not intended) The frustration was intense as I would witness fellow passed to fire cleaners much junior to me in overall railway service moving out of the depot on engines whilst yours truly was left with a cleaning rag in his hands, my pride would not show hurt.

I was heartened however by many of the registered firemen and some drivers who had sign posted me to Yeovil and had heard over the grapevine of my Crewkerne situation. All however was not lost especially on the money earning stakes as I would be regularly asked to fill the boilersmiths mates berth. Dirt and dust prevailed but the lining of the pocket was the order of the day. OK I put my hand up to the charge. "Typical West Countryman"

Yeovil Pen Mill MPD viewed from Wyndam Hill, shortly after closure in 1959 - John Day collection

Yeovil Town MPD and station, viewed from Summerhouse Hill. 30.07.1961 - Photo by E. Fry - R.K. Blencowe collection

CHAPTER 7

THE GANG GET A BLASTING FROM THE FOREMAN

The spring of 1953 was now in the air and I was crowned 18 in February, this proved to be a unproductive period as far as the cleaning brigade was concerned as up grading to cover regular fireman's berths were sparse and far between. There would be an occasional vacancy when additional trains to the booked service were required, this occurred usually at weekends when track maintenance took place. The usual grilling of the senior recipients would take place when they returned to the fold. I heard of their experiences with more then a touch of envy. The number of engines to be cleaned and serviced remained the same but as the gangs were of a full compliment the quota was soon exhausted, each chargehand was acutely aware of the adage "Idle hands make mischief" and so would invent all manner of tasks such as scrubbing and making the mess rooms tidy, also the store areas were given a spring clean. Even with these additional chores there was still ample time and space for young men to explore.

I recall many occasions when three or four mates would take it in turns to vacate the depot. Undoubtedly had we found ourselves in trouble away from our place of employment it would have meant the final curtain descending on our railway career. This was years before the advent of the mobile, the only way to find a colleague should he be required would be to get on the cycle, strain every muscle to get the return transport to him.

Newton Road connects the village of Stoford and the town via station road bridge, the depot staff using this route would report to all and sundry "I tellee what they be the biggest badgers these ever zaw". Five of us took the bait. We decided that a reconnoitre be attempted. Late one night the cleaning gang crept up the roads steep incline, then joined a path through the woods which would take us back to Summerhouse Hill. Whether we imagined ourselves to be attached to 45 Commando I don't know but we tried our best to give a like impression. The outcome was tremendously exciting for we never saw a single Brock, but as the intrepid five wriggled towards the end of path stile hoping to see our quarry on the other side we were stunned to hear the distant but unmistakable voice of chargeman Saunders giving us a severe broadside, "Come down Wally (Radford, Senior Man) I know you're up there, you're wanted". The man in question was lying beside me. The action we took was not of our making for at that precise moment an apparition appeared silhouetted against the lights of the town and depot, the shape of a lady was climbing over the stile and when her foot came down it would be on one of us, all could see immediately that we had to scarper, as if on cue we rose as one, the result was the most piercing scream imaginable, the call of nature if that was the reason had probably came at an earlier stage then envisaged! As we stampeded in all manner of directions I caught a sight of a large man moving to the rescue, we can thank our lucky stars that our eyes were accustomed to the light, the advantage was ours and we made the most of it. I distinctly recall rolling down the steep bank hitting the road and breaking the record back to the depot. Our discomfort had only just begun, as we had to endure a blasting from our foreman, especially Wally who had been required to perform a firing duty. In retrospect I am amazed at the number of inane risks normally responsible young people were willing to take as a group, again an adage comes to mind. 'Safety in numbers' certainly not on this occasion. This episode marked an end to any further ambitions I may have had to venture away from base, it was assisting on disposal and preparation plus a game of cards from now on in.

CHAPTER 8

SKILL OF MAIN LINE DRIVER PREVENTS A DISASTER AT CREWKERNE

On the 24th April 1953 I was quite by chance to witness a most extraordinary railway scene, it was early evening and I was cycling from Crewkerne to visit my girl friend at Misterton, approaching the road bridge which goes over the main line I was surprised to see a small gathering, my surprise catapulted into astonishment when I saw the reason for their presence, the bridge affords a panoramic view over the countryside towards the east but on this occasion everyone's attention was drawn by the tide of humanity that was making it's way up the steep incline towards the station, most were labouring under the strain of their personal luggage, my attention was also drawn to the state of the up side station veranda which had partly collapsed, it's cast iron supports close to the bridge had completely buckled from some sledgehammer like blow. The cause of this astounding scene was clearly visible, as a up fast with its attendant full load of coaches was at a standstill approximately three parts of a mile from the station, its boiler safety valves were giving full vent to the heavens, that was the only thing that was not surprising as it must have had a full box of white hot fire. My curiosity was fully aroused, so in a trice I was back in the saddle and pushing peddle in a frantic endeavour to get as close to the train as possible, through the village of Misterton I sped when I suddenly remembered the promise to see the young Lady, quick detour, breathless explanation and we were both away to the railway bank on which "Merchant Navy" "Pacific" 4-6-0 No 35020 "Bibby Line" stood, this magnificent specimen from the stable of engines which were the pride of the Southern was looking decidedly morose, her middle driving wheel on the drivers side (left side facing) was off the track and resting inside the rail, the either side coupling rods were grotesquely bent, even my half an eye on technical matters could see that had one of those rods broke, and it could have been at speed, there would have been a major disaster. I could not curb my eagerness to assist, up the bank I scampered. The driver, standing by the tender, having with his fireman experienced a footplatemans nightmare must have wondered what on earth this young lad was about, my spluttering explanation is lost in the excitement of that long off moment, but without a doubt I introduced myself as a Yeovil Town engine cleaner and volunteered to assist his fireman in throwing out the fire, my offer to assist however was wisely declined, he had enough on his mind without me adding to those concerns. Before descending the bank to the road way I vividly recall standing transfixed by the close up enormity of the damage and, I reiterate, the unbelievable good fortune that the engine and coaches had not come off the track.

We were to learn via the press however that the train staying on the track was not in anyway marked down to, as I believed, good fortune, but to the skill and vast experience of the engine driver. I give you the following quote from my ex - governor, Crewkerne Station Master C.W. Cobley as printed in the Pulmans Weekly News. He praised Charlie Lodge a "top link" experienced driver for halting the train as he did "I don't know how he did it, but he did a wonderful job" he also added that he did not think the passengers realised how lucky they were. The train the 4.30pm express from Exeter to Waterloo with 400 passengers on board had previously stopped at Axminster and was booked to stop at Yeovil Junction. The axle of the middle pair of driving wheels had snapped at high speed on the bend just before Crewkerne. As the train belted through the station a heavy engine brake block became detached and smashed against the underside of the bridge before ending up on the platform, the collapse of the up side platform roof was attributed to either the engine rocking at high speed or a piece of metal from the engine scything through the cast iron support pillars. There was severe damage to three quarters of a mile of track, single line working was set up between Chard Junction and Sutton Bingham, repair gangs were shortly on the scene and in spite of the intensive damage as portrayed, double line working was resumed at 6 am the next morning, this was

achieved without the aid of anything like the present day technology, and guess what, there wasn't a private contractor in sight, sorry, I should not show my prejudice. Following an investigation into the cause of the axle fracture, all "Merchant Navy" class engines were withdrawn from service and subjected to ultrasonic inspection. In a surprisingly short time however all apart from three were back on front line duty. As you can imagine by the time I booked on duty next morning all was abuzz with ideas and calculated reasons on how the events at Crewkerne had come about. In fact celebrity status was attained when modestly I let it be known that I had been on the embankment talking with the driver. I was asked by senior footplatemen into their sanctuary, and questioned on what I had witnessed. I realised that all had a great respect for their Exmouth Junction colleagues and the Lodge brothers in particular, evidently the fact that there was three

The damaged caused to the 4-6-2 MN 35020 at Crewkerne on 23rd April 1953
- M. Clements collection

Crewkerne station staff examine the damage to the station canopy after the 4.30pm Exeter to Waterloo had passed through at speed. 24th April 1953 - M. Clements collection

brothers in the same top link of twelve sets of men had made footplate history. They were unique and separate characters. I was to learn much about them and the vast range (Salisbury - North Devon - Plymouth - North Cornwall) of route knowledge covered by their depot further along the path of my career.

The conclusion as agreed by those experienced men was that Driver Lodge on recognising the acute danger represented by the sudden violent rocking motion of his engine did not panic and slam the brake handle down, but applied his vacuum 'through the train' brake in a cautious manner, also the consensus of opinion had it that had he acted in any other way there would have been a major disaster.

As a sequel to this event, upon the withdrawal of the main line fleet of "Merchant Navy" engines a confusion of motive power had to be loaned from other regions. A few of these novelties found their way into our cleaners patch at Yeovil Town. This naturally exited our curiosity which in turn led to four of us getting a blasting from the Shed Master, Mr Galliford. We had found the whistle tone of a "Britannia" class (akin to a deep fog siren) irresistible. I remember there was no familiar wire attached to the upper cab framing to pull but a curved lever which when pressed down would give vent to this, to us, majestic tone, I suppose the fact that we were in the confines of the small engine shed whilst satisfying our lust added many decibels to the crescendo of sound as it thundered out across the Station and into the town. Unsurprisingly the office telephone was hot and so in particular were my ears, the fact that I was the junior in seniority cut no ice, I was the elder and should have set an example. At the time I cried "Rough Justice" but on reflection he was dead right. Towards the end of May the "Merchant Navy" fleet began to return to the fold, the sigh of relief was so tangible that it even filtered down from the lofty ranks of the main line gangs to us on the bottom rungs of the promotional ladder.

CHAPTER 9

APPREHENSION AT LOOMING NATIONAL SERVICE

On a personal note I was becoming aware that my days of freedom were ebbing away, to be honest I had tightness in the stomach when the notification dropped through the letter box demanding that I attend a National Service Medical. It had to happen but as I was enjoying such a contented and carefree vein of life the thought of anything pulling it asunder had been cast aside. My immediate family at this time was my guardian Grandparents and Father, my pride kept the gloom under wraps as both men had served in the infantry. My Father had been awarded the M.M. for gallantry as a stretcher bearer. The stiff upper lip was the order of the day. I felt free however to unburden my frustrations to my work mates, they gave me the support that had been afforded to so many others that had been forced into a situation against their will. The Medical took place at the Territorial Drill Hall in Chard, the rail travel warrant routed via Chard Junction was used. I found myself in the company of many more of my age group all with the same bewildered expression. Told to fill in a form stating one's preferred branch of the forces I gratefully appended Railway Branch of the Royal Engineers. Back at work determined to make the most of this now limited period I was seldom in the mess room, whether a engine had to be prepared for a duty or to be disposed after one yours truly was on the footplate asking if he could be of assistance, filling sand boxes, cleaning out smoke boxes, down the pit into the ash pans or what ever I was eager to oblige. This lunatic activity relieved the melancholy and restored the positives and I was able to accept the inevitable future.

There was a ruling that all motive power staff must state a preference should a promotional vacancy occur during their period of absence on military service, I knew of this and had given the matter much thought, the two years and nine months of lost seniority whilst on the traffic had put a stop on any ambitions I may have had of obtaining my registration as a fireman at my home depot, as this decision could ultimately seal my future I discussed it with the lady I wished to share that future with, the application form allowed for three preferences, therefore my first was Yeovil, second Salisbury and third Basingstoke, I put Yeovil first as I knew I would at the end of the day get back there, but in all probability Salisbury would be my depot on return. The information I required was gleaned from the Southern Region application for footplate grades vacancies and their results which was published on a regular basis, this made clear the seniority of each individual depot from Dover to Wadebridge. In the London area for instance fireman positions were filled as soon as the cleaners reached the age of sixteen and men attained their driver status at the qualifying age of twenty three, whereas at Exmouth Junction and Bournemouth the top main line gangs were operated by fireman in their early forties, men of twenty three driving trains in one area and colleagues of over forty and unable to even get passed to drive trains, and all working on the same Southern Region of British Rail, incredible but true.

Expecting the usual welcoming smile after my cycle ride from Crewkerne Station to home, I knew my call up papers had arrived as my wonderful gran who had so unselfishly brought me up from the age of four could not look me in the face. Opening the dreaded mail I could not believe my eyes, my hopes were that the choice of Army unit given me would be honoured, no way was that to be, as I had to report to a Royal Artillery basic training regiment at Oswestry in North Wales. When I told my Fathers sisters who lived either side of me of my posting they quickly saw the possibility that my Dad and their Father would go to Town at my expense as nearly all the lads from Crewkerne had been drafted into either the Somerset's or the Duke of Cornwall Light Infantry. I was also advised not to rise to the bait and bite. How right they turned out to be. "Col is that right that you be going in the long range snipers?" was just one crack, all was good natured and I knew as with all parents that if they could have prevented us collectively from going into the colours they would have done.

So it was to be June the 25th, my reaction was not as I thought it would have been, I did not feel dejected but was resigned to the next two years, all except those that were employed in agriculture had to fulfil their National Service commitment.

On reporting at the depot office next day I was told that I had to take the one week's leave owing to me, this gave me two more weeks of engine cleaning duties. The summer timetable was now in operation and with it the resultant prospect of up grading, three occasions during the next two weeks the shed turners mate was promoted to driver and as the only passed cleaner available I was only to pleased fill that berth. It was the responsibility of the shed turner to position all departing engines in their correct order, it was a complicated remit especially in such a confined area as Yeovil, there was a regular inward and outward flow of motive power. Engines were designated a duty particular to their capabilities, also a strict to the day periodic examination by the depot boiler smiths and fitting shops was strictly adhered to, hence as turners mate I found myself having plenty of practice with the screw coupling as often engine shunts had to be made to accommodate a newcomer into the correct sequence for departure. Activity in the ranks of shed turner fluctuated, a period of frenzied activity when my work was cut out keeping up with my driver's reasoning let alone running between engines, climbing onto footplates, releasing hand brakes, pulling points levers, giving hand signals etc, there followed a complete reversal when one withdrew from the front line and found ample sanctuary in the drivers mess room. This enhanced my prestige as in our tight knit community word travels mighty fast, it seemed that every driver that came in the mess room went out of his way in bidding me God speed and best wishes for my impending absence. I felt both sad and proud, as a few of those well wishers who were close to retirement had served in the First World War. Then it was back to reality as empty coal wagons had to be replaced, a load of sand to be positioned, the Head fitter or our "Frankie" the boilersmith would require an engine movement and so on.

Should there have been a need to cement my commitment to the motive power department the happenings of my last day on duty would have sealed it, I was barred from cleaning duties, the Shed Master bade me to report to his office where he insisted on sharing a cuppa, he had served in the army and was able to offer me good common sense advice based on his personal experiences. The whole management team at Yeovil were gentlemen and all of the young lads were privileged to be a part of that team. It was then a tour of the depot. All made a point of wishing me, all the best and a speedy return.

A great last fourteen days, that, although I did not realise it at that moment, would terminate my status as an engine cleaner and find such a niche in the memory stakes that I find little difficulty to recall.

CHAPTER 10

NATIONAL SERVICE

Two years, it seemed a life sentence to the country's eighteen year olds. Apprehension was very much to the fore, we from the country areas were at a distinct disadvantage when compared with our big town cousins, on leaving school we mostly found local employment, so had no need to travel, to say we were not street wise is no exaggeration. I had drawn the short straw, my mates on been drafted into their County Regiment would at least find companionship among their own kind, I did not have that good fortune, in fact I was not to meet anyone from Somerset for the entire period.

Although now divorced from railway employment there was a constant reminder of my career, as the mode of transport chosen for each move was Rail. The initial travel warrant from home was via Chard Junction to Oswestry in Shropshire, changing services at Taunton, Bristol and Newport, the diversity of motive power noted by this unaccustomed eye gave me little time for melancholy, I had never ventured on (foreign) other regions of British Rail so could be forgiven for thinking the Southern stabled the most attractive and powerful locomotives, my thoughts along these lines had to be adjusted.

The last episode of this first day however was of a completely differing hue. The subdued atmosphere in the packed coach was such that you could cut with a knife, the reason became apparent as on arrival at Oswestry we were herded like cattle into so many army lorries. At the camp there was complete bedlam as the intake was kitted out at tremendous speed, boots and all types of equipment been literally thrown at the startled recipients. If that harsh introduction was meant to install discipline it had the adverse effect on so many of the young fellows. They had been terrified.

As I had predicted that low was not to be repeated, but any sign of tardiness throughout the initial four weeks training period was severely dealt with. After basic training I was drafted to Rhyl in North Wales for an eight weeks signaller's course. I was often asked if I thought the harshness of the training regime had harmed me in any way, well I could only speak for myself and at the end of the day I recognised that I had gained in self assurance, respect for others and personal alertness and fitness. No it did not harm me in any way.

It was then off via the London Midland Railway to Euston and the main artillery depot at Woolwich. Here we were to learn of our final postings. Two of our now Artillery signals detachment were to have a Far East posting. I was one of them, Singapore here we come.

My intake was granted three weeks embarkation leave during which my fiancé and I arranged that our association should be of a permanent nature, we got married, it was, and it has remained the most pleasurable day of my life.

Setting off from Liverpool on the 29th of October 1953 our journey, by kind permission of the War Office, was aboard that most luxurious yet capricious of Ocean going Liners, Her Majesty's Troop Ship "Captain Hobson". I apologise for deviating from the main gist of my story, but the happenings as experienced by many thousands of young National Service Men, the majority of whom had seldom if ever left their own back yards may be of interest. The ship was a one 'Stacker' built I would suggest in the twenty's and was at that time employed carrying passengers on the New Zealand governments immigration scheme, it was fitted out as such and in that respect we were fortunate as we had cabins. I was never to learn the reason of it's commandeering for the troop run, I would hazard a guess that it may have been associated with the Malayan insurgency of that time.

We embarked in dense fog, which was just as well as had we seen the ship from stem to stern many may have been tempted to desert before they had trudged up the gang way. As well as my gunner mate the four berth cabin was shared with two Malay military police personal. We were

Luxury conveyance to Singapore - Authors collection

allowed on deck to witness our departure. As we made our way out of the Mersey I found myself depressed, we had only just been married and this was my last sighting of England for at least twenty months. My mental turmoil however was soon to fade as it was to give way to a depression of an alarming category.

We were to endure a trip down through the Irish Sea and across the Bay of Biscay that was made in hell. After the first day our Malay companions never uttered a single word, they lay motionless on those bunks, we reported this fact to the orderly officer, he came down, gave them a poke with his baton, "They're alive" he said, and that was that. The old lady had been re-fitted for her new roll, the lounge area that we other ranks were allowed to visit was very tastily furbished, settees and their like were secured firmly to the side panelling, or they were until the tossing, pitching and sheer violence of the storm tore them free. I remember

most vividly my first sight of that wrecked lounge and so many other areas, we lads were petrified. For four solid days we never wavered in obeying the order to maintain life jacket order, of course sea sickness was rampant as the vast majority had at the most only experienced a trip in a rowing boat. I was not sick but suffered a constant migraine the like of which has never revisited. We were informed via the speaker system that an unscheduled stopover in Gibraltar was to take place. The master at arms (charged with running a good and disciplined ship) had sustained a heart attack and other injured crew members were to be put ashore. There were other reasons as well, for as soon as we came along side the ship was invaded by dockyard maties sporting all matter of make and mend tools. Thankfully the elements thereafter were more then kind as we made way through the Mediterranean, blue skies, calm seas cleansed the trauma of that first leg from the mind. There was such a well rehearsed programme of continual activity that all the young lads on board were fully occupied, physical exercises, small arms practice from the stern aiming at towed targets, bayonet drill and educational lectures made sure we had little time for mischief.

We were constantly informed via the ships speaker system as to the daily progress and that on arrival at Port Said we would be part of a south going convoy through the Suez Canal. My one abiding memory is waking to a crescendo of shouting and excitement urging all to come upon deck, evidently there was ships to be seen stuck in the sand. Certainly to our unaccustomed eye it appeared to be so, ships of differing types and sizes were in line, it was of course an illusion, there are two channels, the sight that caused the stir was that of a north going convoy, this caused great humour at our expense among the senior personal on board. Once through we were in the Red Sea and the next port of call, Steamer Point, Aden. We were warned that any cases of sunburn would be treated as self inflicted and the recipient would be put on a charge. On arrival we were allowed a short period on shore, a few of us found the R.A.F. camp which had a safe protected area for swimming, a minute period of exposure caused a angry blister on my friends back the size of a tea plate, next morning it was on deck exercises. I will always remember Eric going through the routine with tears of pain coursing down his face, the regulars concocted a liquid that I'm sure prevented the "self inflicted wound" turning septic. Next on the itinerary was Colombo, Ceylon, now Sri Lanka, where moored in the outer harbour we were to watch small children diving to retrieve change thrown from the deck. Then across the Indian Ocean to Singapore, our base was the island of Blakang Mati which forms the breakwater for Singapore Harbour.(It is now the theme park isle of Santosa) I was so fortunate, it was a most beautiful area to find oneself posted. Many of my County Friends were in the Somerset's and were in the Jungles of Malaya at that time. I could expand on experiences in Singapore City and a hair raising trip by train over the causeway into Malaya and on north through the capital city of Kula Lumper into the Cameron Highlands. A hundred yards to the fore of the train travelled an armoured rail car, presumably to set off any explosive devise attached to the rail. Between each carriage there was an open lit area where at night armed guards had to be seen from the adjoining jungle. As soon as the officer of the guard disappeared along the train, so did we away from that suicidal light – but more is for another day. Eric and I were the only two National Service Men attached to The 1st Singapore Regiment, Royal Artillery, and apart from the British Officers and Senior N.C.Os. supported by the R.E.M.E. The Regiment was Malay.

It was an experience of a lifetime and all at the poor British tax payer's expense, regular trips into the City and many more to view the intriguing array of motive power at the main station and depot hastened my service along. Two Christmas terms away from one's family is enough for any young person.

Colin Robins during National Service. 1954
- Authors collection

CHAPTER 11

SO THRILLED TO BE ON OUR WAY HOME

In March 1955 we had our return to the U.K. Notification. The sailing date was to be the second of May.

It was "good bye" to the Far East and "hello" to Her Majesty's Trooper "Dunera" for the return leg to Blighty. No cabins this time round, all, and there must have been well over a thousand of us were berthed on four separate troop decks sleeping on metal sprung bunks, three high and grouped in blocks of eighteen, securely welded to the upper and lower decks. In rough seas they were not for moving. It was an uneventful three weeks, although I remember shore leave of a few hours in Colombo for all the wrong reasons. We were permitted to view certain designated areas. I suppose it was inevitable that some, probably those that had been in Korea and up country in Malaya decided to make use of the freedom time ashore to have more then enough liqueur, this led to big trouble, the high spirits gendered by the shore leave suddenly shot out of the window for there moving towards us was a large group of American Sailors in their all white uniforms, a few words were unfortunately exchanged and in a trice a pitched battle erupted, our American cousins, vastly out numbered took a beating. The Military and Regimental Police were quickly on the scene, it was a sickening scene to witness so many handcuffed soldiers been herded up the gangways. With friends I had spent many an hour in Singapore with American servicemen and always found them to be most congenial.

The voyage was an exact reversal of the outward journey and thankfully without the bedlam in the Biscay. There was a tremendous bonus for me for at its conclusion we were to berth in the Southern Regions Ocean Terminal of Southampton. The emotion and excitement among so many hundreds of young men on that Troop Ship deck as we tied up along side was incredible. Loaded up to the gunnels with kit bags, big and small packs plus suit cases we made way to the head of the gang way. On descending the view presented to me instantly put the clock back as the twelve coach Troop Train that was destined to carry many of us to Waterloo was headed by a "West Country" class Engine. Indeed, Home at Last. I was to spend three weeks clicking my heels at the Royal Artillery Depot in Woolwich before eventual release on 3rd of June 1955. Then armed with three weeks leave payment and my discharge papers I was expecting a non complicated journey down to Somerset, after all I had made it from the Far East with little difficulty, but on arrival at Waterloo the seriousness of a situation of which we had been vaguely informed came to the fore.

The country's train drivers and fireman were on strike and the only services operating were crewed by either men from another trade union or a small minority who decided to ignore their Trade Union decision. At that time I was completely ignorant as to the history of what proved to be in the long term a most severe and crippling blow to the railway industry. Eventually the designated platform disgorged its hordes into a fourteen coach train which had been assisted onto the blocks at Waterloo by a pilot engine with the train engine, undoubtedly a "Merchant Navy" class on the rear.

My home town of Crewkerne was reached after countless additional stops. The family iron road connection had deduced from the phone call we were permitted to make, the time of my arrival.

What a never to be forgotten and yet emotional home coming was afforded me, I was truly privileged.

As my enforced chapter so similar to that experienced by the vast majority of those of the National Service era came against the stop blocks, so the starter cleared for the long run in. I remember allowing ourselves fourteen days of bliss before reporting to the depot at Yeovil.

CHAPTER 12

FOOTPLATE REGAINED

My perceptions warned me that I may not find the same "together" atmosphere that had been so evident at my depot when I had left. I had wished that my return to my chosen profession would be one of spontaneous pleasure. The continued industrial action denied me that moment and in its place a chasm of apprehension opened.

I had avidly read media reports, they did not auger well for the future, indeed many industries that had substantial contracts for haulage by rail which by way of default had been broken were readily agreeing long term road haulage arrangements. It was not realised at the time, but the loss of freight from rail set in motion a decline from which to the detriment of the overall transport system rail freight would never recover. That however was for another day.

View from the bridge towards Hendford during the cold winter 62/63. Only the right track was running - John Day collection

It was therefore a rather chastened young man that arrived at the depot he had left two years previous. As the train services were so drastically curtailed the journey was made by bus, this fact added to my gloom. The station and its railway surrounds presented a vision of surrealism, all was breathtakingly quiet, I felt like an interloper as I made my way through the engine stabling sidings, not a movement let alone a breath of steam was to be seen, and yet the yard was full of the depots and many foreign (other depots) engines. Not a footplate crew was to be seen. I did not know what to expect on ascending the stairs to the office. Much to my relief the chief and assistant clerk gave me a generous welcome, which greatly lightened my despair. Over a cuppa it was explained to me that during my absence the preference promotional transfers made prior to my enlistment had been activated, I was no longer an engine cleaner. My third preference had promoted me to fireman at Basingstoke, and then my second preference had kicked in with the result that I had on paper become a fireman at Salisbury.

Arrangements were made and a date agreed for me to commence work. This information had literally hit me for six as I had received no prior knowledge of the change in my status and had in my innocence assumed that I would pick up where I had left off, at Yeovil. Before once again taking my leave of the Town depot I wanted to feel the companionship of motive power staff, this was realised as soon as I walked into the fitters shop, hand shakes and slaps on the back turned the clock spinning in the reverse direction, with the usual beverage at hand I was urged to fill them in on my National Service ventures, I sincerely appreciated their warmth and togetherness, it was indeed a gift from heaven for me after the office news. On the down side they enlightened me to the bitterness engendered by my colleagues strike action, evidently there were some men reporting for duty which would likely lead to an aura of recrimination on the imminent return to the footplate. It seemed to this layman in such matters, that I could not have chosen a more adverse period to make my return. I had much to ponder on the bus journey home.

The young family Robins had now to consider the options. From the railway angle the choice was brutally clear – Salisbury or through the blocks and out onto the road. Well meaning family members urged us to pull the points and go down a completely new siding, even the post office was dangled as an offering. I could understand their reluctance to have us move away from the close family area.

CHAPTER 13

PROMOTION TO FIREMAN AT SALISBURY

There was however only one realistic course that I wished to pursue, so with my wife's full support, as June 1955 came to a close it was pack the case, take the cycle and on the earliest train from my home town of Crewkerne, I was away to the city of Salisbury.

I was afforded a full day to find a lodge. This was my first visit to Salisbury. On arrival I made a correct decision and struck instant gold, entering the parcel office to seek initial advice I spelt out my quest to the leading porter "Look no further young man I'm sure you can stay with us". Archy who's elder brother was a top link Salisbury driver took me to his home, cycle and all. It amazed me that his wife accepted my lodging with them as if it had been previously arranged, another bonus was that it was all down hill from Bemerton Heath to the depot.

My short apprenticeship at Yeovil followed by my sojourn in Singapore was not in anyway an ideal preparation for a competent fireman's position in such a premier motive power depot. On reporting for my first turn of duty I decided to put my cards face up on the table. This bona fide confession extracted a concession to lack of knowledge and experience. I would be booked a spare turn of duty for one week. Each day I would be required to report to the running Foreman who would allocate a list of engines to be prepared and disposed. Then it was away to the stores for a full issue of clothing, bib and brace overalls, unique footplate headgear (pour oil on it and give it a polish) hat. ¾ heavy top coat (reefer) and rain coat. All done and I was urged (sic) told to use the remainder of the day familiarising myself with the depot's ten shed roads, coaling and disposal sidings, turntable and most importantly the standing orders regarding safety and designated walk ways. All was completely new to me, the immensity of this main line shed with its chorus of sounds, steam spewing from opened cylinder cocks, warning whistles prior to movement of seemingly many loco's, shouts of instruction from men on the coaling stage and engine tenders, to this newcomer it seemed as if I had signed on for a period in a mad house. I did however detect a certain excitement in the challenge, also a discovery of note was the depots unofficial refresher point, one Staff Association club, in the convenient location of immediately opposite the shed. It was later to cost me a few bob in its fruit machine, aka (one armed bandit). These happenings I recall with distinct clarity. I cycled to my lodge feeling confident and over brim with expectancy. Second day and I was to be brought down to earth with a thump, gaining the footplate of a "West Country" class loco to fulfil the task of disposal I realised with a sinking feeling that I was lost. I had no true idea of the correct method to be adopted, reliance on memories of observance from more then two years past would not suffice, swallowing my pride I dejectedly reported this to the running foreman who much to my relief sympathised with my plight.

There was I a registered fireman under the instruction of a passed cleaner two years junior in age, I admitted my embarrassment to "Dolly" (nick name) Dawkins, there was no recrimination in attitude at the fact that I had taken a position in his depot that he could obviously have filled with his eyes closed, in fact I was sure he relished the opportunity to show off his prowess as he powered the fire up one side of the box with the clinker shovel then flicked back the holding clip to enable the rocking bar to be attached so as the drop grate could be opened, in a trice the memory cogs had flicked back in place, so before becoming a complete bystander I insisted that I take over and that he should watch out for any mistakes. I had been given a rundown on the procedures and a practical demonstration, it was now up to me. It was not a difficult square up and very soon the residue dirt and clinker had been deposited down the drop grate, then slotting the bar over the appropriate lever the drop grate is closed and secured. Fire cleaning tools back into side channels, fire made up.

Enginemen were not issued with protective gloves, therefore we took great care to hold cloths as a vital protection against severe burns, never the less we all had the scars of our trade upon hands and upper limbs. Now as previously prescribed I do the business at the smoke box end. Regaining the footplate I find it washed down and as clean as a new pin. All was ready for the shedmen to take 34033 Chard around for coal and water. During the activity we had been in constant banter, he, as we all were at that age with the inevitability of National Service looming, was full of prompts as to thoughts on my stint. I could see a lessening of tension at my assurance that I had enjoyed it. Dolly was to remain a one depot man. I would always remember him for that first meeting and his attitude to this complete stranger "Cheers Mate".

Disposals as described to such various classes of Southern plus several types of Western Region engines made my first week a physical challenge.

One particular combatant that springs instantly to mind had me virtually carried back to the dressing room. Western class "28xx" 2-8-0 weighing in at 115 tons was the culprit. The fire on this particular "28xx" was incredible dirty, my driver was astounded that it had made the depot at all such was the state of its nine foot long firebox, what he plus a couple of his mates and I agreed on was that without a doubt I had drawn the short straw.

There was two disposal roads either side of the coaling stage cumulating with the vacuum powered turn table, the system was one of fluidity, as each engine was coaled so it would move down either rank, the fireman would have to hoist his fire cleaning tools onboard at each movement, coal was shovelled by hand on to a conveyor belt which off loaded it onto the tender, on the main line side of the coaling stage the tenders were fed via wheeled and tipped tubs, the whole area was one of frenetic activity and yet somehow order from the appearance of utter chaos was achieved.

It was usual that fires would be cleaned by the time the engine was in place to take coal, but not on this occasion, in fact we had so little boiler pressure that it was necessary to make an attachment to the next in line, our "28xx" now reduced to a cripple was propelled onto the coaling position, the conveyor belt apparatus was set in motion topping up the rear of the tender, and after a pause while the assisting engine was given the tip to ease us forward the front of the tender had its share, with the full supplement of six tons, we were then shunted further forward so as the coupled engine's fuel needs could be satiated, whilst these activities were in hand I was as ever endeavouring to throw out the now near dead remnants of the firebox.

We eventually found ourselves on the turntable with tender hand brake firmly applied, our assistance was now detached, the table was laboured around and further assistance was coupled to our "dead un". Up to the water column we jerk, in goes the bag and we top up the 4,000 gallon tender. Finally a spare berth with pit facilities for me to bring this saga of clearing the firebox to its conclusion was provided. I somehow managed the smoke box and ash pan ritual without having to call in the local first aider. Back in the cabin my spirits were lifted no end when, as I attempted to wash off in the sink enclosed bucket full of hot water, which was constantly topped up from the ton weight iron kettle, I heard a "Well done young Yeovil". There was no doubt my baptism under fire had received acknowledgement. In retrospect I was never to experience a more difficult square up.

Throughout that first week I was used in a spare capacity, cleaning fires and assisting in preparations. I had at the weeks commencement felt as a fish out of water having little idea what to expect. Training courses had yet to be conceived therefore the running foreman had little alternative but to throw me in at the deep end, any old rate I knew now what to expect. I had gleaned a wealth of basic knowledge on a diverse breed of motive power. Procedures, equipment, differing boiler injectors, lubricators, ash pans, replenishment of types of engine oils, tools and their housing, sands and smoke boxes, all utterly variant. The additional bonus from my perspective was that I was now cock-a-hoop in my own ability. Another encouraging aspect was the feeling of acceptance by my new colleagues.

I made use of my staff travel facility to enjoy a short 36 hours with my family, but to be honest I felt a wrench when parting. Then it was back to the grind stone to occupy my position as junior fireman. I was booked a first turn out of the depot and onto the main line, as my rostered driver was on holiday his vacancy was taken by top link driver Walter Clissold. Our engine was a Maunsell 4-6-0 class "S15" mixed traffic engine, during preparation Walt advised me not to make up a large fire as we were to go light engine to Milford Goods Yard, "How far is that drive?" "About five minutes around the corner" was the good humoured reply. When Walt regained the footplate I had the boiler pressure around to 180lb per square inch, this allowed me to top up the boiler to ¾ full while giving the footplate a good swill down with the pep pipe, as we were going tender first I asked "Put the sheet up Drive" his reply, "Not worth it, the fresh air will do us good" I check the sands and whack the tail lamp in position, smoke box end. My mate had

accomplished his spot of oiling, we were ready for the off. The procedure for movements from the departure roads from Salisbury motive power depot was via a loud speaker instruction from a control point at the depot exit, so on the announcement "Engine for Milford Goods to the depot exit" my driver touched the whistle, and reminding me to keep my eyes skinned lifted the large vacuum ejector thereby releasing the engine brake, a touch of regulator and we were on the move through the depot exit and passing the large and impressive Salisbury West signal box.

The tenders meanderings as it twists and jerks through many crossovers seemed to suggest a distinct objection to the fact that it was leading the way, Walt is telling me what to look out for as we clank along the up main platform, I had when waiting for our instruction to leave the depot taken the opportunity to fill Walt in on my raw experience, he had told me and that all I had to do was keep a ½ a glass of water in the boiler and 160lb of steam and all would be well. We are now through the Station and on a left curve, the substantial marshalling yard is my side and I notice carriage sidings to the right, grinding along at approximately 20 mph Walt informs me the maximum speed allowed for tender first running is 45 mph so we have plenty in hand, I enjoyed the quip which helped me to relax, the track now aligns to the right. My attention is drawn to the signals and their significance. I'm all eyes and ears. I am told that the signals on the gantry ahead read Andover - London to the left - Eastleigh - Southampton to the right. Approaching Salisbury Tunnel my tutor informs me that its correct title is Fisherton and is 443 yards in length, we pass through giving the obligatory whistle warnings. Branching to the right we pass Tunnel Junction signal box positioned in the triangle formed by the convergence of the Basingstoke and the Eastleigh and Southampton routes. Walt informs me that the maximum speed through the junction is 20 mph, and that it's only a short distance to Milford Goods where the shunting is a snip. The home signal is off, under the road bridge and Milford yard is on the right, the line curves severally to the left, we stop over the controlling signal for the yard. A standard class 4 rattles past with a Portsmouth to Cardiff service, Walt advises me.

Ground signal off and we move engine first into the marshalling yard. Coming to a halt the head shunter and his mate are there to meet us, their good humoured banter confirmed my impression of Walt C as a good natured and very popular individual. Making our shunt movements Walt tells me he would normally when booked on similar duties go for a wander allowing his fireman to get on with the job in hand and that if when I had more experience we got together again that is how it would be, this unfortunately would never come about.

We went about our duty attaching to and pulling up strings of wagons, responding to our shunters frantic hand signals we sort out the empties from the loaded and place the required in position. The amount of leverage the shunting pole had to bear from lifting the couplings and pinning down brakes to being thrown to the deck when a wrong move has been made was phenomenal. Eventually a mixed train of grouped empty and loaded wagons would be assembled for despatch.

This like operation would be re-enacted in goods yards both large and small all over our country. I felt for Walt as the "S15" was not a shunt engine, the reverser was a long wind from forward back to reverse and then swinging to forward, the reaching across so as the right hand grips the bottom of the regulator handle, the continual pushing open to the required position, pulling it shut, brake on, reverser again, the instant reaction to the shunters signals, all had required team work of the highest quality. Our meal break was taken in the shunters cabin, leg pulling and warmth was the order of the day with my driver telling me, much to the amusement of all present that every time he came to Milford Goods this same set of novice shunters made him move every wagon in the yard.

A pair of WC/BB 4-6-2s stand in the disposal area of Salisbury shed - R. Davies collection

As we had time to spare I decided to make a visit to the signal box, arriving at the top of the stairs I attempted to make an impression by thoroughly cleaning my boots on the outside mat, as I knew all signalmen abhorred coal dust left by fireman on their pristine linoleum covered floors, the ruse paid off. I introduced myself to the most congenial of signalmen and explained that as it was my first visit to the yard I could think of no better way to initiate myself into the history and workings then inquire at the signal box. I struck gold. He told me of the 1930s when as many as 40 wagons would be loaded in one afternoon. How the yard was suited to sudden inflows on its 17 roads, all of which were named as opposed to the more normal numbering. The yard was also unfortunately unique in as much as owing to the slope of the ground wagons would run out of every road except one unless braked, so it is not in any stroke of imagination a gravity yard. There were a dozen coal pens for unloading coal through the bottom of trucks, a ten ton crane was provided for handling heavy and awkward loads from a wide loading dock, the every day work of the yard consisted of sorting out 250 vehicles. My chance visit had unearthed a mind of information, so engrossed was I, that after shaking his hand in appreciation I had to run like the scalded cat back to our "S15".

With the tail lamp in place we are stood at the yard exit signal waiting for our diagrammed departure time. After a Southampton to Salisbury service had cleared our signal comes off, a touch of whistle and we are away on the reverse trip joining the Waterloo to Exeter main line at Tunnel Junction. Through the tunnel Walt was explaining to me that we would be checked and stopped at signals prior to the Station as the platforms would be occupied, this proved to be the case. Home signal off and we were away over a sleeper crossing and clanking along the down local platform, subsidiary signal off we follow through the cross over's onto the engine disposal siding nearest the down main line. After carrying out engine requirements and topping up the tender we get relief. I had very much enjoyed my outing with senior driver Walt Clissold. This had been my first duty away from a shed for over two years. Now a registered fireman I could look forward to progression via seniority through the link and into the next where there were running duties. The career of driver Walter Clissold was terminated in a violent and bizarre manner.

4-6-0 Grange backs onto a GWR train at Salisbury. 1947
- Phillip Brown collection

CHAPTER 14

INVOLVEMENT IN MY DRIVERS NEAR DEMISE

My regular driver was a very senior man who because of a medical condition had been relieved of duties on the main line. Arthur Rattue was a gentleman. There was many a slack period during shunting. I would never miss a chance to bring the conversation around to Arthur's motive power career. Born in the 1890s he was very articulate and would enthral me with his vivid recall of life and railway experiences from that far away period. Although young at the time of the major Salisbury railway disaster of July 1st 1906, he spoke with uncanny clearness on his observations on that day. The Salisbury driver was named Robins, "Spelt with one b like yours Colin" he told this gob smacked and attentive young man. The "Ocean Special" had set off from Devonport at 11pm and had changed engines at Templecombe, evidently the engine whistle was heard for a long period before the train came off the rails whilst taking the reverse curve at the east end of the station at high speed, it had then struck a train of empty milk tanks which was approaching Salisbury east end from the London direction. 24 of the boat train's passengers died. Driver Robins and fireman Gadd were instantly killed as was the fireman of an engine on an adjoining track along with the guard on the empty milk train. My mate rattled these facts off as if he had just read them from his regular Telegraph. I did at a later juncture read up on this unexplained mystery disaster. Why did an experienced driver take his train through a permanent 30mph speed limit at 60 probably 70 mph. Arf recognised my interest and the next day brought along an album of photo's for me to savour.

I would always remember Arthur and he would never forget me for engaging him in a near lethal incident., We had just taken coal and had arrived at the water column for a top up, the engine was a 4-6-0 "King Arthur" (no pun intended), the water point did not sport a swing around arm but a rubber tube, which we fireman had to reach out for from the rear of the tender, grab and pull onboard. The tender water filler on this breed of Arthur was situated in the centre of the bulbous rear section. I put the tube in and shouted for Arth to turn the control wheel on, which he certainly did, he gave it full power. After a short time I felt it straining to ease out of the tender. Frantically trying to keep it from jumping out of the tender I shouted at the top of my considerable range for the surge to be lessened. Imagine my predicament, to release my pressure so as I would be able to lean over the side and bellow would be suicidal. Suddenly the inevitable happened - out it jumped! My much admired driver was dealt a completely unexpected blow which knocked him off his feet, thankfully there was a pair of men alerted by my lunatic rants that were instantly on hand.' I felt wretched and useless.

By the time the water flow had been checked Arthur or "Old Cocker" as he was affectionately known was as wet as if he had come out of a bath with his clothes on. He would attach no blame to me. As we assisted him to the mess room, he scolded himself for having turned the water pressure on to the full power position. The weight of that falling tube of solid water could have killed a man. In other like situations, for instance, had it been me at the wet end, this episode would have been viewed with hilarity, but such was the concern for Arth and his well being, every Salisbury man present showed a sincere desire to assist him in some way, as if by magic towels in various levels of cleanliness were produced, so in next to no time backed by the blessing of the running foreman, and looking as snug as a bug in a rug with ill fitting overalls, ¾ reefer jacket and instantly dried hot socks my popular driver was escorted to his home. Next day same duty, he was as kindly as ever – what a man!

Yeovil engine 145 Drummond K10. Yeovil Town shed on Table Road. (L to R) G. Lazenbury, J. Lambert, E. Leaworthy, W.Radford and T. Jennings. 1932. - D. Brown collection

CHAPTER 15

CHANCE MEETING LEADS TO CHANGE OF DIRECTION

It was the following week, my third at Salisbury when a situation came about that would shape my entire future. Good fortune, coincidence, happen I was in the right place at the right time, we have all heard the clichés. I had prepared an engine and was on my way to have a cuppa when for some unknown reason my attention was caught by a Maunsell's 'U' class 2-6-0. Suppose it could have been the Yeovil connection. There leaning over the side was a fireman I knew, over I went and climbed onto the footplate. "Look who's turned up" and "How's it going young Crewkerne?" was the greeting. I was naturally chuffed. News travels very quickly in a small depot, they were fully aware that I had been made up to fireman at Salisbury and because of my low seniority they considered that I had made a wise move. I concurred but explained to them that as I was now married I was at a disadvantage and would have to stay in lodgings for some considerable time which meant only been able to see my family for short periods. I was just about to take my leave when the driver one Harold Ham (who incidentally I was to find myself rostered with in the future) informed me of a possible way to solve my concerns. He was sure that on the present Southern Region vacancy list there was a fireman's position advertised at Yeovil Pen Mill. I was staggered by this snippet of information and countered by asking why with my low seniority he should think that I stood a chance. Harold had the answer. Evidently as there were very few Sunday duties to be worked and it was on the cards that the ex - Western depot was earmarked for closure, his hunch was that no one would bother to apply. So wet was I behind the ears that there is no doubt that had it not been for this chance encounter, scrutiny of the regular vacancy list would not have occurred to me. I recall running the width of the shed to the main offices, sure enough there pinned on the enginemen's notice board was the vacancy list containing the discussed topic.

With very little pre-thought I inquired if I was eligible to apply, I was made aware that as I was already in the grade I could only apply for an accommodation move which would entitle me to the vacancy providing no one seeking promotion applied. I noted the office staff looking perplexed, after all from their angle I had only been there five minutes and wished to scarpur (run). I explained my reasons, only ten miles from home etc. The governor urged me not to make a hasty decision that I may regret in the future as there had always been an influx of men from the west and none that he had heard of who were disappointed at their decision. I was also urged to consider the earnings potential at Salisbury via working rest days (extra 12 hours) and regular booked Sundays (eight hours at time and ¾). The calibre of work and route knowledge emanating from Salisbury was phenomenal, all these factors should have been taken into consideration. But for better or for worse, heart ruled head and I applied. I told Arthur of my decision and reasons, his reaction was one of understanding but I sensed his disappointment in me. After a further three weeks by which time I was enjoying the togetherness of this 'A' classified shed my name was on the successful applicants list and I was given a start date at Yeovil Pen Mill.

The special feeling of being part of such a professional and experienced clan had not been considered. Now with the dye cast I soaked up the atmosphere with distinct purpose, every spare moment when I was not disposing or preparing engines was spent in the mess room where there were sets of top link men from depots as diverse as London (Nine Elms), Exeter, Bristol, Bournemouth, Portsmouth and a host of smaller sheds. There was talk of rough trips when engines had to be nursed to conserve steam, keeping to time during inclement weather, what a wealth of experience was at hand. I was told that slowness in the promotion stakes at some localities meant that many did not become registered drivers until they were well over 40 years of age and could be 60 years old before attaining the top link, so what they collectively did not know was not worth knowing. There was one other amazing fact noted, that not once did I discern any reference to their fireman having to shoulder responsibility for poor steaming, in fact the adverse was portrayed with gambits such as " If anyone could make that ******* brass up it would be my mate"!

The industrial action that these committed proud trade unionists had rightly or wrongly taken was via a democratic vote and they had adhered to that decision. Yes they had taken a bloody nose in defeat, but they had stuck together. I was only a nipper but didn't I feel good to be associated with such a unique body of men. The scene as portrayed would forever be etched in my memory. There was a contrast so opposite to the one described waiting for me at my chosen depot that made me query whether I had made the right career wise decision.

YEOVIL DUTY No. 518.			
4 P./4 F. (57 X X Class)			
21/6, 5/7, 26/7, 9/8, 12/9.			
—	Yeovil Loco.	...12.20 p.m. ‖	
12.25 p.m.	Pen Mill	...12.50 p.m. V	
28/6, 12/7, 2/8, 16/8, 23/8 and 6/9.			
—	Yeovil Loco.	...11.25 a.m. ‖	
— **	Yeovil T.	...11.40 a.m. E	
11.44 a.m.	Yeovil Jc.	...12. 7 p.m. P	
12.11 p.m.	Yeovil T.	...12.20 p.m. ‖	
12.25 p.m.	Yeovil Pen Mill	...12.50 p.m. V	
19/7 and 30/8.			
—	Yeovil Loco.	...11.25 a.m. ‖	
**	Yeovil T.	...11.42 a.m. P	
11.46 a.m.	Yeovil Jc.	...12. 5 p.m. P	
12. 9 p.m.	Yeovil T.	...12.20 p.m. ‖	
12.25 p.m.	Pen Mill	...12.50 p.m. V	

YEOVIL DUTY No. 518—continued.		
EVERY SUNDAY.		
12.58 p.m	Yetminster...	... 1.20 p.m. V
1.38 p.m.	Yeovil Pen Mill ...	... 1.50 p.m. V
1.52 p.m.	Yeovil Town	... 2. 5 p.m. V
2. 7 p.m.	Yeovil Pen Mill ...	... 2.20 p.m. ‖
2.25 p.m.	Yeovil Loco.	... 3.45 p.m. ‖
3.50 p.m.	Yeovil Pen Mill ...	... 4. 0 p.m. V
4.17 p.m.	Thorney & K.	... 4.50 p.m. V
5.30 p.m.	Yeovil Pen Mill ...	... 5.47 p.m. ‖
5.52 p.m.	Yeovil Loco.	—

Yeovil Men.
(1) 1st set on duty 10.40 a.m., work and dispose.

4-6-2 7MT Britannia class 70013. Oliver Cromwell enters Sherborne Station on the 13.05.2009, 56 years after the incident at Crewkerne, which replaced the Merchant Navy class that had been temporarily withdrawn.
- Richard Duckworth collection

2-6-2 7P/6F class V2 60800 Green Arrow on the 07.08.1999 at the Yeovil Railway Centre, Yeovil Junction. Several members of this class were used to help replace the Merchant Navies that were temporary withdrawn after the incident in Crewkerne in April 1953.
- David Brown collection

4-6-2 WC/BB Class 34067 Tangmere runs through Sherborne on a Cathedrals Express.
- Richard Duckworth collection

4-6-2 8P Merchant Navy Class 35028 Clan Line stands on the disposal pit at the Yeovil Railway Centre, Yeovil Junction. 08.05.2010.
- Richard Duckworth collection

4-6-2 7P/5F WC/BB Class 34067 Tangmere, leaves the turntable at the Yeovil Railway Centre, Yeovil Junction, after being turned by members of the Southwest Mainline Steam Company. 14.02.2009
- Richard Duckworth collection

One of the original name plates from 4-6-2 7P/5F West Country Class 34004 Yeovil. Held be Pete Goodland, Vic Rigden, Dave Brown and Ron Weston on the 09.10.1994 at the Yeovil Railway Centre, Yeovil Junction.
- Glennis Brown collection

CHAPTER 16

I RETURN TO HOME PASTURES

After a weekend at home I was again on the platform at Crewkerne Station departing on the 6.48am service to Yeovil Junction, on the branch into the Town then across to Pen Mill on the 6.45am ex-Taunton.

The first impression of my new abode from the A30 over bridge is its compact neatness, so quiet and tiny in comparison with the vast and bustling Salisbury Depot, the thought must have occurred, "What have I done", but for better or for worse I resolved to be positive. Making the acquaintance of the Shed Master I was introduced to his Chief Clerk, both made me welcome. Again I was to be the junior hand, my third move each to a junior position, some hat trick!

The motive power at the depot was provided by the pannier and prairie tank engines, I was also informed that although the depot had been transferred from the Western to the Southern Region it had been able to retain the condition of employing the grade of fire dropper. On reflection this was a terrific plus for footplate crews as it protected the eyesight and health of its future front line men, although the balance between which railway company gave superior consideration to the health of its footplate staff was countered by the fact that the packing of the glands with what at a latter stage would be proven to be the killer substance asbestos, was the prerogative of the Western Region Driver, conversely on the Southern this duty was the remit of the fitting staff.

After the obligatory local instructions, which I digested in a fraction of the time it had taken those few weeks ago at Salisbury, I was allocated the advertised vacancy. My first roster would be on the following Sunday, which unbelievably would

2-6-2T No.4591 at Langport West with a Yeovil - Taunton train. 12.05.1964
- John Cornelius collection

be the only Sunday duty in the entire link, I mentioned that as I had been lodging for six weeks I would prefer to be excused that duty. I was assured by the chief clerk that this would be no problem as he would easily find a substitute for me, this pleased me no end.

Did I have reason to regret this decision for it led me into a position of conflict with my new colleagues. This clerk knowing I was completely ignorant of the political situation gave this solitary Sunday to a man who had worked.

What an invidious predicament this utterly innocent was placed in, I was to be challenged regarding my attitude, and then the truth circulated. This episode was a wake up call to me.

As suggested I utilised this first day to familiarise myself with the admittedly spartan surrounds of small shed and stabling points, walking into the mess room I met the two man cleaning gang, immediately I felt at ease. Explaining my brief footplate experience there was no rancour at the fact that I had taken a vacancy that would otherwise have gone to one of them, in fact the opposite as they suggested that we climb aboard the only pannier tank engine on shed. Every item of footplate control equipment from injectors through to the supply of steam heat was pointed out to me, taking water was not as straight forward as I would have perceived as the pannier tanks had a filling point on each side of the tank top, the expected procedure was to unclip and lift each cover so as the levels could be checked as full, the tanks were in effect separate entities connected via an under pipe so as the weight of water held either side would always be exactly balanced. Another for me "novelty" was that each engine had a locked tool box positioned on the side framing, the key was labelled with the corresponding engine number and kept in the stores, my mentors were under the impression that locking away tools was the norm, they honestly thought I was shooting a line when I told them that at Salisbury one had to watch their engine lamps, firing irons, shovel and everything else as some fireman looking for tools that had been nicked from his steed would be up on the first vacated footplate to restock his larder. I owed a debt of gratitude to my new found mates as without their volunteered assistance I would have been at a loss the next morning as my duty was a 4am as ordered start.

A few years down the line the close relationship formed on that first day at Pen Mill would lead to one of a more permanent nature. Those two passed cleaners would be with me at Yeovil Town as Firemen. I was at Yeovil Junction one evening to meet and escort a cousin to our home, as I was greeting her who should tap me on the shoulder and request an introduction, but my Pen Mill buddy Ken Fay. I was only too pleased to oblige. This "again" chance meeting led to wedding bells. Here the family "railway" kicks in, the Son of that union is now a Standards Manager with South West Trains based at – wait for it – Salisbury and what a railway family he represents, father, grandfather, (The uncle who signed me on) and great grandfather, The Crewkerne Crossing keeper.

Next morning to the ring of the newly purchased alarm I am up and away on the cycle for the ten mile stint to Yeovil Pen Mill. On arrival I am allocated the preparation of one of the depots pannier tanks, the coaching from the previous day is now enacted as I collect the appropriate keys from the storeman and return with the empty containers for recharging, wanting to start off on the correct foot I top up the drivers feeder (oiling can) and make sure there is a plentiful supply of paraffin in his flare lamp, then its up on the tiny footplate, opening the firebox door I jerk liquid from the duct lamp onto the embers of the fire and light the lamp from the resultant burst of flame, this same action would often lead to the perpetrator receiving singed eyebrows, now having a proper look around I spy an iron sleeve that obviously has to be placed over the bottom ring of the circular fire hole so as the baffle plate (plate that deflects outside cold air away from the boiler tubes) can be placed over it, I could see there was a knack in applying it to its correct position.

I proved the knack had evaded me as my first attempt landed it in the firebox – what a start, and what a struggle extracting that heavy and solid shape back onto the footplate via the fire dropper's long shovel. The fire is made up under the door. I can not help but compare the tiny tank engine's five foot four inch firebox with the carnivorous box's of the Salisbury fleet where I had witnessed an experienced hand having heaved a lump of coal so large it had jammed in a "Merchant Navy" class" firehole door "Bit big init Mate?" I enquired "No it ******* well ain't" was the reply as he belted it in with the coal pick. Flare lamp in hand I check the sand boxes and top up where necessary, examining the tightness of the smoke box door, cleaning and displaying the paraffin filled head lamps and leaving one on the framing bracket. Now it's the turn of the bunker, so with coal pick at the ready I am up and at it breaking up any large lumps and generally tidying it to so as the chances of any rolling down the sides and causing injury will be minimal.

Writing this the mind has suddenly shot forward several years, I am walking from Yeovil Town motive power depot shed to the drivers and firemen's mess room, a "West Country" class locomotive is moving into the Depot on the road that is immediately adjacent to the main office block. Our accident prone chargeman, one Alfie Saunders having just recovered from a broken arm is walking towards me

between the building and the lumbering mass of engine, we are both looking to gain the same entry point, suddenly as if in slow motion a solitary oval shaped briquette, (block of compressed coal dust) known among loco men as donkey b******* detaches its self from the untrimmed over loaded tender, bounces onto the side panel and lands on top of dear old Alf's head, I did yell "look out" but to no avail, his eyes glazed over as I ran towards him, and as I held him his flat cap slid off to reveal a badly split head wound.

Back on the footplate I am well satisfied with the results of my fledgling efforts, testing the injectors and topping up the boiler to ¾ full I use the pep pipe to lightly swill away the residue coal dust and give the boiler front and all within sight a good old clean up with the stores supply of cotton waste. The Southern Region issued the as explained rusty cloth. My driver gains the cab has a look around and conveys his satisfaction. Hand brake off and we move out for water. To reiterate, it was of vital importance that these small capacity side tanks be filled and equalised. I was to discover that the thought of the injector's blowing out owing to the tanks been low on water induced a state of paranoia in a minority of this depots drivers. With side tanks topped up to the gunnels we leave the prepared engine ready to be taken off shed.

That first week would not see me progressing beyond the confines of the depot until the Friday when I was allocated to a very senior driver for a three hour shunt duty in the local freight yard.

This driver's attitude upon learning that he had this Southern newcomer who had never fired to a pannier tank as his mate was frankly disgusting, he played merry hell with the shed foreman so as all within hearing range was party to his vociferous objections, apart from being astounded I recognised he was uttering a disservice to his badge as driver and I instantly compared him with my Salisbury top link man on that shunt duty to Milford Yard. On our way along the up island platform at Pen Mill to the controlling ground signal for entry into the down yard I kept my thoughts and tongue quiet – he came over my side to check on every signal such was his confidence in me and I thought in his self. Not a word of recognition was uttered. Whilst the shunt moves were taking place I took stock and was concerned as to whether there were others of a similar vein, thankfully my apprehensions were unfounded.

There was a calming sequel to this event, for after our return to the depot the foreman tactfully beckoned me aside and apologised for Charlie O's behaviour, he also advised me of his own embarrassment. A small Depot is much akin to a village, both are tight knit communities, all are aware of each others strength and weaknesses, word of this confrontation between driver and foreman soon spread, thankfully my part was portrayed as piggy in the middle. I was urged to put the matter to rest. I thought – enough said.

CHAPTER 17

PAIRING WITH A REGULAR DRIVER

The following Monday I was to attain my rightful position in the link structure, taking the position vacated by a fireman who had successfully applied to be made up to driver in the London area. My regular Driver was Frank Smith, this was to be the first of two separate driver, fireman pairings. Frank was in his mid fifties and had begun his career at Westbury towards the end of the First World War. He had a wealth of main line experience from his period as a fireman. I am sure from the onset he recognised he had a bona-fide audience in yours truly as he recalled footplate activities with all types of G.W.R. Motive Power from fast passenger mileage through to freight and banking duties. He would lament on the promotional system which banished him to the colliery town of Aberbeeg when he had yearned to stay the course as driver in a main line depot.

It was the prerogative of the Footplatemens democratically elected Local Departmental Committee 'L.D.C.' to place the duties allocated to the depot into a link structure which alternated each week. Twelve mid day was the demarcation between early and late turns, signing on times of 9am was known throughout the trade as office hours and was a rarity indeed. It was fortunate for me that I was not adverse to using peddle power prior to the commencement or termination of a shift as the earliest booked passenger service from my home station of Crewkerne via Yeovil Junction was 7.20am and conversely on late shifts I would have to be on the peddles and away from Pen Mill Shed by 8.30pm at the latest to enable a connection to be made with the 8.40pm branch from the Town Station to the Junction for the days final train home.

Yeovil engine 2-6-2T taking water at Yeovil Pen Mill after arriving from Taunton. Guard Charlie Rodber talking to driver Frank Smith and fireman Colin Robins holding water column.
- Authors collection

YEOVIL DUTY No. 518.
4 M.T. (45 XX Class)

—	Yeovil Loco.	5.30 a.m.
5.35 a.m.	Yeovil P.M.	—
	F—Shunting 6.15 a.m. to 6.45 a.m.	
	C—Shunting 6.45 a.m. to 6.55 a.m.	
—	Yeovil P.M.	7. 5 a.m. P
8.17 a.m.	Taunton	9. 0 a.m. P
10. 1 a.m.	Minehead	10.50 a.m. P
11.51 a.m.	Taunton	11.55 a.m.
12. 0 noon	Loco. Yard	4.10 p.m.
**	Taunton	4.22 p.m. P
5.37 p.m.	Yeovil P.M.	6.14 p.m. F
(10.55 a.m. Severn Tunnel Jn.)		Bank
6.44 p.m.	Evershot	6.58 p.m. F
7.18 p.m.	Yeovil Pen Mill	—
	C—Shunting 7.20 p.m. to 7.50 p.m.	
	F—Shunting 9.30 p.m. to 12.15 a.m.	
—	Yeovil Pen Mill	12.15 a.m.
12.20 a.m.	Yeovil Loco.	—

Yeovil Men.
(1) Off No. 520 (M.O.), No. 514 (M.X.), prepare.

(2) 1st set on duty 5.15 a.m., work to Taunton, change to No. 60 (W.R.) at 8.35 a.m., work and assist requirements for 1.55 p.m.

Taunton Men.
(3) Off No. 60 (W.R.), change at Taunton 8.35 a.m., work to depot.

(4) Off No. 60 (W.R.), prepare for 4.10 p.m.

Yeovil Men.
(5) Off No. 60 (W.R.), work 4.10 p.m., relieved at Yeovil Town 5.25 p.m. (M.O.) as ordered, (M.X.) pass. to Yeovil Jc., relieve No. 561 at 6.20 p.m.

(6) 2nd set on duty 5.10 p.m., relieve at 5.25 p.m., work and dispose.

It was imperative that the driver fireman team developed a genuine understanding. The vast majority of drivers would instinctively recognise should his mate be having problems, for instance with getting his fire to cooperate, in footplate parlance "Having a ruffin" and would as far as practical ease back on his consumption of steam endeavouring to make up for any time loss on the easier gradients. Frank and I did as they say "knock it off" but even the best of teams have their off days and our relationship over the two separate pairings was no exception. The motive power supplied to work the diagrammed duties throughout the depot comprised the 0-6-0 pannier and the 2-6-2 tanks, the sole exception was a heavy Bristol to Weymouth freight which Pen Mill men relieved at Westbury with either a 2-6-0 Manor, Hall or Grange class engine on the front end.

This difficulty persuaded me to pull out all the stops in an endeavour to find rented accommodation in Yeovil. Before we lift a shovel in my episode away from Pen Mill shed I will now recall a situation that is relived in mirth but at the time caused me much anguish and frustration. There was a 4.04am regular freight from Exmouth Junction Marshalling Yard to Salisbury Yard which was booked to stop at Crewkerne to enable what was termed as "Road Box" to be off loaded from a designated box wagon, (van) if however there was nothing for my home town the guard would advise the driver accordingly "Nothing for Crewkerne Drive" and if the up distant signal was off, my lift to Yeovil would sail through at a rate of knots, or it did so when a certain Signalman was on nights. Word soon got around Yeovil Town Depot that young Robins ex-junior porter come engine cleaner was now a fireman at the Town's Western Depot, each and every one of those senior drivers in the link that worked the said freight let it be known to me that should I require a lift all I had to do was ask the signalman to keep his up distant signal on. So many early duties I would arrive on the platform, put my quest to the signalman – "No problem Col, any time Son", but not when Freddie G was on that shift "More then I dare, they will give I the sack" was the rebuke afforded me. Even so I would stay expectantly beside that small long gone signal box as some drivers would apply sufficient vacuum brake to engine and fitted head of wagons to allow a pick up should I be there. I vividly recall the gesticulations of despair from the footplate as they sped through knowing I then needlessly had ten miles of cycling to endure.

2-8-0 28xx 3819 shunts under A30 road bridge at Yeovil Pen Mill - John Day collection

It was as well that the vagaries of chance when intending to use the freight came into the calculation, I allowed sufficient time to cycle, so as I would not be late for my turn. From my tentative start at Crewkerne all three Signalmen and their relief counterparts were like uncles to me, especially Freddie, but hidden behind that carefree façade however was a fear of repercussion that must have been stifling.

At this present time when one observes the chaotic state of the line side it is difficult to believe that then, such was the inbuilt culture of safety bred into track maintenance that at rare times I would cycle those miles to Yeovil Junction along a clear ballast free cess. Using the track side was not authorised and if reported I would have been in hot water.

I was to learn that the turns in the link with Frank followed

a distinct and unvaried pattern of diagrammed work consisting of preparing engines, shunting, banking and working stopping passenger duties across the Branch to the county town of Taunton, and plying freight across the extent of the depot's route knowledge. There was no dispensation for fireman to be granted familiarisation trips upon filling a vacancy. It was in at the deep end and no arguments. By far the majority of drivers accepted this situation and my new mate fell in to this category. I was however to be rostered with the unwelcoming brigade, their nervousness at having a young stranger booked with them was tangible. The brotherly greeting would take the form of "Hope you can manage the job". This confidence builder would be followed by the pure pedigree of their regular fireman.

CHAPTER 18

THE ENIGMA OF 'BANKING'

My inauguration into the mysterious world of banking came about on an early turn. The pannier tank prepared we make our way via the appropriate signals and points to arrive at Pen Mills down side east yard. "Screw her down Colin" and we make our way to the shunters cabin, I am introduced to the head shunter. Very soon we are enjoying his excellent company with a cuppa to boot. This ritual was as if it was devised from the rule book and was likewise adhered to.

The so recent footplate industrial action had led to a reduction in the volume of freight moved by rail, but even so, by far the bulk of the nation's goods relied on the unobtrusive railway for its distribution.

The shunting period allowed on this particular diagram was a short one hour from 4-45am until 5-45am. "Into it" with a vengeance, the regulator was used in open aggression to conform to the shunters frantic arm signals to pull up or knock "em off". This pulling up and sorting out was constant in keeping with the previously explained shunting at Milford.

The follow on part of the duty was yet another initiation. We were booked to assist the 10-40pm ex-Paddington freight from Pen Mill to Evershot. Frank advised me that the standard procedure would call for an attachment to be made to the rear of the train as the incline did not commence until we reached Yetminster. His expert explanation of the distances and gradients involved left me in no doubt as to where the power and boost of a full head of steam would be needed. I had half a box of good fire stored mostly under the door. My driver appreciated the fact that as it was a first time for me I wished to explain my plan to enable a more substantial spread to be achieved without standing in the yard wasting steam to the heavens via the safety valves. Frank concurred.

The practice was that should the freight be running behind schedule the footplate crew would be so advised. We had received no such advice. I was full of anticipation and over my mate's side as the 22.40 ex - Paddington freight with a 28xx class 2-8-0 at its head rumbled past with what appeared to this novice as an endless stream of mixed freight in tow. Frank had no need to inform me that our quarry had a full load indeed. The elements this August morning were perfect. I eagerly await my first venture beyond the confines of Yeovil Pen Mill and out into Great Western territory. The down yard exit signal is off, we make our way towards the now stationary guards van. To the critical southern footplate man with his inbuilt prejudice to anything Great Western, the box like small western tanks portrayed the epitome of ugliness. I was about to learn that the unattractive exterior camouflaged a strength out of all proportion to its size.

The track ahead swung to the left, the high dome and chimney made the forward view difficult for the driver, so in the time honoured way I verbally and by use of hand signals guide my mate onto the van. We make contact, bounce off a little then finally ease up. The guard is between making the attachment. Frank gets down onto the cess and collects the freight load ticket. The classification for engines was on the scale of 1 - 8, the Western 28xx class was one of the most powerful heavy goods locomotives in the country and was therefore categorized as eight, the maximum load it was permitted to haul up Evershot bank was equivalent to 43 of loaded goods, which could be made up from a maximum length of 60 wagons. When calculating a load the "Equivalent to loaded goods wagons" table had to be consulted which shows that each wagon had a Marked Carrying Capacity, i.e. 13 tons and under was equal to 1, and at the top of the scale 50 tons and over was six, therefore it is feasible that a load of 7 wagons carrying 50 tons each would constitute a full load, conversely our 28xx was permitted to take 60 vehicles over the top, as a empty wagon counted as ½. The goods guard was certainly a good customer of the pencil and rubber stockist. For Evershot bank the pannier had a loading of 3 which was equal to a load of 24 so it was on the cards that the load for both engines could be a maximum of 66.

To enable the severity of the gradient of this short but steep incline to be appreciated I give you the following comparison. On the Southern Region the highest freight numerical classification was afforded to the 4-6-0 "S15" locomotive which was six, this would allow a maximum load of 55 for the toughest incline between Waterloo and Exeter, the mostly 1 in 70 to 1 in 80 Honiton bank. Evershot however has a three mile section of between 1 in 65 and 1 in 51 hence the previously quoted 43. I cannot recall the load Frank quoted me from the load ticket, but can quite remember it was close to the upper limit for

both Engines. We were now all but ready for the assault in earnest, the guard has removed his tail lamps, and I have placed a lamp on the front buffer beam bracket and the mandatory one to the rear. As in accordance with rule 133 clause (c) of the 1950 British Railways Rule Book the guard is giving my driver the signal to start. My driver now calls the attention of the train engine driver that the banker and train is ready to proceed by giving two "crow" whistles, this is acknowledged in like fashion by the front engine after the driver of that engine has satisfied himself that his advance starter signal is off. Until these crows have been exchanged neither engine must move. We receive the crows from the front both loud and clear, the thought occurs, on a peach of a morning such as this so does half of Yeovil!

Our little power house is in full forward gear, my mate has opened the regulator and we are urging our charge forward but as yet there is no sign of progress, suddenly there is a lessening of tension from the front, Frank makes it clear from across the footplate "Hang on Colin". I did not have to be told for although we were straining into the seemingly immoveable bulk the tug presented by the enormous pulling power of the 28xx jerked us to the fore with such violence that had I not held myself taunt I would have been thrown backwards. This, Frank informed me over the din, should not have happened, a pull, yes, but the lead driver should have shown more restraint and caution in easing away. He then added that he was not a bit surprised at the rough treatment afforded us, as the guard during their chat had told him that the driver on the front had worked during the strike. Frank reasoned, that he, as a well known trade unionist would have been noticed at the yard exit. Another pull has me realising that our importance at this stage is secondary, my mate has his reverser pulled up towards mid gear and has the regulator half open, he tells me there is no alternative but to let the train engine dictate the initiative. This is my first meaningful duty out on the road as a fireman booked with a regular driver. I remember making sure nothing was going to spoil it. I am pleased to find on yanking open the fire box door that we have a mass of near white hot fire.

I was never to feel at ease when firing up on this class of engine as either side of the shovelling area there is the raised platform of the driver and fireman's position. There is no clearer sign to a footplate crew that near perfect combustion has been achieved then the telltale marker of white exhaust from the chimney turning deep grey in response to each round of coal applied, also there is a distinctive odour, this is happening. I did not recognise these symptoms as any other then normal, but a little later career wise I would endeavour to create the latter with very little success.

Our speed is increasing as we pass under the Southern Region Waterloo to Exeter main line. I attempt to keep the gauge glass reading at ¾ full. Use of the injector does not reduce the boiler pressure which has me thinking I must be having 'Beginners luck'. I am leaning over the side checking that the injector is not wasting water and then peering to the fore endeavouring to get a clear sight of the lead engine some fifty plus wagon lengths away. The curvature gives me the view I have been seeking. The motive power on the front is really putting it's self about, it is an inspiring spectacle. Turning off the injector I again bend the back adding five or six rounds to the white hot mass, must have been feeling confident as instead of opening and closing the fire box door between each firing I am lifting the chain which in turn places the half door into the fire box aperture. The track adopts a more level profile as it cuts through an area of outstandingly beautiful countryside. We are now over the Somerset boundary and into Dorset, ploughing along at I guess 30 mph, it seems to me that every nut and bolt is straining to break free such is the vibration created on board this bucking bronco, I also reflect that fitments which are firm will be shortly dancing a jig. Frank bellows across that I should expect an increase in pressure from the front which would intensify as the lead engine drops in speed on encountering the lower reaches

Halt a 1 in 53, followed by a final hurdle of near two miles at 1 in 51. Frank in true partnership tradition shouts across to me that in his opinion our charge has been miss calculated, and he doesn't mean under weight. The regulator is fully open and the reverser lever is in full fore gear, the pannier is giving her all, and so, as we can see from the height of its blast is the lead engine. The farming community here about have more common sense then grow cereals as the molten rockets would without doubt set them ablaze. We continue to make sluggish but determined progress into and through the 1 in 52 barrier. Acting on the my drivers experienced advice I had ceased firing and let the boiler contents gauge reading drop to half a glass. We are now piercing a range of hills via Evershot tunnel. In response to the gradient Frank has eased the regulator to its closed position, we feel a tug as the couplings take the strain and

4-6-0 6800 class 'grange' about to enter Holywell tunnel, being banked by a Yeovil 0-6-0 pannier tank up Evershot bank - Phillip Brown collection

YEOVIL DUTY No. 519.

4 F.T. (57 XX Class)

—	Yeovil Loco.	4.40 a.m. ‖
4.45 a.m.	Yeovil P.M.	—
	F—Shunting 4.45 a.m. to 5.45 a.m.	
**	Yeovil Pen Mill	6.25 a.m. F
		(Bank) M.X.
	(M.X. 10.40 p.m. Paddington)	
6.53 a.m.	Evershot	7. 0 a.m. ‖
7.20 a.m.	Yeovil Pen Mill	
	F—Shunting 7.20 a.m. to 10.10 a.m.	
—	Yeovil Pen Mill	10.10 a.m. ‖
10.25 a.m.	Yetminster	11.20 a.m. P
	(8.20 a.m. Paddington)	Bank
**	Evershot	11.45 a.m. ‖
12.10 p.m.	Yeovil Loco.	2.25 p.m. ‖
2.30 p.m.	Yeovil Pen Mill	2.56 p.m. F
	(9.45 a.m. Bristol)	Bank
3.30 p.m.	Evershot	3.55 p.m. ‖
4.15 p.m.	Pen Mill	—
	C—Shunting 4.50 p.m. to 5.10 p.m.	
—	Pen Mill	5.45 p.m. P
6.50 p.m.	Taunton	8.20 p.m. P
9.19 p.m.	Pen Mill	9.30 p.m. ‖
9.35 p.m.	Yeovil Loco.	—

Yeovil Men.

(1) M.O.—Off No. 480, (M.X.) off No. 512, prepare for 4.40 a.m. ‖.

(2) 1st set on duty 4.25 a.m., work and dispose.

(3) 2nd set on duty 1.40 p.m., work, relieved in depot.

(4) Off No. 546, dispose.

of this severe climb. Yetminster down distant signal is off and to my left I have my first sighting of the down holding siding which is able to accommodate a full length freight plus banking engine.

In the time honoured way Frank consults his time piece and makes the point across the clamour "Doing well Col" which lifts me no end, we are now into the incline. I would forever remember this first realisation of the power which was out of all proportion to the size of the pannier tank breed. In quick time we are down to distinguishable exhaust beats. I am chuffed, no pun intended, as by luck more then judgement, after firing and closure of the firebox door the exhaust erupting to the heavens is near black.

The boiler pressure needle is near the red, I open the injector water valve, turn on the live steam, gently cut back on the water supply until the matching pick up sends every drop into the boiler. I would very soon recognise this portion of the bank as the onset of its most severe section, three short spans of 1 in 73 and 65, then abreast with Chetnole

once again tighten. I have the injector on, the firebox door half open with the blower valve off its face to arrest any tendency of a blow back.

The train engine now fully in command makes its way to the Evershot advanced starter signal. Now at a stand I am off the footplate and in between lifting off the coupling, we are again separate entities. On the platform the guard is confirming Frank's prediction that the load had been miscalculated. Via the distinctive whistle we draw the attention of the signalman and the train enginemen that the banker is detached. The advance is pulled off and we listen for the acknowledgement from the front. We get it all right, a long high pitched note followed by a deep shorter version administered by the 28xx class brake whistle. Of course in my innocence I did not conjecture the significance, seeing Franks countenance turn to undisguised outrage, I enquired "What did that code mean?" "What did that mean" he snorted, "A** H***, that is what that B***** blew". How I did not collapse in hysterics was an act beyond compare. If I had done the regulator handle would have been twisted around (Somerset phrase) "Me neck".

Later in reflective mode, I reasoned that had I participated and fully supported an action which had cost my household three weeks wages and a bloody nose in the bargain. My reaction to the insult hurled at us by the Weymouth man would have been in the same vein. The unique sound of sudden extended couplings and my first bout in the field of assistance from the rear is over.

We move forward pass the starter, ground signal clears and we cross over to the up road. On the platform I reverse the tail lamp to the smoke box. The rear ash pan damper is closed and the bunker is given a soaking. Evershot up starter is off, a blast on the whistle, touch of regulator and into the tunnel we go. We emerge with regulator shut, engine brake rubbing and for good measure hand brake on, we descend this harsh gradient. That first bunker leading trip was weird, stood looking ahead through those square windows with their outward protection of prison cell like iron bars with the small coal carrying capacity to the fore. I make a promise that I would look up the history of this so ugly but immensely strong pup. No worries re battling with a storm sheet with the pannier. The distant signal for Yetminster is off. I sit arms folded on the tip up seat. I recall feeling pleased and confident regarding my families future in my home area, this optimism would sadly prove to be an illusion. Now back alongside the Yeovil Town to Junction branch we attract an exaggerated whistle from the resident Drummond "M7" push pull tank as it propels its charge from the Town, the fireman one Dave Cook is extending his arm in a gesticulating manner, what's this?. He has a match box held between his forefinger and thumb, my mate laughs but for some reason I am annoyed, is there an affinity in the making for this unsightly little powder keg? I should have taken this little wind up in the same jocular vein as it was intended.

We are back at Pen Mill and have taken water. The starter is off, we move past the signal box and stop over the crossover ground signal, thence it clears and we are back in the down goods yard. The duty continues with a period of 'Shunting', but first a can of nectar - tea, and breakfast. Ron Whittle the head shunter makes his appearance, pulls himself aboard and proceeds to enforce the impression I was forming, that the combined footplate and traffic grades here at this outcast Western enclave were an exceedingly likable and together breed.

The evenings outgoing freight made up of merchandise from the area's industry and farms plus many not required empty wagons is assembled. We take leave of our impressive shunter and make our way to the yard exit signal. In accordance with the diagrammed workings at 10.10am the road is cleared. A customary tug on the whistle cord, and we are away light engine to Yetminster. 15 minutes for the 4½ mile jaunt. The niche in the duty that we are about to fulfil has me full of expectancy but tinged with a degree of apprehension, we are to assist the 8.20am Passenger ex-Paddington up the bank. I went across the footplate and enquired as to how the procedure with the passenger on the bows would vary from the goods. All I got from my mate was "You will be alright Col".

Arriving at Yetminster we move into the down siding where I screw our engine down. My mate opens the cylinder release cocks, (this allows residue high pressure steam to escape) Frank is now away for a chin wag, left with time on my hands I decide to clean the fire. My mate duly returns, climbs aboard after nearly burning the bottom off his boot as he stood on the hot debris and announces his surprise at my actions. I remind him that my Southern breeding taught me to throw out dirt at given opportunities. Things are working out a treat as I have a good base of clean fire and the boiler gauge glass is ¾ full.

At the booked arrival time of 11.20am we hear the unmistakable blast from the whistle of the approaching train engine, simultaneously the observed board (in my Southern breeding, stick) drops off. We are up and raring to go as the 8.20am ex - Paddington with a 4-6-0 Hall class on the front cruises by. The maximum passenger train load allowance for the 49xx class is 288 tons, which equates to nine coaches. We count eleven, two over the top. In accordance with the "Sectional Appendix to the Working Timetable" applicable to that period the Signalman has pulled his starter off allowing the train to be brought to a stand on the Evershot side of the box. The ground signal comes off and we move forward to stop under the signal box window, the load is now communicated to my driver by the signalman, "Eleven Frank for 352 tons". The Bible, sorry appendix reads, it is not necessary for the guard of a passenger train which is being assisted from Yetminster to ascertain the number of the assisting engine, this pleases my trend of thought as Frank will not get to hear the lead engine drivers pedigree. We ease forward, touch and push into the rear buffers. As a novice I marvel that with the engine at a stand and the regulator open something between us and the rear coach does not give. Frank gives the mandatory double crows, the advanced starter must be off as we clearly hear the rejoinder from the front. The boiler gauge glass shows the water level as just under the top nut.

We try but do not shorten the length of that rear coach. Suddenly with a lurch we are away pushing with every ounce of power at our disposal, the exhaust beats increase in frenzy and frequency. I'm thinking, when is he going to pull her (reverser) up? He does, to about 60% cut off, still sounds as if he is hammering the daylights out of her. The steam pressure much to my amazement is right on the button. I had put a pint of engine oil on the firehole door hinging and sliding equipment during my unofficial engine requirements back in the siding, now it is paying dividends, it slides open to the touch as if on ball bearings. Our regulator is fully open and the cut off is back to 40%. On a left hander I find an incredible view to the front. The majority of coach windows were open and a wave of humanity was leaning out and jockey wise slapping the side of the coach in encouragement to us. I bellowed for my mate to come over and have a look, which he did, he then decided to prick my balloon by informing me that the same had happened on the right handers from his side, but he had decided he would leave me to discover this gem.

It turned out that this on fine days was the a usual occurrence, so usual in fact that enginemen on the up road would on sighting a passenger service struggling up the bank give an urgent and prolonged series of whistle warnings for obvious reasons. My firing as previously described is to be in short bursts. Keeping an eagle eye on the boiler contents gauge I do not let it drop below ½ a glass. Frank shouts over the rumpus that we are approaching Chetnole Halt which would be all but half way to the tunnel, and just to lift proceeding to a higher level, the caveat "We've got the steepest part to come Col and I'll probably have to drop her over" I utter a silent "****". Just then we gave the impression of endeavouring to demolish an over bridge span as our exhaust mixture of steam and fire gasses slammed in to its underside engulfing the perpetrator and entering the cab, now into the 1 in 51gradient with ½ glass of water in the boiler gauge and holding our steam pressure at not far short of maximum we look to be sitting pretty.

This is the middle of the summer and I'm just realising that I was perspiring to this same degree just that short time ago in Singapore at this same time of day whilst lazing about killing time, what a waste. I'm feeling a little puzzled as each time I catch Franks eye I discern a unabashed grin, I call across "What ya laughing at mate?" reply accompanied with a full laugh "You wanna to see your face" I had without a thought been wiping the sweat off my dial with the back of the hands, all I needed according to my mate was a sweeps brush as we had the chimney. My answer was "Just".

Our speed was well below 20 mph, reverser dropped forward to 60% on full regulator we keep banging away, I put the injector on, as we have less then a ½ a glass, before we enter the tunnel. The penetrating echo of the lead engines whistle, no lewd innuendos this time, more an acknowledgement of our assistance, pervades the ears. I can sense the 8.20am ex - Paddington is about to say farewell, as we exit the tunnel the gap between us quickly increases. As per instructions we follow forward and come to a stand at the signal box. Had we been assisting a stopping service we would have been attached, therefore the detachment would have taken place in the platform. The points are pulled over, the ground signal is cleared, and we move over the cross over as previously described.

My driver puts forward the theory that the train engine we had just assisted must have been having a rough trip steam wise as the load was only two coaches over the limit for the "Hall" class he knew that we had propelled more then those couple of coaches. Years later having a chat and a laugh with fellow footplate men from depots who had diagrammed work on the front of duties with booked bankers, it appears that it was often the case that the front end crew would consider, that providing there was not a danger of the train becoming stuck, (term for inability to move forward) they would as far as possible take it easy. I suppose their reasoning had probably been that the banker crew had been sitting around on their butts while they had been slogging their proverbial out, so let them earn their corn.

While we are on a nostalgia trip I give you this little nugget. 40 years on from these events I found myself near the village of Chetnole heading for Batcombe. Memories I

did not wish to suppress came to the fore. A look at the map (please do likewise) decided my parking lot, in a gate way. Explaining to my wife the sortie I had in mind extracted a look which made me think she doubted my sanity. Undaunted I was across a field and peering over the railway line side fence, it had long been down graded to a single line. Up the track was my quest, a bridge, down the bank and a short walk had me examining the underside brick work. After all those intervening years the scorching ballistic blasts from countless steam chests and firebox's had left an indelible crust, I was not in the least surprised.

We are on the up road with tail lamp reversed. Spot on time at 11.45am the signal comes off and we are away. We cruise down the bank in the previously described vein with the fire well down in size compared with my first trip. At 12.10pm we are in the tiny depot, our day is up, I screw the handbrake on, as I climb off I'm met by the fire dropper with a "hope the size of that fire don't melt my shovel nipper" I tell him that it had been cleaned at Yetminster, and off I went. One quick glance back caught him gazing after me with his mouth open. Trevor Dunn and I were to become the best of pals.

Into the small mess room for the ritual scrub up I gave myself a jolt, looking into a cracked mirror made me realise why my mate took the rise out of me. Lucky that I had gone into the cabin, as had the Southern brigade at Yeovil Town and beyond seen the state of me I would never have been allowed to live it down.

Every evening the alarm was set at 3am. There was three inter related families in that three bed roomed council house at Misterton, my in-laws were truly kind and generous folk and must have been saints to put up with us all.

In the saddle by 3.30am gave me ample time for the ten mile ride prior to the start time of 4.25am. As on Monday the early freight was, with minor variations and loadings, to keep time as would the 8.20am ex - Paddington. From my introduction as the utter novice on Monday I felt justified at feeling more then satisfied with my progress, my gain had been in confidence and hands on experience, but no way would I fool myself, there was recognition that my position was very much on the bottom rung and there was much climbing in the craft of firing to be done.

The following week found us diagrammed to work the second part of the same engine duty No 519 as the previous early turn, signing on at 1.30pm. Although the engine had been prepared I was astonished that my driver had me hoisting myself from the framings to the tank top checking either side's water contents, nothing like making sure, but in my book your mates must be trusted.

Depot exit signal off and we are let loose in the yard. Our first task is to assist the 9.45am ex - Bristol freight, which Frank informs me is a Pen Mill duty, but on this occasion, for reasons that escape me (Probable due to special traffic arrangements) it is crewed by Weymouth men. Making our way down the yard I am told that the procedure will be the same as last week regards attachment etc. In ran a 43xx class 2-6-0, classified as four in the freight loading chart, which was half the loading of last weeks 28xx class. The

The unlikely duo heading out to Yetminster for banking duties are U class 2-6-0 31637 and 57xx 0-6-0PT 3671. 25.08.1962 - John Day collection

As I have mentioned before the nastiness was beyond my comprehension. How an industrial dispute could engender such ugliness, was beyond my understanding. My mate was a thick set and sturdy individual and was to reveal to me a side of his nature I was never again to witness, for after making the bunker leading trip back to Pen Mill he nearly broke the securing chain off the water column such was his continued annoyance.

After a booked period of carriage shunting I was in for my first trip over the Western branch to our County town of Taunton, on reflection I am sure the fact of my admitted inexperience in passenger train firing did not cause any qualms but I did harbour an uneasiness regarding handing over the staff to the signalman when leaving each single line section and collecting the authoritative replacement to enter the next section from the same signalman, all performed when leaning over the side of the in motion cab. I had enjoyed an adolescent giggle with mates when observing this to us decidedly dodgy antic from the western platform at Yeovil Town. We were without a doubt wishing to observe a mishandled change, but through sheer expertise we were thankfully disappointed. My mind set was probably suggesting "Chickens coming home to roost" as now I would be the one to make sure the change over was correct. I had been keeping my passed cleaner mates abreast with my experiences and progress, in the place of expected resentment there was genuine interest and sincere friendship, they had several firing turns under their belts and were only too pleased to put me through rehearsals, which hand to hold the staff that had to be collected by the signalman whilst making sure the other arm was correctly aligned to make the collection, I was a willing pupil to my junior instructors.

loading was to the capacity of the maximum tonnage for both engines of equivalent to 48 loaded wagons. The trip was a near repetition of the previous ventures with one alarming exception. The distant signal at Yetminster was at caution, next thing we knew we were thrown forward such was the check encountered, Frank had warned me of this possibility so we weren't hurt, we both feared for the guard who gave us a reassuring wave.

There was a similar situation towards the end of steam and the beginning of my driving career at Fratton when a heavy application by the train engine actually put the guard through his window and onto the van veranda causing lacerations to the face.

We were now one tightly buffered up unit. I instinctively knew that the situation we were in would call for exceptional skill from the front man, anticipating the possible snatch my mate applied minimal brake pressure which would extend the couplings, suddenly there was a violent tug, had the slight brake application not been made we would have been literally at a loose end. My mate did not apply power until he was certain the train engine had the clearance of Yetminster advance signal. My drivers actions confirmed my respect for his competence. He now gave her the gun, again she brassed up well and had me thinking that I had mastered the art, which in these ideal conditions with a clean fire I no doubt had. Arriving at Evershot I uncoupled from the van, having a word with the guard I mentioned that my driver was concerned for his safety, I was not prepared for his lamentations regarding his drivers well known pedigree as the most erratic in the Weymouth depot, he added that I should inform my mate of the freight drivers name, when I regained the footplate I passed the info. The effect caused Frank to turn purple, evidently of the very few that had worked through the strike we had the misfortune to encounter two in such a short period.

Yetminster station 4-6-0 hall class, starts to climb up Evershot Bank. 1948 - Phillip Brown collection

CHAPTER 19

OVER THE WESTERN TO MY COUNTY TOWN OF TAUNTON

At 5.30pm we are on our three set Taunton train standing in the departure platform. Frank now introduces me to the, and here I use the correct phraseology "Auxiliary Token Machine". It is the remit of the fireman to withdraw the single line token in the case of a passenger train, and by the shunter in the case of a freight. My mate advises me thus – permission to withdraw must first be obtained from the Signalman, when this is given the token has to be lifted through a machined column and then pressed forward as if turning a key in a lock, it must then be turned from right to left when it can be withdrawn. We are now back on board, the token in its carrier is hung on the engine handbrake, our guard makes his appearance and notifies my mate of the loading, "Three for 96 tons Frank" has a friendly quip and is away back to his van, as the up main at Pen Mill curves to the left my mate joins me to observe the guards green flag "Right Away". All doors closed, at the booked

forward its 'Jack in the box' characteristics are explained. The display reads 'Down branch', the facing crossover takes us to the left onto the down Weymouth line and then an immediate set of points transfer us onto the down branch, the track layout bends to the right, the advanced starter and Yeovil Town distant signal is first viewed from the drivers side, we are now along side our home depot and there giving me the thumbs up is my young guru Ken Fay. Frank has the regulator open to the first valve and the lever pulled back to 30% cut off, (percentage of steam admitted to the cylinders when the piston has completed 30% of its travel) feeling confident that my fire is adequate I resist the urge to have a shufti, we follow the River Yeo whilst to the right the bank steeps away to Wyndham Hill. (The track bed is now a designated walk way). The regulator is closed, touch of blower and the injector is on. Home signal off we go under the road and foot bridges

2-6-2T 4593 typical example of motive power used on Taunton branch from Yeovil
- Nick Wiley collection

TAUNTON DUTY No. 59.

4 P./S F. (45 X X Class)

—	Taunton	...6.50 a.m.	P
7.54 a.m.	Yeovil Pen Mill	—	
	C—Shunting 8.0 a.m. to 8.45 a.m.		
—	Yeovil Pen Mill	...9.56 a.m.	P
10.53 a.m.	Taunton	...5.50 p.m.	P
7. 0 p.m.	Pen Mill	...7.45 p.m.	P
9. 0 p.m.	Taunton	—	

Taunton Men.

TAUNTON DUTY No. 60.

45 XX Class.

—	Taunton	...9.45 a.m.	P
10.45 a.m.	Yeovil P.M. ...	...11.47 a.m.	F
11.52 p.m.	Yeovil T.	...12. 5 p.m.	F
12.10 p.m.	Yeovil Loco. ...	... 1.55 p.m.	∥
2. 0 p.m.	Yeovil P.M. ...	... 2.32 p.m.	P
3.40 p.m.	Taunton	—	

Taunton Men.

(1) Work and change to No. 518 at Taunton 8.35 a.m., work to depot.

Yeovil Men.

(2) Off No. 518, change at Taunton 8.35 a.m., work, assist requirements for 1.55 p.m.∥.

(3) 1st set on duty 1.0 p.m., perform requirements for 1.55 p.m.∥, work and relieved Taunton 3.40 p.m., work No. 518, 4.10 p.m.∥, etc., and relieved Yeovil T. 5.25 p.m.: (M.O.) as ordered: (M.X.) passenger to Yeovil Jc., relieve No. 561 at 6.20 p.m., work and relieved 8.15 p.m. and home passenger per 8.25 p.m.

Taunton Men.

(4) Prepare No. 518, relieve at 3.40 p.m.

departure time of 5.45pm the guard gives us the tip. My driver is across the footplate and creates his 25 inches of vacuum, as the brakes release their grip his left hand lifts the regulator, 0-6-0 pannier tank No. 3733 takes steam and we are on the move. Having swatted up on the engine duty I am confident that as the run to Taunton is only 65 minutes I should be able to cope, although the thought niggles away that I have no inkling as to the gradients, the length of sections, placement of signals and uppermost that changing of the single line "Authority to enter the next section" staff antic.

The starter signal when moving from the up platform at Pen Mill to the Taunton branch is my mate's side, As we pull

into the platform. Application of the vacuum brake and its gradual release has the brake gauge needle lifting as we come to a smooth halt.

The Town to Junction Branch is to our left in Number 2 platform with the resident "M7" tank in the shafts. No worries re exchanging the single line token as my mate informs me the signalman is walking down the platform from his box to make the swap in a relaxed manner. At 5.52pm my mate receives the tip, lifts the "big jet" (term for large vacuum ejector) the needles shoot up to 25 inches, touches the whistle, opens the reg. and we are off. Gazing across the tracks towards the Yeovil Town motive power main offices and train crews mess room it seemed incredible that it was less then three years ago that I signed on the M.P. dotted line.

The former LSWR main line to Yeovil Hendford reduced to a siding in the 1880s accompanies us as we move up the gradient to Hendford Halt. Throughout this initial trip

I am briefed on all aspects of layouts, gradients, signal posts shut off points and distances. This information will assist me in my deliberations as his fireman. This is my first brush with the term, that in future years would be so paramount, namely "Route Knowledge".

I see on pulling back the firebox door that the contents has burned through nicely, now is the time to put a few round her. "Shutting off for Hendford" warns my mate, on goes the injector and the firebox door is eased open, then "The bobby will be standing in the six foot to exchange the staff, I'll take it as slowly as I dare" I stretch over the side of the pannier, right hand holding the staff at six o'clock with left hand in a position to bring aboard the authority to enter the following section to Martock, all went well. Off the halt at 5.56pm we are on a rising gradient, to the drivers side is the Westland Aircraft Company's extensive works and airfield.

Although the old girl with the 96 tons in tow is vibrating in effort to respond to the demands of the regulator, my main concern is her steaming qualities which to my relief are giving me no problem. Cresting the top of the bank the reverser is pulled back to near mid gear, we arrive at Montacute Halt at 6.04pm. The platform is my side. I get the green flag and convey the tip "right away mate". Next stop Martock where Frank informs me we pass the Taunton to Yeovil service. I am informed that all the branch single line distant signals with the exception of Montacute are fixed at danger. The home signal is off, we clank over a level crossing, complete another exchange with the signalman, this time I find an iron shaped hoop containing a key in a pouch on my arm, I think what next? Martock has the distinction of a two platform layout. I also note a sizable freight yard with goods shed to match on my left. One minute station time and we are away. Four minutes from Martock and we arrive at Thorney and Kingsbury Halt with its adjacent milk concentration depot. Here Frank tells me is where the key within the single line token which I had received at Martock comes into play, it allows access to the milk factory siding which is gained via a set of points operated from the ground frame. There is a daily engine and brake van booked service departing from Pen Mill at 3.27pm solely for the collection of this depots milk and by products. At the waggle of the green flag. I call across the tiny footplate "right away mate". As per laid down instruction I look back along the train until we depart the platform. A short burst of power and in four minutes we are inside the Langport fixed distant. The Box is on my side. Frank comes across (no deadmans handle to bother him) beaming a smile and points out the catching apparatus that I have to dispatch the circular token and pouch onto, instinct wished me to toss it fun fair style. Leaning out, frame in left hand pannier tank in right I place it dead centre over the catcher for the bobby to collect.

It is 36 minutes from departure at Pen Mill, four single line sections and seven stations and halts have been served, total distance near 13 miles, true, doesn't seem that important, but you would not have suggested that to the hundreds of Somerset users who viewed this branch as not only a way of life but hugely critical in the field of transportation to the larger areas of employment.

This is 1955, the station of Langport serves a small compact Somerset town, its importance however to the large farming community cannot be overstated, this railhead handles the vast majority of incoming farm machinery and animal feed, transported in an array of differing wagons. The area supply of coal and oil is sated by rail, out going loaded traffic is considerable. Spinning the enemy, i.e. time, forward to the present, I often motor from our adopted town of Fareham to our county town of Taunton via the A378 which tapers to its narrowest passing through Langport. It takes two medium sized road transporters from opposing directions to affect a full stop. The expedience of decisions with precious little thought to the future was surely wrong when it was decided to cut off the life blood from the railways to such country communities.

Our little tank engine is more then cooperative, short bursts of firing around the box has the boiler pressure gauge needle hovering just short of the "Lifting the safety valves" red line, now full of confidence in the use of the injector my aim of not allowing the boiler contents gauge level to fall below three quarters is achieved, regular use of the, linked to injector spray, i.e. pep pipe keeps the dust to a minimum. Later in my firing career I will encounter situations where it is impossible to stifle choking coal dust.

The departure time from Langport West is 6.21pm. I get the guards tip. "Right away mate". Frank responds by giving our steed steam, we pass the starter, my attention is now drawn to the advance starter and Curry Rivel distant signals that are located on the same post, both are off. Now flying at all of 25 mph, our impetus takes us on and through the Junction passing the signal box which stands on the down side to our right, and out onto the direct Great Western main line from Paddington to Plymouth. Next stop Athelney which all students of history will recognise as where King Alfred burnt the cakes. Now well and truly onto the Somerset levels, the country either side is bisected by drainage ditches and Willow trees and is prone to severe flooding, hence the distinct elevation of this section of track. We are now cracking on, I am in my element sliding open the firebox door and firing up as if there is no tomorrow, Frank however brings me back to earth with the caution that we did not want to arrive at our county town with a box full of fire, I must curb the enthusiasm. The track is as one would expect, in keeping with the countryside, apart, I am told, for a short up gradient just prior to Taunton. I have just put the injector on, when a shout across the footplate warns me "Wouldn't like to argue with this one Colin" one stride and I'm across, in time to view the smoke box of an up fast as it blasts past. The rush of air is so tremendous that I am impressed that we had not been buffeted into the marshes. "What service is that?" "One of our Kings with 12 on" is the haughty reply. I realised that Frank would have been as proud as a Peacock to have being on that footplate with the regulator and responsibility in his hands, at that moment I felt for him as I recalled his stifled retrospective ambitions.

We have now been travelling full pelt at around 35 to 40 mph for all of four miles. The "Wooper", (name given by me to the "Woop, Woop" call sign of the western automatic train control device) informs us that Athelney down distant is at caution, the driver lifting an ATC equipment attached toggle cancels the warning and in so doing nullifies an automatic brake application. The sticks, sorry, forgot we are on the Western, boards, both inner and outer are off, the regulator is closed and the train vacuum brake is gradually applied, to enable my mate to have a clear field of vision I have the fire box door cracked open with the blower off its face thus lifting any smoke drift.

The 1950s time book allows nine minutes for the five mile section from Langport West to Athelney, hardly ground shattering, but suitable timed for a 0-6-0 tank engine that was way past its sell by date. But as I have intimated, weighing in at less the 50 tons but exuding a tractive effort of over 22,000 lbs their strength was out of proportion to size, however their ungainliness was not becoming in passenger mode. Bringing our train to a halt Frank comes across the footplate and points out the holding bracket that contains the single line staff which I have to collect as we pass the signal box. I under go an instructive brief on the deviation we are to take from the London Paddington to Exeter via Castle Cary main line to link up with the main Paddington to Exeter via Bristol line at Durston. At 6.31pm I relay the guards tip, slam the firebox door shut and look back along the length of the train as we pull out of the station, gathering the staff which gives us possession of the single line from its prop adjacent to the signal box I note its location, give the thumbs up to my driver and secure it. Frank shouts over the racket that I should take note of the signal post positioned between the down and up main line, it held aloft three boards, the right side one was off and cleared our pathway to the branch whilst the higher and centre controlled the down main, the exit from main to down loop was authorised via the left board. We go over the level crossing (Location check, the road is a spur from the A361 and links the villages of Athelney and Stoke St Gregory) and branch off to the right. No sooner

has the reverser been pulled up then the regulator is closed, ½ mile and we arrive at the isolated single line halt of Lyng, not seeing any sign of habitation I enquire as to its significance, evidently it serves the two hamlets of West and East Lyng. As the single platform is the driver's side he accepts the guards tip.

Before we make our getaway, a humorous, at least from the footplate viewpoint, true incident which occurred a few years latter comes to mind concerning this small halt. Yeovil Town driver Harry Churchill and his mate Mick Guppy whilst working the earliest service to Taunton came to an abrupt halt at Lyng, it was mid summer.

Many ladies wearing their much admired late 50s style flared dresses on their way to their employment at Taunton stood on that platform. Problem was the engine tanks had been fed with an overdose of water softener pellets and to bring the matter to an embarrassing crescendo our mate Mick had allowed his boiler control to go decidedly awry. As the service jerked to a halt the safety valves fed by the surge of brown boiler water lifted to the heavens, what chaos ensued. The cloud of spray, thankfully much cooled by the height it had been propelled fell onto the innocent and unsuspecting intending passengers. After taking the footplate crew apart with their justified criticisms it was about turn and off home, dresses and hair ruined. The claims department were put on overtime such was the deserved compensation.

Five minutes later and 1¾ miles further Frank is indicating for me to come across to his side, "Durston Col, signalman is going to be leaning out of his box to collect the staff" slowing with the clanking of the side rods getting more defined, I reach up and hand it over. We move out from the branch onto the down main side of the island platform,

Mr Tom Hall, the last shed master of Yeovil Town MPD in 1963. During his time as shed master he managed over one hundred and fifty staff.
- D. Brown collection.

Reg Barllett - Roster clerk at Yeovil MPD retired 1964 - Mike Cement collection

having joined the Great Western Paddington and the midlands to Penzance via Bristol and Exeter main line. I am informed that should the down main be occupied we would have been routed into the loop therefore occupying the other island platform face. I remark on the friendly acknowledgement I had received from the one porter. Frank tells me that Joe Brett is a lovely chap and the following week I would likely meet him as our duty would involve shunting the yard, I said that it would be a pleasure.

I was always to remember that so innocent introduction with in the context of the following week. Showing apprehensions as to whether I should fire up again, the information is supplied that we have less than six miles with Creech St Michael Halt intervening before the county town. The line we now occupy is the down Bristol, with a mischievous grin I am told that we would almost immediately part company with the adjoining up Bristol and pass over the up and down Paddington to Penzance via Westbury main lines. In answer to my look of astonishment. "Yes Colin the same set of tracks we left at Athelney, you are in for an engineering treat". We are climbing an embankment which gives way to the metalwork and girders of Cogload Flyover, sure enough from my side of the footplate I am looking down on the double track West of England to Paddington main line stretching away to the east, I catapult across the footplate to view the continuation of the afore mentioned view with the up Bristol combining to it's right, we now descend, ahead I see an array of junction signalling. Frank noting my confusion clears the air thus, we are on the down relief, to our right the roads run down main, up main and up relief.

The impetus gained covering the down gradient from the flyover has us getting up quite a lick of speed, the A.T.C. bell gives a shrill ring confirming that the down relief distant for the junction is off. A pull back of the firebox door lever has me deciding not to fire up. "Come across, you won't see the like of this on your Southern, Creech water troughs" then "Our fast's don't have to stop for a top up we pick it up at speed" how could I counter that. The bristling pride at being an G.W.R. engineman was tangible, the troughs positioned in the centre of the tracks stretch for over 400 yards, I am told that when on approach the fireman lowers his engine's scoop over 4,000 gallons is deposited into the tender, evidently the troughs are replenished via a pumping station from the near side canal. Water troughs were not an option for the Southern as the main line motive power had sufficient water carrying capacity for the mileage involved. I do however recall an incident involving a foreign (Other region) 4-6-0 Standard class "5" that had been serviced in Yeovil Town depot, who ever had screwed (put the hand brake on) her down had chosen the wrong wheel and in so doing had lowered the water scoop, along came the preparation set of men and were surprised to find the tender hand brake off, they found out why when the driver blew off the brake and opened the regulator, the effort to move was thwarted as the lip of the scoop lifted the track.

I return to the duty in hand. My mate slams the regulator shut and announces "running into creech" on goes the injector with the ever coupled slight opening of the firebox door we coast for some distance before the vacuum brake brings us to a halt without a hint of a jerk. Since leaving Pen Mill I have made a point of noting our volume of passengers, it has surprised me how popular this service is. It makes me realise that although I am now attached to a depot that works a branch line, this route is as important to its customers as the main line is to theirs. Our guard waggles the green. I call across "Right Mate". Away on time at 6.44pm we are booked in Taunton at 6.51pm. The reverser is pulled up and the rattling door rattles no more. The ATC gives off its cautionary siren for Taunton East Junction, regulator shut, firebox door opened etc. Injector on and cut back, Frank explains the signals as we come up to them, every signal appertaining to ourselves on the down relief is repeated in like on the down main, the cross over signals down relief to down main with the left signal to Taunton East Loop plus the distant for Taunton West and vice versa on the main is expressed on gantries, the home signal is off and we are running in on the down relief.

Had attention been given to happenings on my doorstep during my basic education it would have been obvious that Taunton was an important rail head as it had heavy freight and passenger connections to Barnstaple, Minehead and Chard, it was also a prominent calling point on the Great Western main line route to the West of England. Our guard pulls me back to reality by announcing that he will see us in the mess room. Frank fills me in on the procedure, firstly under the jurisdiction of a passenger shunter we pull forward to the water column for a top up. On the tank top to receive the arm as it is swung around and getting use to the equalisation of water content concern, I have both side tank lids open before the request is put. I am surprised at the quantity of water used and begin to understand the drivers concerns. With both side tanks full to the brim and the boiler gauge glass level at ¾ full we prepare to run round the empty stock. Detached we move forward over a ground signal, it clears, bunker first back through the station and up over the cross over, ground signal clears and we are back engine first to be re-coupled to our charge. Shunter takes up position in the leading brake van and relays via arm signals the authority to propel forward. Over the ground signal that controls the movements from down relief to up relief. It clears and we repeat the previous movement. Given the stop signal when our tail end is over the ground signal, we obey the tip to propel the stock back into No. two carriage siding.

Each single shunt movement is controlled by subsidiary ground signals. I recognise that a driver's route knowledge had to be comprehensive. At certain points there is more then one ground signal positioned on top of each other, they read ground signals top to bottom apply to lines left to right. Should an extremely unlikely event occur, such as a signalman pulling off the wrong route movement, the driver would not take it, it would be recognised why the engine is stable, on will go the signal, the footplate men would observe the points move as the correct road is set up and signal cleared, often a signalman will pull back his sliding window and acknowledge the error, after all when the chips were down we were a complete team.

Here without hesitation I leap forward 40 years. I am completing a fast electric service from Waterloo to Portsmouth and have had problems with the braking system, subsequently having been brought to a stand at Havant home signal I decide to request advice via the signalman. I enact the conversation. "signalman, would you please get in touch with the mechanical and electrical fitters and ask the following" signalman "sorry mate, I'm Railtrack and you're South West Trains and I'm reminding you that the longer you stay at that signal the more it will cost your company". Togetherness? Can anyone come up with a more detrimental vital industrial contrast?

We make our way to the platform mess room for a scrub up. After grub and a shared can of tea I feel pleased and confident that my first short passenger trip had gone well. We are rostered to work the last service which departs Taunton at 8.20pm back to Pen Mill. My mate is well into a chin wag as I make my way back to our pannier, on the footplate I'm chuffed to bits to find my plan has worked a treat, one side of the small firebox has burnt through, pulling the clinker shovel aboard the residue is quickly despatched, clean fire thrown over and the worst of that side follows, then on the floor with firing shovel I rake away the dead ash leaving little evidence of misdemeanour (The head shunter would have gone bonkers had he seen me dumping ash on his six foot). "Frankie" boy back on board creates the vacuum, our guard drops the tap. (testing the brake by destroying the continuous brake from the guards van) Frank has no idea how clean my made up fire really is. The two exit ground signals giving us access to the up relief are cleared and at 8.10pm we are stood in the up relief platform waiting for the off.

As the return leg is to be bunker first I give the contents a severe soaking. Even though this is mid summer I have a lit head lamp on the centre buffer beam. At 8.20pm he receives the tip and opens the regulator. The return leg of this duty is, apart from the novelty of running through the halts of Creech St Michael and Lyng, a reverse repetition of the 5.45pm out. My apprehensions at firing to this class of engine whilst working bunker first are proven to be unfounded. Throughout the trip I am subjected to a much appreciated running commentary, particular importance is attached to location points, e.g. "See that tree just before the over bridge? that is where I shut off, she'll run in with time to spare from there" also " I'll have to drop her over here as there's a bit of a bank for a mile or so" all these snippets are vital regards familiarising ones self with a route. I could not have been booked with a better tutor. We are across the Somerset levels, have left Langport and Thorney Halt in our wake and are running into Martock with four stops and eight miles to go, maintaining boiler pressure has been no problem, suppose it could have been had I not sorted out the dirt on the fire bars. Martock Level crossing gates closed to road traffic, starter signal off and as the guard gives a blast on his whistle Frank creates the vacuum and responds with a pull on our whistle cord, the lever is in full reverse gear, the regulator is opened to the first valve.

I am in position over my mate's side in order to exchange the single line token which has been our authority to have sole possession of the section from Langport to Martock for like jurisdiction over the section to Yeovil Hendford. As we gather momentum I allow my fire to run down for cleaning on arrival at the depot. Sat on my small tip up

seat it's up the bank to the village station of Montacute, injector on before the regulator is closed. Receiving the tip "Right away mate" and we are into the steepest gradient of the trip. I think Frank had second thoughts regarding my fire as he belted the day lights out of our little beast only pulling the reverser up three notches from 75% cut off, this act to my amateur mind had an adverse effect, as I imagined this treatment would have resorted in a depreciation of steam with the pressure gauge waltzing back, no way, for as soon as we hit the top of the bank and the regulator was closed our old lady lifted her safety valves to the heavens. Remark from across the cab. "That woke her up Col". Again the staff is exchanged, Hendford Halt starter is off, as we pull away our exhaust beats are crisp and singular but become rapid. This section is a short down hill run into Yeovil Town, the dampers are closed, the firebox door is partly opened in an effort to knock her back in steam, we are soon racing towards the Town signal box for the speediest token changeover yet, the signalman is standing on the platform edge to the far side of his box, leaning over the cab side we make a clean and in my case much relieved change over, as we slow to a stop my mates face is a picture of mirth, he explains that I had shown contrasting expressions, one of deep concern and the next second when I glanced at him with the incoming staff in my hand my face was beaming.

I remembered this change over when some years later I was booked a Taunton duty, my driver was a passed man (passed to drive fireman) and a close personal friend, we decided to try a not very responsible experiment. Basically it was to see whether the signalman would pull out of a change over at an over the top approach. The Town box was chosen, I hung over the side staff in hand determined not to flinch, our speed was such that Ken would have to drop the handle as soon as we passed the change over spot. We certainly had our comeuppance as the signalman quite rightly withdrew from our silly game, which left me in the deserved position of having to run cap in hand back up the platform to make a chasten apology and the change over. Think I made the lame excuse that my driver must have mistaken his braking point.

On arrival at Pen Mill the single line staff is given up to the platform foreman, now under the authority of the passenger shunter we deposit the empty stock into the carriage sidings for over night cleaning, shunter breaks the vacuum pipes, driver responds to the bellowed request "ease up", followed by "pull away". Still light, no need of a lamp on the front, we pull up, on the deck pull a set of points, jump on as the footplate comes level and we are through the yard and into the depot. The fire was about right for cleaning so fair dues I have reason to be satisfied with this first Taunton trip. The ten mile cycle ride to home will bring this eventful day to closure.

Duties to Taunton were to become a regular feature during my nine years as a registered fireman at Pen Mill and Yeovil Town motive power depots. Not all trips were to be such a snip as my first one. However, it seems to me that the "Ruffins", as they were so endearingly called, occupy a receptive niche in the memory stakes.

CHAPTER 20

'DOWN THE PAN' FOR STEAM

One in particular springs to the fore. Relieving a pair of Taunton men that had worked the first leg of a Minehead to Yeovil duty, came off the train at Taunton for engine requirements and the mandatory top up, the usual change over banter was exchanged. We had a preferred engine a class "2" 2-6-0 Standard tank, known within the fireman ranks as a "Mod piece of kit". On this occasion however I was to curse my luck. We were booked 4.10pm light engine from Taunton Depot to work the 4.22pm passenger back across the branch. Opening the fire box door had me suggesting to my driver that he should think about requesting a fresh engine as the fire seemed to be deficient of brightness, his comment after having a look was "All that wants is a good lifting with the dart". I had a few years firing under my belt and my perceptions were that this fire had not been cleaned and that we were in for a mauling, also the fact that the bunker had been coaled with the dreaded egg shaped briquettes did not auger well for the trip in hand. We were now attached and waiting for the off, although it was not the done thing whilst in the platform I had the blower well off its face. Thankfully for a reason we were ignorant of we had a delay, so by the time we had the right away I had boiler pressure up to the red mark and a glass full of water, first stop a stones throw at under three miles, with the amount of coaxing that fire had she should have been blowing her head off, fact was she had come back in steam, as soon as he shut her off, I whacked on both the blower and the injector, and in that order.

We left the up Bristol at Durston and cut across the branch to join the up Paddington at Athelney. By this time even my "all she needs is a good lifting with the dart" driver is showing signs of throwing a wobbly. Stood in the station at Athelney he unbuckles his pride and confesses that "It looks as if you were right". My retort is "Only one thing for it mate you will have to nurse her all the way to Yeovil, and if you insist on me using the dart all it will do is disturb the top of the fire which is the only part that is giving us steam". My thinking that the bed was dead was confirmed at Yeovil when she was eventually squared up. What a struggle ensued, talk about nursing her, the Standard was pulled up on 15% cut off as we trickled along the main to Curry Rivel and Langport, at every station we delayed our start until we had sufficient fuel in the bin to set us on our way with hope, by the time we got to Yeovil Hendford we had all but given up the ghost, it was as previously explained all down hill, but we had to wait as we had sufficient pressure to release the brakes, booked relief at Yeovil Town my driver used the signalman's phone to request a change of engine.

Did we cause disruption, running 30 minutes late was enough to blow the strict timing of a single line branch completely out of the water. The powers that be arranged for us to stop short of Yeovil Town Box, the requested fresh engine with the crew that was booked to relieve us on board reversed onto our front end, I did the attachment, the brake was created through the train, then destroyed, I then split the vacuum pipes between engine and train, next agreed move was for our failed engine to be pulled forward, points reversed and with ignominy we were propelled forward and unceremoniously cut off. We fortunately had sufficient steam to move forward onto the depot disposal pit. The episode was an embarrassment to ourselves on the footplate, but in all honesty we were on a sticky wicket from the moment my driver came to his ill considered decision, there is no way other drivers would have taken that chance, in fact the majority would have walked into the shed foreman's office at Taunton and played merry hell.

There was always that element of rivalry between the Great Western and the Southern and the query remained, were we set up? I was not made privy to my driver's report, but I was perplexed when the redoubtable footplate inspector Sam Smith had a word with me. I told him the exact truth. His response put me at ease "I've read the report of the disposing set, the fire was in such a state that it had to be thrown out and the engine relit, my opposite number on the Western will have to do a bit of digging." Good old Sam. I was to endure other pairings with this particular driver, one such duty makes me break out into a sweat such was his poor route knowledge over a section he had signed as being fully competent.

My Driver Frank Smith had advised me in all aspects of the Taunton road and at the end of that first week I felt fully confident.

The following week we are on the roster that Frank had alluded to when we spoke of the porter at Durston. The signing on time of 8.55am, in fact any time between 8.00am and 9.30am would be known throughout my career as "office hours". This duty I was assured would be a little snip, also there would be an added bonus for me, I would be able to use the train service from my home to get me to and from work. However the happenings during this 'snip' day would have ramifications that are still very much with me as I write.

The date, 27/7/55. the weather was perfect. We are "light engine" to Castle Cary. Our 0-6-0 pannier tank No 3733 is as diagrammed prepared for us. All I had to do was push the fire over the box and liven it up. At the booked departure time of 9.05am the depot exit signal is cleared, a touch of the whistle and we on our way bunker leading. This is yet another first time route and duty for me, Frank again excels in his running commentary on all points from a route learning aspect, the distant signals for the two intermediate stations of Marston Magna and Sparkford are off so there is no hesitation in our progress. The ATC gives off its cautionary warning as we approach Castle Cary distant signal, outer and inner home signals are cleared on approach, coming off the up Weymouth to Paddington we move across the junction and join the up main west of England to Paddington, we pass the signal box which is positioned to our left having covered the 12 miles from the depot well inside the allotted schedule. Now at a standstill my mate calls me across to his up platform side and introduces me to, what he describes as a "Backing Signal". It has a rectangular indicator box set below the signal arm, with the signal in the off position a indicator will prescribe one of four set routes. Down goods loop, down Weymouth, down Taunton and goods shed. Frank reckons it's a rarity. The signal arm drops and the "Jack in the box" reads "Goods Shed" now looking to the front our regulator is lifted off its face and we move with high pitched creaks forward, coming to a halt outside the shunters cabin. The family 'railway' kicks in and I am introduced to the resident head shunter and his mate. The duty allows 40 minutes to sort out the compact goods shed and yard, this accomplished our engine and tea can is topped up and we are at the yard exit signal ready for the off. Our load is a mixture of coal, box wagons and war department traffic for the government sidings at Dimmer, there is also an additional member of staff in the guise of travelling shunter. The road is cleared and hand signals are exchanged as we move from the Castle Cary up goods yard through the crossover onto the down Taunton.

requirement to enter the Dimmer sidings meets that criteria. Our shunter operates the ground frame and in conjunction with the signalman we receive the authority to make what can only be described as a decidedly dodgy and grinding entry, to say the spur and siding was in a sorry state would have been an understatement. After cutting off the van and non government traffic we leave the spur road and literally creep forward into the depot, off shunt the two government wagons and reverse on to the van. In my entire footplate career I was never to encounter such an unstable length of track, although I was to happen upon privately owned sidings at Chichester where yours truly exploded two box wagons loaded with flour into the atmosphere.

Pulling forward over the ground signal we then propel our short freight onto the down main, all aboard, Alford starter is off, the usual exchange of hand signals and we are away. On our journey to Durston we shunt the small yards, which are situated on the up sides at both Keinton Mandeville and Charlton Mackrell, their layouts are identical and comprise a dock (short end road), goods shed and a further siding,

0-6-0T 3733 on the Durston Castle Cary pick up goods trains at Somerton. 23.05.1959
- John Fox collection

YEOVIL DUTY No. 520.

4 F.T. (57 X X Class)

—	Yeovil Loco.	...	... 5.45 a.m. ‖
5.50 a.m.	Yeovil Jc.	...	... —
F—Shunting 5.55 a.m. to 6.50 a.m.			
—	Yeovil Jc.	...	... 7. 5 a.m. F
7.30 a.m.	Hendford	...	... 7.53 a.m. ‖
7.58 a.m.	Yeovil Loco.	...	... 9.10 a.m. ‖
9.40 a.m.	Castle Cary	...	... —
F—Shunting 9.40 a.m. to 10.30 a.m.			
—	Castle Cary	...	...10.50 a.m. F
1.18 p.m.	Durston	...	..., 1.30 p.m. F
4. 0 p.m.	Castle Cary	...	... 4.10 p.m. ‖
4.35 p.m.	Yeovil Loco.	...	... 9.23 p.m. ‖
9.50 p.m.	Castle Cary	...	... —
F—Shunting and banking 9.50 p.m. to 3.45 a.m.			
—	Castle Cary	...	... 3.45 a.m. ‖
4.10 a.m.	Yeovil Loco.	...	... —

Yeovil Men.

(1) 1st set (M.O.) on duty 3.5 a.m., prepare Nos. 521 and 518, prepare for 5.45 a.m. ‖, work and prepare and work No. 503 and work and relieved in depot 7.50 a.m., prepare and work No. 503 and relieved 10.50 a.m.

(2) M.O.—Off No. 536 (Sun.) perform requirements for 9.10 a.m. ‖.

(3) 1st set (M.X.) on duty 4.15 a.m., relieve in depot, perform requirements, work and change to No. 514 at Yeovil Jc. at 5.50 a.m., work and dispose.

This first leg to the W.D. sidings is what I would term as a 'short shunt'. During it as Frank gave me the run down on this Castle Cary to Durston route and its history, my mind focused back to my learned Driver Arthur Rattue and his résumé appertaining to the doomed Plymouth to Waterloo boat train crash at Salisbury on July 1st 1906. I am informed that this line, termed as the "New Line" opened to traffic on the day after, namely the second of July of the same year, thus reducing the Great Western route mileage from London to Plymouth via Bristol by 20 miles from its original 246 miles. The LSWR distance was then almost on par at 230 miles. The understandable rivalry between the two companies over the lucrative Transatlantic Liner Passenger and Mails was acknowledged but on no account could it have contributed to the Salisbury disaster.

The box at Alford opens on an as required basis and our

plus for me an unexpected feature for such humble yards, namely two ground signals which give excess via crossovers to both the up and down main. All of ten miles along the new line and we are shunting at one of the many ancient capitals of Wessex, the town of Somerton, there is a down and up goods loop, we stop over a ground signal controlled crossover, it clears and our guard hand signals us back into the up platform line, ground signal off Frank throws the reverser into fore gear, opens the pannier's regulator and we pull forward into the up yard, a sharp bout of shunting ensues, each road has its empties sorted out even the padlocked Dorset Farmers siding is invaded, we leave the, sorted out loaded and empty wagons in the up sidings for the latter in the day pick up freight. Now stood at the yard exit signal I prepare the fire for the ten mile section along the down main to Athelney. During the shunting operations I felt an unimportant bystander as the cream of the Western Region motive power thunder along both sets of track with their full loads.

Looking back towards the station my eyes are riveted on the cab of an approaching "Castle", I am in awe, it appears to oscillate as it roars past us heading towards Taunton. Frank brings me back to earth with the shattering gambit "We follow that one". Ground signal clears, whistle touched, reciprocal wave with the guard and we pass through the crossover onto the down main, our 0-6-0 and six wagons get into a canter as we leave the cleared advanced starter and with a long

4-6-0 Castle Class, 7020 Gloucester Castle on the 12.15pm Plymouth - Paddington passing Somerton. 23.05.1959 - John Fox collection

whistle blast pass through the 1,054 yard Somerton Tunnel. Our load is so light my fire needs little attention. The boiler water level is kept at the ¾ glass mark, leaving behind the halts of Long Sutton and Langport East we pass through Curry Rivel Junction and are united with the Yeovil Pen Mill branch line. The Somerset "flat lands" abound either side. Athelney and with the pick up of the single line staff we are into the previously described scenario to Durston.

Into the goods yard we have a relaxed and together banter with the shunters, after which we are into the shunting with a vengeance. The adage "Sooner we get the job done, the longer we shall have for tea" was much to the fore. However the at hand situation of normal and standard practise was about to be shattered by a most horrible and violent episode.

CHAPTER 21

AWFUL TRAGEDY AT DURSTON

Lyng Halt viewed from the last train in operation. June 1964 - Nick Wiley collection

Yard cleared of unwanted empties, loaded goods placed in order for latter despatch and we are having a relaxed brew up on the footplate, Durston down bay platform is two roads over from our position, all is peaceful. Suddenly we are aware of an eerie cry or howl emanating from the platform area. Frank expresses the thought that it is kids playing about but agrees that I should investigate, onto the ballast and across the foot crossing I look along the island down main platform edge.

There is a shape which I initially discern to be mail bags moving in the breeze, walking up the four foot I get closer and instantly freeze in panic. Lying between the platform and the running rail was the person that only the previous week my mate had described as a lovely man. Porter Joe Brett. The dear man had lost both his hands which lay crushed on the line, one leg was also severed, and the other was still attached but clinging to his trunk via his long pants. Glancing along the track and observing a down fast heading our way dispelled any tendency to numbness. Lifting Joe's broken body I heave it up on to the platform, jump up and pull it in clear then straight back down onto the track, race across both sets of roads, onto the up platform, straight into the Station Masters Office. I can see him now sat at his desk mouth wide open. I grab the phone off its cradle and call 999, "ambulance and police, emergency Durston station" plus short description. The S.M. goes white as I quickly explain my panic and haste, as I leave his office the down fast is disappearing towards Taunton. Over on the down platform two platelayers are beside Joe with the signalman approaching, we kneel beside him but there is little we can do. The Head shunter who according to the signalman is a St Johns Ambulance Gold Medal holder takes one look and passes out cracking his head on the platform. Incredibly Joe is repeating in a faint voice "What have I done?".

Durston Porter Joe Brett died on his journey to the hospital. The Ministry of Transport Enquiry which I attended was held at Durston on the 29th of September. It was never established how Joe came to be on the track. It was however a fact that the 11.21am ex-Yeovil Pen Mill to Taunton service departing Durston at 12.13pm was the last train that Joe saw away. An addition to the conundrum was that he practised a strict aversion to crossing the track, always taking the long way around via the authorised foot and barrel crossing. Whether he saw a carriage door on the catch or door handle not in the horizontal position and in securing it as the train was moving out, he somehow got entangled, or another theory was that in turning a two wheeled platform barrel he may have swung himself against the train? All would remain a mystery. Had however the rule appertaining to observing from the footplate until the train has left the platform been carried out, the accident could not have been prevented but it would have been witnessed. We were all deeply shocked and sickened by this awful tragedy. The reverse trip with the 1.30pm freight to Castle Cary and the subsequent return to our depot with the light engine was a subdued venture indeed.

British Transport Commission

BRITISH RAILWAYS

WR8701/56

XXXXXXXWXXXXXXXXXX

WESTERN REGION

DISTRICT MOTIVE POWER SUPERINTENDENT

TEMPLE GATE, BRISTOL

Telephone
BRISTOL 21001
Extension

Your Reference

W.1   7th. October 1955

Please quote this Reference :-

20950

Memo. to Fireman C.J.Robins, Yeovil

Porter Brett fatally injured
DURSTON, 27.7.55

       The District Motive Power Superintendent, Newton Abbot has informed me that at the Ministry of Transport Enquiry held at Durston on September 29th. the Inspecting Officer expressed his appreciation of the prompt way in which you acted after finding Porter Brett injured.

       Mr.Hall also wishes to add his appreciation, and I may say that I am pleased to learn that a member of the Bristol District Motive Power Department staff acted so promptly.

. . . .
Dist.M.P.Superintendent

Copy of complete memo

Durston station viewed from the last day of service of the Taunton - Yeovil branch. Showing where Porter Brett was fatally injured - Nick Wiley collection

CHAPTER 22

AN EERIE NIGHT BANKER EXPERIENCE

A further Cary duty I favoured which carried through on the same engine workings as the Durston goods was the night shunting and banking turn. Young Robins and cycle would leave Crewkerne on the 5.18pm ex-Sidmouth to Waterloo milk and parcels Train at 6.48pm, across Yeovil Junction up platform, into the van of the 7.14pm branch to the Town, over the foot crossing onto the Western up cess, burn rubber like some one possessed, and "Bike" and I would be by the cabin by 7.30pm. This would give me ample time for either a pint at our B.R. Staff Association Club, which was and still is conveniently positioned adjacent to Pen Mill station, or to a get to know you better session in the cabin. To be honest it was a snip. Engine prepared, it was a repeat of the first part of the previous week apart from utilising the lit head, tail and gauge glass lamps. Light engine to Cary, our booked freight shunting and banking period was diagrammed from 9.50pm until 3.45am. The "as usual" plan was to square up the yard shunting post haste. This achieved I would pull the fire back under the door, leave the rear ash pan damper open, ½ a glass of water in the boiler gauge, and much to a certain signalman's annoyance we were all three in the cabin having our unhurried supper. I was much the junior in age and therefore experience, but how clear I can recall those cherished memories of humour and togetherness, when we had talked ourselves out we would, as they say, "get our heads down".

The shunters cabin in the up yard at Castle Cary was sited next to the war-time built 85 lever signal box. (The previous box was demolished, with the signalman and the driver of the Durston goods losing their lives during the bombing and machine gunning of this strategic junction by a lone junkers 88 at 9.15am on the 3rd of September 1942). During our period of tenure we may be required to bank booked freight traffic on the up between Cary and Brewham, there is I discover an agreed procedure, whereby should assistance be required the signalman would open his sliding window and in "Wake Up" but amicable mould of voice inform us and the surrounding area that, i.e. "The Tavie's off Somerton and wants the banker". (for Tavie read Tavistock) The shunter would with equal clarity reply "Thanks Signalman". This week however we were warned by the shunter to keep our wits about us as "Mr Grumpy" was on nights and he would only give us one low key warning and if we didn't hear, then tough. We would be woken from the land of nod by the rumblings and vibrations of a braking freight in need of immediate assistance. I remember deciding that the scenario described was not for me as I could well imagine the impossibility of getting our little pannier around and on the mark in an instant.

Before the signalman had closed his window after giving the subdued warning I was out of the cabin and on the footplate, flare lamp lit and throwing shadows. I have pushed my fire over the grate. In no time she is making steam. Stood behind the signal box, looking to the rear and over the bunker, I have a good view as the paraffin lit head lamps make their seemingly lone appearance from under the road bridge, now the unmistakable silhouette of a Western 28xx class 2-8-0 escapes the gloom, as the engine comes level with us there is a shaft of sheer brilliance, akin to a searchlight, that lifts to the heavens at 45 degrees emanating from the footplate, shading my eyes the light cuts the drivers effigy to perfection, can not see my opposite number, he has to be sat over his own side, one thing is crystal clear, his fire must be white hot to give out such a glare through the open firebox door.

The heavily loaded goods of mixed traffic rumble by, I am thinking the procession is endless, then the guards van makes its appearance, I can just make out the guards image leaning over the van veranda. We are primed and rearing to go, the yard exit ground signal comes off, Frank gives her steam and we ease out from the yard onto the up main, moving gingerly along side the platform, my driver comes across to check and put me right regards the cleared calling on arm, which is attached to the starter and up goods loop signal gantry, the goods loop is utilised as a refuge should a freight be required to be "put away" pending the passing of a more critical service. The guard is down beside the ballast, swinging his lamp from side to side he guides us onto his van in the time honoured way, he is my side so I am relaying my perceptions of distances in wagon lengths as we close the gap, also as the van tail lamps have yet to be taken in Frank has the advantage of judging his easing on to the van to perfection, encountering pressure my mate eases forward until any slack between the wagons is absorbed. Frank has told me that the maximum permitted load over this section for a 28xx class is 392 tons with the proviso that should a driver consider it necessary the banker could be utilised even though the load is less.

I queried this and was given as an example, the train engine having steaming difficulties, slippery rail head conditions, sands not working, and with a grin, making sure the banker crew did not kip all night, and lastly, the crew wants to make a little "ovie" overtime. I scoffed and put it down as a joke but was at a later stage to realise my mate had meant it! Down at track side the guard hands me the loading, both having regained our respective positions, Frank reads out 55 for 460 tons. "Ready then" more a statement then question, simultaneously the whistle wire is pulled and the rendition of two crows exudes, we have not attached as we are parting company, as at Evershot, at the top of the bank, we strain and hear the answering call, the advance signal is off. Our regulator is half across its full travel with reverser in full fore gear, we are not moving, suddenly we move forward and gather momentum, my mate is making sure that contact is not lost and sure enough very soon our dash is arrested as the weight of tonnage makes itself felt, the incline to Brewham Box is a little under seven miles, it varies in intensity culminating with a section of 1 in 81. Thoughts of an easy trip are shattered as we are soon throwing up the rockets, looking to the front on a left hander the flashes of sharp beams as the lead engine fireman opens and closes his firebox door between firings light up the night sky, these panniers seem to relish the challenge. I must be doing something right as the boiler pressure hardly wavers when the injector is put on. Over the crescendo of clattering sounds Frank's raised voice informs me that "We're now on the level through Bruton station". I look over the side, we are along the platform and I note the starter is off but whether we are on the flat or not I haven't a clue. "How much further" I bellow "Another 4 miles, I'll tell you when to throw the shovel down, enjoying it?" I look up to answer but he has his head turned away, I reckon he's having a giggle. We plod away in the same vein with the regulator fully open and the reverser pulled up to about 40% until I am advised, "That will do Col". We keep going and I curb my desire to put more on by giving the footplate and bunker a swill down, we have ½ a glass of water and as the regulator is shut I nearly have a heart attack as the water level in the gauge glass all but disappears. I had not made allowance for the down gradient, the injector is on before we come to a halt. The guards van tail lamps are already fading as we hear the distinct whistle of the 28xx as the freight picks up speed on its way towards Westbury. I look back from my side and see a bright white light at buffer beam height, also a ground signal, pleased I didn't ask as it is an obvious ground signal controlled short up siding. Ground signal off and we travel a short distance along the cross over and stop – Brewham isolated signal box, can't believe it but the signalman is a mate of Franks and they decide to have a chin wag, the fact that we are still on the crossover does not matter one iota, then with a "Try and get us a rabbit before Friday" we are away whence we came, and we wonder why the Western lads called it 'Gods Wonderful Railway'.

After the bunker first rattle down the bank we get relief from

another can of nectar 'Tea'. We would bank as required until our booked time of 3.45am when we would return to the depot, where already washed off from the tank capacity test cocks it would be on my trusted steed for the ten miler back to home.

I was to enjoy many such diagrammed ventures at Castle Cary during the following nine years including the instance when stood in the centre of the shunters cabin with a freshly brewed can of tea. I unthinkingly swung the can with arm extended in a high circular motion, which was the habit, but NOT in a confined area, the gas pipe which fed the mantle lit lamp was snapped off as clean as a whistle as my high velocity can of tea belted it, the light from the fire and shunting lamps showed the dust been moved from the floor, seeing the inherent danger the shunter quickly shut off the gas main as my mate and I got stuck in the door frame such was our panic to exit. It seriously shook us when we contemplated the consequences had the cabin fire ignited the atmosphere. The head shunter had to make a report which we all signed. I remember it well, it read "Dear Sir, as the heavily laden (train number) up freight passed at speed by the shunters cabin the vibration was such that the gas pipe to the cabin light broke off" and he insisted that he sign the letter off in that condescending vogue of the time "Sir, I remain your most obedient servant" I sated my exception by signing below the other signatures.

Another situation of mirth was Yeovil Town driver Maurice Jerrard, known as "Laugh a minute Man" he knocked the blocks down at Brewham. His fireman whilst inspecting the residue spotted wood worm, Jerry agreed to his suggestion and put a piece of the rotten timber in with his report to support the claim, that he only touched them and they fell down-true!.

CHAPTER 23

FOOTPLATE CORDIALITY SPLIT ASUNDER

There was a solitary heavy freight booked to the Yeovil Pen Mill depot, namely the previously mentioned 9.45am ex-Bristol. My introduction to this duty stays in the memory stakes for all the wrong reasons. On the week in question Frank and I had to part company as we were both booked to cover holiday vacancies. Travelling pass to Westbury I found myself with a most amicable driver, Jack R, who like my regular mate did not show the slightest concern when I unburdened myself with the admission that I had not fired to a Western main line engine. "Don't worry about it son you will be O.K." was his reassuring comment.

Arriving at Westbury we made our way to the relief cabin, on entering my mind did a somersault back to the mess room scene at Salisbury, the warmth and togetherness of a closet of motive power men. I know memories play tricks but I'm sure there was upward of a dozen sets of men in there, evidently many were spare awaiting orders while the other sets were waiting to relieve. The taken for granted procedure was that the driver phone the Traffic Controller, which Jack did, and learnt that our charge was running

late and he would be informed as the freight was running in. Managing to find a couple of seats and settling to play the waiting game I noticed a distinct change in the level of banter and humour, not having the slightest clue as to why this should be I looked over my Daily Mirror and could not help but notice that many of those present were looking towards us in a hostile manner, feeling uncomfortable and apprehensive I just did not know how to handle the situation, and yet something told me that it involved my driver as my perceptions were that the anger was directed his way. The ice was well and truly broken however when I handed Jack my paper. Up shot a giant of a (I was later to learn) Westbury driver, across the cabin in a trice and glaring down at me, he demanded if I knew who I was offering the paper to. Now completely bewildered and decidedly alarmed I some how found my voice to answer "My driver who else". This man had lost control of himself and it was only through shouts of caution that he managed to find restraint, I recognised this slight relaxation and asked, "what the hell this was all about"?, the answer was thrown with terrific venom. "You son called that man driver, every man in this cabin knows him as a blackleg" This had me dumbfounded. Had I tried to eat a sandwich it would have been impossible to swallow it. Jack sat without saying a word, but I had a distinct impression that he was shaking in his shoes.

It was walking to the relieving point that he apologised for being the cause of such hatred. I could not find a satisfactory reply, but consoled myself with the knowledge that I was not part of it, another plus for my National Service.

The news from control has us on the departure end of the down main platform, our mood is sombre compared with the pre relief cabin buoyancy. The emergence of a grimy 49xx class "Hall" increases my apprehensions, climbing onto the footplate the fireman I'm relieving really makes my day by announcing "Best of luck nipper, she's a *******". I did not feel in the least offended by the 'nipper' remark as he must have been a good ten years older but the "expressive" bit hurt. We take water as I get the coal forward. On the footplate I am told that we have a full load. Now a familiarisation trip as the footplate layout is explained. My mate learns of the prophet of doom warning and suggests I get the irons down off the tender and give the fire a good old lift up. I resolve not to moan again as I reckon my mate wishes he had gone sick. She's right on the mark as the starter and distant for the next section clears. Long blast on the whistle and we take the strain, I heed my drivers advice and move over to his side so as to exchange hand signals with the guard.

```
        YEOVIL DUTY No. 521.

           4 F.T. (57 XX Class)

    —         Yeovil Loco.    ...   ... 5.30 a.m.  ||
5.35 a.m.    Yeovil Pen Mill ...   ... 5.50 a.m.  F
6.10 a.m.    Hendford     ...   ...   ...    —
        F—Shunting 6.15 a.m. to 8.10 a.m.
        F—Shunting 9.0 a.m. to 11.0 a.m.
    —         Hendford     ...   ...  11.20 a.m.  F
11.25 a.m.   Yeovil Town  ...   ...  11.35 a.m.  ||
11.40 a.m.   Yeovil Loco. ...   ...  12.35 p.m.  ||
   **         Yeovil T.,   ...   ...  12.43 p.m.  F
           (12.29 p.m. Yeovil Jc.)
12.48 p.m.   Pen Mill     ...   ...   1. 5 p.m.  ||
1.15 p.m.    Hendford     ...   ...   ...    —
        F—Shunting 1.15 p.m. to 6.0 p.m.
    —         Hendford     ...   ...  6.55 p.m.  F
8.40 p.m.    Westbury     ...   ... 9. 0 p.m.  F
11.17 p.m.   Yeovil P.M.  ...   ... 11.25 p.m.  ||
11.30 p.m.   Yeovil Loco. ...   ...   ...    —

Yeovil Men.
(1)  Off No. 520 (M.O.), No. 514 (M.X.),
     prepare for 5.30 a.m. ||.

(2)  1st set on duty 5.15 a.m., work, perform
     requirements for 1.10 p.m. ||.

(3)  2nd set on duty 12.20 p.m., work, relieved
     at Yeovil Town 7.0 p.m. and as ordered.

(4)  3rd set on duty 6.45 p.m., relieve at 7.0 p.m.
     work, dispose and as ordered.
```

The gradient from Westbury to the west via Castle Cary initially falls away for a mile at 1 in 170 which allows an impetus to be set up for the undulating climb to Brewham summit. Jack is filling me in on this in short snatches of conversation. I have used the feeder with intent slapping warm oil to every moving part of the firebox door, the lifting of the fire has had the desired effect, my mate has a shuftie and announces "Put some round her, she's burnt through a treat" I look back along the jinking 40 plus wagon load

and experience a beginners thrill, another plus is that I feel balanced and confident when lifting coal from the tender shovelling plate and despatching each load to its intended place. (I would shortly be brought down to earth with the realisation that getting back into the routine of firing left handed to Southern engines would be an entirely different kettle of fish).

Our route takes us through Clink Road which is the Junction for Frome, Woodlands, Witham and its branch connection to Merehead stone quarry and Cranmore. Between bouts of firing, pulling coal forward, injector usage, keeping the footplate tidy and general observations, particularly back along the length of the train on left handers, my curiosity is aroused in observing my drivers technique in usage of the screw operated reverser and the regulator. I am made aware of the differing gradients but in spite of the considerable slack between wagons should they be allowed to buffer up I have not felt the slightest snatch. Later with experience I would recognise this as good driving skills, coupled, 'No pun intended' with an equally skilled brakeman. Suspicions founded on the remarks made when I gained the footplate at Westbury have been unfounded, in fact the opposite is occurring as she lifts her safety valves on the Brewham incline.

Having passed the 108 mile post (from Paddington) we breast the summit. Jack explains the advantage that a vacuum head of wagons has when working in conjunction with the engine brake in controlling the rate of descent, and also, should the guard be a proficient performer with the vans brake, thereby aiding the load to the rear of the brake controlled front portion to string out. (taunt couplings) The danger of a snatch or a more dangerous brake away when power has to be applied would be minimal. We are now dropping down the initial section which is one of 1in 81. The complete scene is an utter contradiction to the terrific flaying that our 4-6-0 was enduring just minutes ago on the reverse gradient. The whole purpose of my drivers concentration is now focused on retardation, and this is my first brush with it. I would in time form the view that the braking element required a greater skill then the opposing application of power when hauling.

Watching the vibrations of the vacuum gauge needle as it registers the applied application, I recognise that the progress of our load is as harnessed, should a distant signal be observed at caution there would be no sweat in bringing our charge under complete control to affect a halt at the stop signal. Bruton distant is off. Jack noticing that I am watching him like a hawk, calls me over and gives me an insight (which would forever stay with me) into his particular braking technique. I have a demonstration into the art of gradual brake release which is described as critical, especially in this particular location, as the descent of 1 in 93 terminates abruptly and changes to one which is dead level on gaining Bruton stations eastern boundary, this continues through to its western extremities, when it drops away again at 1 in 98, therefore a freight could occupy three conflicting gradients, I am set a conundrum "What do you think would be the consequence of releasing the engine and vacuum head brake application in one action?" My reply was probably "big trouble".

The consequences were described in graphic detail thus "blowing off my brake" (creating, on W R locomotives 25 inches of vacuum) with the large ejector would enable the head of the train to literally run away, this would cause such a massive snatch to the rear, which is held in a anchor like grip by the screwed down guards brake van, that there would likely be a brake away". The vacuum brake gauge train pipe needle had shown me that we were applying ten inches of brake, it had now been gradually released to five inches, and was held steady at 20 inches allowing five inches of brake application through out the engine and fitted head.

We have now left Bruton and its level segment, there has been no discernable check, pull or pressure from the rear in spite of the three differing gradients. When in future I would find myself propelled against the boiler front or jerked back, at times with violence, against the tender through lapses in either the guard or drivers braking techniques, I would remember Jack R.

Keeping our tonnage under control is the main priority as we continue the descent. As the gradient levels out Jack gradually lifts his vacuum and as Castle Cary Junction distant is spotted in the off position the brake needle is at 25 inches, there is I notice hesitation until the slightest of tugs is felt from the still braked guards van, then with the train well strung out and speed therefore reduced the regulator is opened slightly and closed, opened and closed, until he recognises that the slack between the wagons has been exhausted, then the regulator is lifted to half of its full travel or to the first valve as constant power is applied. We are now advancing alongside Castle Cary down goods loop and adjacent sidings.

Winning the football pools would have given me no more satisfaction then I felt at that moment, I had just put down the shovel, my mate has taken a seasoned shufti at my firebox contributions and given it the thumbs up. Sitting on my tip up seat and leaning over the side I take in the view along the framings, the home signal is off as is the left of the two high gantry positioned starter signals to the west of the station. A hearty tug of the whistle wire extracts acknowledgement of long standing friendships betwixt Jack and the Cary signalman. The whole situation is a "buzz" for this 20 year old as we leave the Paddington to Penzance via Taunton main line at Castle Cary Junction and thrust into the near 40 mile branch to Weymouth. Apart from the fact that we are heading a fully loaded freight as opposed to my previous experiences of running light engine, I feel confident that at least I know where I am, never the less my mate advises me that we are a dozen miles from Pen Mill and that the road was easy running. We would, and this is going to be an about turn for me, require the banker. I recall thinking in an adolescent vein "Great". My initial nervousness when having to use the injectors has now evaporated and I feel confident.

The cleared distant signals give us an unhindered run through the intermediate stations of Sparkford and Marston Magna. Jack is now bringing his ship under control by slightly bringing down his large vacuum brake handle thus allowing air to enter the train pipe thereby applying appropriate brake pressure to engine and vacuum head.

There is no discernable pressure from the loose fitted portion of the train for reasons as explained. We pass Pen Mill down distant, with progress curbed to around 15 mph, the outer home is dropped as we near it, I note that the vacuum is allowed to drift up to 25 inches, this induces the semblance of a tug as the tail strings out and is checked by the guards slight brake application. The down goods and marshalling yard is making its appearance to the left, now on the severe left curve Jack calls across that spotting the next board, the inner home, is vitally important. It's off as I sight it, "Inner home off mate" is bellowed across the footplate, we rumble along the down platform, the water column is my side placed inside the yard exit. Jacks first sighting was the delivery end of the column, he then had less then the length of the tender to make his "On a sixpence" stop. To this, at the time "novice", stopping a heavy tonnage of freight with a just adequate assisting vacuum head was close to the uncanny. In actual fact to the vast majority of experienced driver's it was routine.

Into the tender I receive the column sleeve as its arm is swung towards me. Concern that the tender should not overfill (all but drowning my gentleman driver at Salisbury would forever haunt me) has me chasing to and fro betwixt shovelling forward and checking the water level. "Coming up mate". Jacks there spinning the shut off handle. We, driver and boy are back on board and I am told to look out for a shunt movement. The yard shunter has cut off the wagons five or six back from the braked portion, the starter is off and we pull away, up over the yard to main points. I am relaying the shunt signals. Stop! Points over. And before the front end recoil they are cut off, vacuum head and engine coming to a near instant halt. I watch the cut off wagons disappear under the A30 road bridge thinking "There's going to be an almighty crash" I would latter appreciate that these guys were, and I kid you not "Professionals in their own rights" We are given the tip to pull up a couple of lengths, signals stop when we're clear, points over, ground signal off, shunter on his way back to the yard gives us the tip to fall back on to our train, we are being waved back, until "Nearly on em mate" then we "Clunk" buffers with our rear end. The fire by this time has burnt through a treat and is red hot to across the centre of the firehole.

The guard comes up with the revised load, off comes the left board. Jack takes his time pulling away allowing sufficient time for our guard to regain his van, then recognising the slight relaxation in tautness from the rear as the sign that the van brake has been released he lifts the regulator and we bark away towards the advanced starter. The following would be a retake of my initiation banker trips with my rostered driver, apart from the fact that I was the fireman on the engine leading the procession instead of providing a helpful leg up from the rear. I thought we had a problem for at the instant the regulator is closed the safety valves lift. On went the injector, the valves close and we manage to hear the bankers two crows. The advance drops off. Jack cements an unforgettable niche in my memory when he invites me to respond, hardly believing my ears I grab the whistle wire and pull the double 'Cock-a-dood-el-oo.' Later that evening I would burst into the front room of my in-laws three family council house and explain this honour, only to extract a bland response from my wife's dad of "Get the boy a cider there's something wrong we in"

I note that the footplate conduct adopted by Jack and my regular driver Frank Smith was similar in as much as they did not close themselves off. I was to encounter drivers who for long periods would not even glance your way unless you were having a "Ruffin" for steam, and then it could be a cutting "What's up, in the **** are we"? or some other unprintable innuendo. Later in my career as a driver at Fratton, not only would the young crew share a near equal status but would also share their respective duties performing the driving on a day about basis.

Apart from the novelty of my first time firing to the train engine the event was as expected with the definite advantage of having ample space and a realisation that you were on the front and most definitely in charge. Also, between bouts of attending to firing and boiler control I did not miss a chance to look back down the bank at the snake like procession we were escorting. Occasionally on a protracted curve there was, as far as I am aware, a never captured view of our support banging away at the rear.

Now nearing the summit my mate suggests that I put the shovel down as after we clear Evershot the gradient will, apart from one sharp ascent, fall to Weymouth.

Looking ahead and I am amazed to see the distant signal for Evershot in the off position. I bawl to Jack "What's the signal doing off" reply "Because we're not stopping" "But what about the banker?" "He is" I think my mate is loosing his marbles, how the ****** hell can the attached assistants come off when we are not stopping. Now with a blast on the whistle we are into the tunnel, there is a distinctive wrench from the rear which I assume is the banker relinquishing its support duties, we speed on through the station and onto the reverse gradient where Jack enlightens me as to how we lost our attached pannier.

The Western goods guards had come up through the ranks of yard shunting and therefore had mastered every trick in the trade with the shunting pole, so should the coast be clear, meaning there was not an inspector in the area, it would be arranged between the drivers and signalmen that the guard when nearing the top of the bank would lean over the rear of his van shunting pole in hand and make the detachment. This had been arranged prior to leaving Pen Mill. I suppose my countenance of ignorance and bafflement had made my mates day, hence the guffaws of laughter.

We are now on a near equal reverse gradient to the struggle up Evershot with varying falls of 1 in 69 to 1 in 150. We are classified as a semi fitted freight, (checked in the Southern Region 'Western Section' speed tables for the relevant period) as such our time allowance Pen Mill to Weymouth is precisely 1 hour one minute, had the freight been, what is described as "Ordinary", meaning loose coupled, i.e. no vacuum head, only the engine brake to the fore, the time allowance is increased to 1 hour 17mins. The third category is reserved for freights with 50 vac-fitted wagons – allowance 51mins.

We are now clanking down the bank, the regulator is

redundant, there is a continuous grinding as the engine brake coupled to the vacuum head check our descent, I note that the tender is vibrating to such an extent that its contents seem intent on invading the footplate via the shovelling plate, an addition to the clamour is caused through my inabilities in the field of boiler control as our 4-6-0 lifts its safety valves, only thing I can take a bow for is the absence of dust through copious amounts of pep pipe water used on the tender.

.

The instant uncompromising clamour of motive power followed by the short intermittent hollow sound of following coaching stock rush past us on the up. The so descriptive running commentary continues, "road levels off here for a mile, Maiden Newton distant is the next board". Distant is off, we pass through the station with its branch line to Bridport peeling away from the up side. "Sharp drop of 1in 90 here then near three miles on the flat", "road drops away again Colin, 1 in 120 for a kick off and then less steep for a couple of miles, tunnel ahead". I shut the firebox door. The blower is applied, Jack harnesses his charge. A blast from the whistle on entry, half way through, and exit. Now on a controlled ascent we pass through "Bradford Peverell and Stratton halt". The vacuum gauge needle creeps up to 25 inches and sure enough there is that tale, tale slight tug as our guard with hand brake takes up the slack. The road levels out then rises. We spot the Dorchester down distant at caution. Jack curses "What did I expect, so far outside our booked slot".

The brake and gradient assists us in curbing our advance into Dorchester 'Poundbury' Tunnel. With restraint we exit, the outer and inner home boards drop off as we near them. The bobby has used his skills, slowing us down so as the service that is holding us back will clear his block, this enables the all important starter to be pulled off before we are brought to a halt. (I would latter recognise this as great signalling.)

Jack "We now link up with your railways Waterloo to Weymouth, or if you prefer, down side". The advance clears, taking the strain we gradually gather momentum, I check to the rear, all is in order. My confusion at our restrained progress is put to rest with the explanation "Our next and last incline is mile and a half at 1 in 90 up to Bincombe Tunnel, we will take it steady down this short drop and when we hit the bank I will pick up the slack, drop her over and get rid of the surplus fire". Thought - "This could be interesting". Jack has another gander at my wasted efforts and tells me that after we turn the top there is a descent of four miles into Weymouth that is pretty sheer with falls of between 1 in 50 to 1 in 74. In my language, if we don't reduce it on the way up then I will have dropped the Western fire cleaners in the cart as well as melting their shovels.

Jack is as true as his word, we are not increasing momentum on the short 1 in 70 slackening to 1 in 117 descent. Observing that the vacuum gauge needle is quivering on 22 inches I watch with riveted interest as the gauge needle is allowed to rise in the most delicate way. My attention is drawn to the track side metal gradient sign which mark the change from descent to ascent. Brakes now off and the technique as previously noted comes into play, short opening and closing of the regulator until we feel that slight retardation which imparts the knowledge that the couplings are taunt, battle is now joined as the regulator is given the double valve "Full whack". Boiler contents gauge glass registers ¾ full which more by luck then judgement is spot on for the amount of pasting planned for my fire. I am sure my mate derives pleasure from explaining his

mastery to this very much "in awe" young fireman. The reverser is wound forward to 75%, the velocity of steam, firebox gasses and remnants of fire tare through the blast pipe and propel there selves skywards, she does not drop back in steam. Then "Put the injector on Mate, I will ease the regulator as we approach Bincombe Tunnel". This is done and as the regulator is eased the gauge glass is showing less then ½ a glass.

My attention is now drawn to the signal box off the up side, there is a central refuge with lead offs from both up and down mains,

4-6-0 Grange has steam to spare after descending Evershot Bank and approaching Yeovil Pen Mill. 1938 - Phillip Brown collection

this I am told is utilised as a sanctuary for the up assisting bankers after their labours from Weymouth. A prolonged pull on the whistle cord announces our entry into the near half mile long Bincombe Tunnel, blower on, firebox door cracked allows partial illumination, we lip the summit and I have an instant bout of tummy wobbles. My novice mind set shrieks "S*** we're dropping a plug". Jack calms my fears by explaining "We were dragging our load against the collar on a severe incline, the boiler contents level was sloping to the rear hence the high reading, on turning the top the regulator is eased and the reverse occurs, i.e. boiler contents flood to the front". On a fall of 1 in 50 to 52 the pressure from the rear makes itself felt even though the guard would have his brake firmly applied.

The fire was now greatly reduced but livened up to such an extent that the safety valves were blowing steam to the heavens. The advice from the "Governor" was. "Hold the boiler contents at a ¼ as when we level off the true reading will be ½ a glass. This will allow space in the boiler to keep the old girl quiet?" Our engine vibrates and grinds in protest at the heavy brake application afforded it. Through Upway Wishing Well Halt, Upway Junction and its branch to Abbotsbury we continue on this shuddering course. The view to the front over looking Weymouth Bay and the Isle of Portland is truly spectacular. Another halt, Radipole, and Jack announces "at the bottom in a jiff". Weymouth distant warns me that my first freight trip is coming to its close. On my side (to the left) there emerges the motive power engine shed with a fan like spread of engine holding and departure sidings. We are joined by two roads extending from and into the depot, our progress is restricted to a minimum and then to a squealing and protesting halt. "How's the fire Col?" "Reckon it's about right Drive" I answer. My thinking is that if I get half a chance I will lift the fire up one side before we get into the depot. Looking to the front from the driver's side I see the reason for our delay, a "West Country" class loco gunning

towards us heading a string of coaching stock. Jack can't resist a quip "Trust one of yours to b**** it up" (get in the way). I'm chuffed that these Western men make such digs, but realise it is all in the best of humour.

We get the road, the whistle is touched and we take up the slack and ease through the cross over. Looking forward to the left I have a view of the main signal box, now with the head of our freight into the goods yard we are under the jurisdiction of the head shunter. We are brought to a halt about two engine lengths short of the stop blocks. Off the footplate, tail lamp on the smoke box end, back, duck in between to uncouple, vacuum pipes split. Opening the lungs I belt out "ease up". Jack squeezes up and I lift off the engine coupling. Out into the six foot I decide to pull the vacuum cylinder release strings on the first box vans directly behind our engine, got to wagon number four when I encounter the assistant shunter performing the same duty from the tail end. "Where've you sprung from?" "Off the train engine where else" I reply. His retort which has stayed with me "B***** me mate you must be in a hurry, never seen a fireman do that before". I made a resolve, which I never kept, to curb my instincts.

Our train is pulled off and we follow in its wake. The signal controlling the exit from the yard comes off. Away tender first, from the up side goods yard via main the line cross over and points onto the disposal road in Weymouth motive power depot. Hand brake on, Jack opens the cylinder release cocks etc and proceeds to guide me to the running foreman's office where he makes his report, and then it's the mess room for a wash up before we take the authorised walking route to the station. On the cushions back to Pen Mill with an hour's overtime in my back pocket there is time to reflect on a day's work that had thrown up such a myriad of contrasts. The atmosphere of confrontation in Westbury relief cabin, my disbelief that the assisting engine had been literally cut loose on Evershot bank, to my hesitant belief that my first time performance on the footplate had been adequate, and all within the space of nine hours. After 47 years on the iron road I came to the very same matching conclusion that assaulted my mind on that ride in 1955. There was no other occupation in the country that was likely to offer such a variance of circumstances in one shift as that repeatedly presented to footplate men.

CHAPTER 24

'ODD BALL' DRIVER

On many occasions during my time at Pen Mill I would be booked on the aforementioned duty and my description of the work will suffice as average. Each driver however had his own unique method of handling his charge to which of course his fireman had to respond. All depots had there 'odd ball' characters and I was paired with one driver that I would have nominated as Yeovil Pen Mill's. Harold S. and I left our train engine at Weymouth shed as previously described. The allotted time allowance for each particular designated walk way was agreed between the depots management and the men's locally elected representatives. As we joined the path Harold remarks that if we got a move on we could make the service back home, to which I stated "Just the job, lets go for it then". His response knocked me out for more then one reason "Hang on a minute, if we hold back we can watch it go out, book back on the next one and make an hours overtime". I

put to him that if we genuinely did not have sufficient time, then what was the harm in getting a move on catching the service and booking back on the next which would give us the best of both worlds" "No, somebody will report I" was the final word. This resorted in me having to cycle the dreaded ten miles. Had I attained the self confidence that was soon to assert its self I would have got on the train regardless. I am not being harsh, but looking back it seems that a discipline built on a premise of fear re dismissal had resulted in individuals been frightened of their own shadows. But on the other hand we thankfully have not witnessed mass unemployment.

At this time the depot provided the engine power for marshalling the Towns main freight yard situated at Hendford, this was accomplished by a 0-6-0 pannier and at times the slightly more sophisticated 2-6-2 prairie tank, my recollections are of a compact yard with plenty of point pulling when shunting and making placements, full attention to front and rear during movements in such yards was the order of the day, tedium was relieved by contact with the terrific group of men employed there. Yeovil Hendford absorbed and despatched nine freight movements on the Monday to Friday basis. The volume and assortment of traffic was immense, and this was when the threat of road haulage was more than apparent, how the yard had functioned years prior when rail was the solitary conveyor makes the mind boggle.

2-6-0 U class enters Hendford halt with a Yeovil to Taunton train on the last day of service. 13.06.1964 - John Day collection

CHAPTER 25

THE HOME FRONT

To matters Domestic. During December 1955 I took the opportunity to occupy a 1800s built terraced house at Yeovil. There was a council imposed closing order on one bedroom. It did not deter us. My wife's wonderful family wished us to stay with them but to be honest three families in one council house was a little cramped. Our rent was 12s = 60p per week. Goodbye to the apprehensive waits on Crewkerne platform and good riddance to the ten mile cycle rides. We felt content with the responsibility of independence.

A little gem, I mentioned in the Pen Mill cabin that I would have to purchase a couple of clothes line posts. A few days passed and there was a knock on the door, there panting with effort was the four man cleaning gang, two on duty, two off, they had acquired two long boiler tubes with holes drilled so as pulleys could be applied, their cycles had been used as carriers. Our coming family member Ken Fay was the instigator. The deed was both kind and thoughtful and typical of the era.

CHAPTER 26

BACK TO SQUARE ONE - MOTIVE POWER DEPOT WISE

Our little family's security was short lived. My depot which had been annexed from the Western Region was to be amalgamated with the larger Southern depot of Yeovil Town, but first a little pruning was to be achieved. This resulted in my position of "again" junior fireman becoming redundant. Less then three months after establishing ourselves the bottom fell out of our hopes. My elected union representatives attempted to ease my concern by explaining the built in dispensation afforded redundant personal, this allowed me to take up any fireman's promotional vacancy in the Southern Region irrespective of seniority, in a nutshell redundant men took preference.

Joy and I with heavy hearts had to re - assess. There was

many senior passed to fire cleaners, many of whom had decided to sit on their hands during their National Service. I was now 21 years of age, had completed my fourth reallocation and again I was to be the junior hand.

Yeovil Town had a structure containing seven links, e.g. two sets of 12 and one of six which were progressive in seniority, plus the early and late turn branch men, early, late and night shed turners, and two further links of two sets of men, totalling 39 pairs of men. Should the shed staff employed as coal men, fitters, storemen, boilersmiths, washout men, plus foreman and office staff be included, the depot had a workforce close to 120 men.

YEOVIL DUTY No. 517. 2 P.T. (M.7 Class P & P.)		
----	Loco. Yard	7. 5 a.m. ‖
---	Yeovil T.	7.22 a.m. P
7.26 a.m.	Yeovil Jc.	7.42 a.m. P
7.46 a.m.	Yeovil T.	7.56 a.m. P
8. 0 a.m.	Yeovil Jc.	8. 7 a.m. P
8.11 a.m.	Yeovil T.	8.20 a.m. P
8.24 a.m.	Yeovil Jc.	8.35 a.m. P
8.39 a.m.	Yeovil T.	8.42 a.m. P
8.44 a.m.	Pen Mill	8.48 a.m. P
8.50 a.m.	Yeovil T.	8.55 a.m. P
8.59 a.m.	Yeovil Jc.	9.12 a.m. P
9.16 a.m.	Yeovil T.	9.28 a.m. P
9.32 a.m.	Yeovil Jc.	9.45 a.m. P
9.49 a.m.	Yeovil T.	10.25 a.m. P
10.29 a.m.	Yeovil Jc.	10.35 a.m. P
10.39 a.m.	Yeovil T.	11. 0 a.m. P
11. 4 a.m.	Yeovil Jc.	11.11 a.m. P
11.15 a.m.	Yeovil T.	11.45 a.m. P
11.49 a.m.	Yeovil Jc.	12. 2 p.m. P
12. 4 p.m.	Yeovil T.	12.36 p.m. P
12.40 p.m.	Yeovil Jc.	12.53 p.m. P
12.57 p.m.	Yeovil T.	‖
---	Yeovil Loco.	1.40 p.m. ‖
---	Yeovil T.	1.50 p.m. P
1.54 p.m.	Yeovil Jc.	2.10 p.m. P
2.14 p.m.	Yeovil T.	2.45 p.m. P
2.49 p.m.	Yeovil Jc.	3.10 p.m. P
3.14 p.m.	Yeovil T.	3.30 p.m. P
3.34 p.m.	Yeovil Jc.	3.51 p.m. P
3.55 p.m.	Yeovil T.	4.19 p.m. P
4.23 p.m.	Yeovil Jc.	4.33 p.m. P
4.37 p.m.	Yeovil T.	4.56 p.m. P
5. 0 p.m.	Yeovil Jc.	5. 8 p.m. P
5.12 p.m.	Yeovil T.	5.18 p.m. P
5.22 p.m.	Yeovil Jc.	5.28 p.m. P
5.32 p.m.	Yeovil T.	5.48 p.m. P

0-4-4T M7 on Yeovil Town -Junction push and pull service. 18.05.1962
- John Day collection

NO choice, either move or throw in the towel. Then an unexpected life line, an amended vacancy list emerged advertising vacancies for two fireman at Yeovil Town. In spite of the leg pulling from Pen Mill men, banging on about going back to cleaning fires, there was no hesitation.

On Monday 9th of April 1956, I was back at the beginning – Motive Power wise. The second vacancy was taken by my mate from cleaning days, Terry Edwards, he had been made redundant at Bridport. The moves were not without controversy as we "knobbed sticked" i.e. jumped in front of, gained preference over

2-4-0WT built by Beattie for LSWR, 30587 stands at Yeovil Town MPD. 31.05.1960 -
John Day collection

I quote from my diary – First day at Yeovil Town, 9th of April 1956, rest day. I was placed in the junior gang of six. The driver who drew the short straw – me, was one Harold Ham. (affectionally known as Hammer, which in his profession he certainly was not). Harold's father Bill was one of the two regular drivers on the Yeovil Town to Junction push pull branch. Bill was proud of his status and in recognition was never without his bow tie, as I recall was driver Cranberry of Salisbury shed. My period at Yeovil was to provide a permanence of eight years which in retrospect was of vital importance. We as a family unit were able to mature and set a structure towards the future. Concerns regarding security of employment did not enter into the scheme of things, although several of the senior firemen transferring to drivers positions elsewhere should have warned us of the impending instability. No one could conjure up the nightmare scenario of the eventual mutilation of the Salisbury to West of England main line that fate had in store. I was and felt at home.

CHAPTER 27

WE GET STUCK UP HONITON BANK AND HALT THE ALL IMPORTANT PAPER TRAIN

The following week came the pairing with driver Ham and the introduction to the Exeter main line. The duty had a signing on time of 1.15am. What a corker it would prove to be.

First part of the duty was to prepare and work a 2-6-0 "Standard" "4MT" light engine to Yeovil Junction. The aforementioned preparation procedure was adhered to.
My first visit to the stores threw up a cracker that will forever stay with me. I shout "Stores for oil" a nondescript deep Somerset voice answered from the bowels of the store. "Wass wake I up var, help yer B***** selv".

Clanking and resounding through the hollow like station, under the foot and road bridge, my mate's consideration regarding the unearthly hour would not produce a hint of whistle. We were routed into Yeovil Junctions up bay platform, engine screwed down, tail lamps reversed, we were over the foot bridge and stood on the down local platform. I was all interest as Harold described the route and gradient we were to encounter. I perceived that the luck of the draw had dealt me a trump in this driver, he was accommodating, relaxed and just up my street, amusing. I was told that he recognised my inexperience and would point out features and give advice throughout.

This calmed my awareness and gave me a lift in confidence, which quickly evaporated, as looking towards Yeovil Junction "A" Box (still there) produced the sighting of a lamp on top of the smoke box and one centre of the buffer beam head code moving towards us. Class "S15" 4-6-0 No 30828 (now preserved) emerged braking and grinding to a stop on the "W" mark, up on the footplate the driver we were relieving explained his 20 minute late start from Salisbury West yard, which incidentally we had not noticed such was the involvement in conversation.

This Yeovil crew had signed on duty a 6.45pm on Sunday, relieved the 5.20pm ex - Exeter at Yeovil Junction at 7.30pm and worked it to Salisbury. Engine off and into the depot. P.N. (Posh initials for meal break) Prepared and worked the light engine to West Yard for the 20 minute late running freight. Thence relieved by us. The load ticket was handed to my mate, and they were away on the ferry engine. I get the coal forward as the tender is topped up, "Water up mate" arm of column is swung back and secured.

The news is that our wagon total is 46 = 55 which is a full load for an "S15" over the section Yeovil Junction to Exeter. At 2.45am still that 20 late, my mate touches the whistle, eases the regulator off it's face to take up the strain, then a more business like opening to the first valve. Yeovil Junction B box is my side. I go over to my mate's side, we are on a left hander, with the spare head lamp I exchange signals with the guards swinging hand lamp, and remark "Train complete mate". This is my first outing on the "S15" since the trip to Milford Yard at Salisbury and I am surprised how working the injectors and keeping an eye on the lubricator sight feeds has come as second nature. Firing left handed is not easy, I have to get used to it as a driver will not allow a fireman to turn his back on him, there have been incidents where such tactics have resulted in a kick up the A**, sorry pants.

My driver is short and thick set. I will learn that this humorous character reacts in good spirits when addressed as 'tub'. Looking across the footplate I am amazed at his method of holding himself in position. The seat's for both men are hinged and top a box area which can be used for oil containers, tools and personal belongings. Harold much to my amusement folds his right leg beneath his bottom and somehow his left leg folds over his right knee and dangles, his body is so positioned that he is able to look over the framing side to the fore, weird, but no way did I make a comment!

Harold keeps me informed regarding reference points, i.e. Sutton Bingham Distant Signal etc. The 4-6-0 is vibrant, the regulator ¾ across its travel, the reverser is probably wound forward to 35% cut off and all to me is performing like clock work. Of course I did not realise it at the time, but Harold Ham was a recognised skilled engineman. We tip the incline at the 126½ mile post from Waterloo. "Four miles of up and downers Colin and then we will be into your home town bank" is projected across the footplate. There is no alternative then to fire left handed and I seem to be getting into the swing of things. I am even operating the ratchet designed firebox door with a flick of the right hand between shovel loads. As a nipper in such magic I am pleased with my progress. Peering over the side I make the momentous decision to purchase a torch so as I can observe that the injector is not wasting water.

Gaining momentum with the boiler pressure gauge needle

near the red, I decide to lift up the hinged half fire hole door flap, the brightness from the firebox is so fierce that it lights up the underside of bridges and overhangs with more clarity then sunlight. I catch a glimpse of yellow, the shut out Hardington signal box. Cutting across country our passing presence must be heard for many a long mile, 40 to 70 loaded wagons carrying 500 to 600 tons, steel wheels on rails with joints every 60 feet. I can now understand how as a junior at Crewkerne, on a clear morning I could hear a down freight from such a distance before sighting it at the bottom of the straight. I know this area well from my cycling experience. 130 mile post and Harold is touching the regulator, observing the exhaust as it flows back over the tender, now opening it further until the exhaust is thick and unbroken, slight pull from the rear is instantly interpreted as "Now we gottem mate" Prior to the 1 in 80 Crewkerne incline the regulator is right over, the reverser is wound well forward and we are into em.

My mind goes back to that enigma of childhood and the devil in the night clanking from this same bank. Surely at this speed we would not suffer that same ignominy, we are on the incline where on the up road the described "Merchant Navy" class broke her axle. Now onto the short section of level track through Crewkerne station our speed has dramatically reduced, the exhaust blasts through boiler tubes and cylinders are speeding skywards. This is a different shooting match with rockets smashing the underside of the Dorchester road bridge as we strain through the station of my birth. Now on a left embankment our exhaust beats are regular, strong and singular. The regulator is pushed across to its furthest limit, with my mates right arm extended with hand closed on it, in fact I am firing up under his arm, former posture abandoned he is stood just to the left of the firebox door, alert to arrest the first sign of driving wheel spin. Going through Crewkerne gates at an estimated speed of 15 to 20 mph we are in the heart of my adolescent exploration area, reflections of who would have thought prevail.

The gradient of 1 in 80 persists as we near the tunnel, we are in a cutting. Suddenly without a trace of warning there is a shattering of normality as pistons and side rods go bananas. Harold shouts "Sands" I have the engine sands operating lever pulled back before his voice checks. The driving wheel spin only checks when the steam is cut off. The loss of momentum almost brings us to a stop. At the split second that the wheel spin is arrested, my mate is feathering the regulator, feeling for the reaction from our load which will give him the assurance that the couplings are extended, and then additional power is applied. The application and concentration shows as my drivers usual jolly expression is transformed to one of acute concentration. Reverser is over on the maximum 70%, gradually the regulator is pushed across until it is fully opened. This is fingers crossed time, and I suspect our guard has more then his fingers crossed, as he, if we did stick would have to do some walking.

We are well over in steam for as we came to a near stand and the power was cut she lifted her safety valves. Our impetus gathers strength as we enter the tunnel. I lean across my box seat, left hand on the sands control lever and peer at the up side wall. Once more I have a flash

back to my last venture in this Tunnel. Our small bond of friends got caught out during a run through dare, it seemed then as yesterday, incidentally it still does. Our exhaust, again strong and regular break free from the restraints of the brick work and burst into air. At mile post 133¼ we are over the summit. My mate remarks that apart from the one slip we managed that a treat, so providing we get the distant for Seaton Junction, Honiton Bank should not be a problem. Gathering speed, we thunder through Hewish Crossing and it's minute signal box and cottage, vibration and utter bedlam is created in an instant, how on earth the occupants of such tight to the line dwellings do not part company with their beds remain a mystery. I have mentioned this in a humorous vein when chatting during engineering works, they maintain that, and I quote "We get used to it me boy". Sorry but I never believed it.

At mile post 135 my driver closes the regulator and brings down his large ejector brake handle so applying two to three inches of brake to engine and vacuum head.

The gradient now falls for 13 miles with variants of between 1 in 120 to 400. This is my first serious brush with the insidious plague, coal dust. Whilst the injector is on the dust is kept at bay via the use of the pep pipe spray, the down side is that we get coated with back spray which will enable coal dust to cling to clothing and skin!

As I write and relive these exact events, I find it incredible that the terrible coal mine encumbrance of emphysema did not have a more profound impact on footplate grades. Chard Junction distant signal is off. Harold allows the vacuum brake needle to drift up to 21 inches, wait for it, and there is that familiar tug. I am told that the check confirmed that our guard was alert with his van brake correctly applied, also explained is the careful approach prior to sighting the distant, as had it been at caution, having the train under control would have enabled a restrained stop to be made at the home signal which protects the level crossing as well as the station. This is a lesson that was to stand me in good staid in the future.

It is a gloriously clear morning, full moon and stars like jewels. I will later learn that we have followed the course of the River Axe from close to its source just east of Crewkerne, shortly it will wind south to meet the sea at Seaton. (maps out) my mate encourages me to build up my fire and to pay particular attention to the back corners, as there is six miles of falling gradient before we take on the challenge of Honiton Bank. I am fed the knowledge that there is the possibility that the control may arrange for us to be shunted back on to the up main at Axminster as the time allowance between the most important "Time wise" train of the day, the 1.15am ex-Waterloo passenger and newspaper service and ourselves had been reduced from 1 hour to 40 minutes by our 20 minute late running. Our booked time passing Axminster is 3.18am the papers are timed at 4.17am. My immediate thoughts are that if we do get put away the boiler safety valves will be blowing their brains out in the centre of that then, none sleepy market town. The descent is now lessened to 1 in 265. The distant signals for Broom and Axe gates are off, the brake is rubbing as Harold strains for the sighting of the controls decision, namely Axminster distant signal. "It's off, we're now in Devon" Harold states. We had in fact crossed the county boundaries of Dorset and Somerset no fewer then five times since leaving Yeovil Junction and now, "Career wise", I am introduced to the cream county. Harold "Thought they would do the obvious, 40 minutes lee way is bags of time" he would regret this prophetic statement, we are on the level through Axminster. The signal box is on the end of the down platform. Lyme Regis branch departs from the bay adjoining the up platform. At m.p. 146¼ the gradient reverses to 1 in 100. We are gathering the slack well before the bottom of the bank, the slightest of pulls from the rear and my mate with gradual but meaningful purpose eases the regulator over. The distant signal for Seaton Junction is sited on the 1 in 100 incline and although the box is switched out from 11pm until 6am it is respected as if open. We are now really into them, under a high bridge, along the down through, it is explained that the gradient through the station eases to 1 in 300 followed by an immediate rise of 1 in 80. 30828 is confirming Harold's predication and is brassing up well. A mile into the bank however our exhaust beats can be counted, we soldier on, my mind is on the button regards the sands. Plodding on with the exhaust gases reaching for the sky, an event occurs that I would never again experience.

Harold has called me to his side and is pointing ahead to a bridge where the track is seen to bend to the left, as a further marker, there standing as sentinel is an enormous tree. "That is known as Snobs Corner". What you mean by that mate I ask. "Where cocky b******* meet their match" he retorts. Our exhaust beats, whilst reaching for the sky have dramatically lessened in tempo. Suddenly horror upon horror we literally STOP! The look of utter amazement on the chubby features of Harold Ham is as clear now after more then 50 years as it was at that incredible moment. We realise our dour predicament. Can we get them going again? Then the root of the fright – the paper train and the agreed financial penalty imposed should it be delayed. At least the infant partnership of Ham and Robins would be recognised, if only in notoriety. Try as try might we could not shift them, the result of gradually releasing the brake so as the load would drift back to become buffer tight against the brake van, then with reverser in full fore gear the engine is given regulator, known as 'snatch' was negative. We have to part them is the decision. I blessed the elements on my journey along the cess to meet our guard. I hardly had need of a lamp. My drivers decision to cut the couplings 20 wagons back is agreed, buffered up, in between, coupling off and I'm out. The tension caused by the urgency of our dilemma is apparent. I receive the guard's pink wrong line order form made out to the signalman in advance. It is the procedural document that will authorise our return for the rear portion. The guard instructs me to inform the driver that six wagons plus the van brake is secured with brake stick applied. Also he will put down three detonators at the prescribed distance in advance of the detached portion. This is for guidance on our tender first light engine return. Young fit and eager I run full belt along the clear track side, on gaining the cab I am told in no uncertain terms to sit over my side and steady myself down, I understand this common sense advice as I have difficulty in getting my words out.

With a long pull on the whistle cord my mate gives her

regulator. There is a mile to the sanctuary of Honiton Incline, Harold gives her the gun, the regulator is eased as we approach the at danger home signal, it is then pulled off. The signalman, alert to our situation is standing with hand lamp displayed in the six foot, we slow to a halt, he clambers aboard, and driver and signalman quickly sort out strategy. He will give instructions via his hand lamp as to when the rear wagon is over the points controlling the refuge siding. My roll is to operate the point's lever and when the front portion has reversed and is in clear I will detach the engine and pin down brakes as required. I hand over the guard's wrong line order which the signalman retains. The front section pulls away, when clear I cross the down road to the points handle, the buffers clang as the signalman's red is seen. I pull over the one way lever, my mate reacts to the swinging lamp and slowly reverses his charge into the siding. With detached section in clear I dash to the footplate steps, Harold hands me down the coal pick and instructs me to pin down the brakes on six wagons, done and engine uncoupled I place a white tail lamp on the rear, points secured, our exit onto the main is made.

We receive the green from the signal box, move back and get the verbal confirmation that the facing runaway spring points some 790 yards to the rear are closed and locked, he also gives us the unsettling information that the 1.15am ex-Waterloo is waiting clearance at Axminster. Nevertheless rules are rules and our progress back for the rear is interrupted as the spring catch points are checked. There is no problem regarding the location of the rear portion as "Snobs Corner" would forever remain a permanent etch. "Shall I sprint in front and pick up the dets?" I ask "No, best to set them off, it will be the signal for the guard to return and at the same time give the farmers an early call. We touch, I make the attachment. On my way to meet the guard, who, much to my surprise has returned from his protection duties. He explains that as the morning is still and crystal clear he had been able to discern with clarity all our moves as the sounds vibrated down the bank. He had retrieved the two inner spaced detonators (often referred to as shots) and left the outer three for the paper train to explode. "I'll come up the front for a chat when we're waiting on the up road", is his parting remark. I'm thinking, what is he talking about, up road, I had a lot of learning to do. The 20 less wagon lengths run allowed a more coherent report to be made to Harold, in return he clears the fog of our guards "up road" gambit. The refuge siding will not take our full length, it is permissible however, as we have a brake van on the rear, to cross over and reverse on to the up line. The signalman shows his intention as he vigorously signals us towards him and then aligns his lamp to the away from him angle. Again the red stop signal, followed by the guards white lamp swinging side to side signal authorizing and guiding us back over the cross over onto the up line. The gradient is such that as the engine brake is blown off there is a simultaneous tug from the rear as the tonnage attempts to dictate our descent, however, this drift is under the control of the engine brake and we reverse in an orderly manner. As the engine clears the cross over the rear portion is brought to a halt, I screw down the tender brake. The guard having applied his van brake joins us on the footplate, there is a easing of tension as the signalman is now able to give

Axminster the section clear signal.

As previously emphasised the elements were perfect, even so the unmistakable beat of a "Merchant Navy" class caught us unawares, Harold and our guard consulting their time pieces agree that the sound must be echoing from the valley floor at least five miles to our rear. Our attentions are now riveted towards the ever increasing crescendo as it takes on the lower reaches of Honiton Bank, the driver is certainly giving her the gun. An additional ingredient of expectation is created for me as the guard remarks that when the three shots he had left down as protection are fired off, he would be away to the rear. He did not have to wait long as very soon there is a detonation of such splendour that would have evoked many of "Yer wass reckon that was?" between hitherto sleeping Devonshire couples. The guard retreats to his van with the understanding that after the papers have cleared the section to Honiton we will be away, leaving the detached portion for collection later. I'm pulling coal forward after making up the fire, keeping my eye open to the rear for expectant fireworks. I am not disappointed, the rockets firing into the air is more akin to a "Roman Candle". Suddenly with much ferocity the engine representing the pride of Southern Regions motive power, the "Merchant Navy" class, with attendant parcel vans and passenger stock thrusts past, seemingly paying scant attention to the adverse gradient of 1in 80. He's getting his fire down as after the summit (153 m p) has been topped it is all down hill to Exeter Central, remarks Harold. I also learn that the driver would have been informed at Axminster that the section to Honiton Incline was clear but that three detonators had been left on the track by the guard.

The three miles to clear the section at Honiton must have been accomplished in near record time as the incline signalman was very soon giving us a green. Blast on the whistle to alert the guard and with a full head of steam we are taking the strain. I use the advantage of the cross over to exchange signals with our Guard. The starter, 700 yards from the box is off, with a reduced load we take the tunnel in our stride and top the summit at the 153 m.p. I am told that we have 16 miles of mostly falling gradients with a late 'sting in the tail' of two miles at 1 in 100 between Broad Clyst and Exmouth Junction. My driver having a quick 'shuftie' advises that there should be enough in the box to see us through, he then resumes his ungainly posture as we clank, rattle and roll through the lace town of Honiton, Sidmouth Junction, (now titled "Feniton") and the Devon cider town of Whimple. The delayed "papers" have long preceded us, leaving a clear path in its wake, now approaching Broad Clyst our descent levels out. The regulator of 30828 is gently eased across and steam is applied, the couplings pick up the slack and our charge is finally strung out for the final two mile ascent through Pinhoe. In spite of the concern my mate must be experiencing regarding the significance of the time delay caused to the eminent 1.15am ex-Waterloo, he continues to give me a briefing on the route.

Now shut off and under control we are approaching the two aspect coloured light distant for Exmouth Junction which is at yellow. Again across the driver's side my attention is drawn to the two arm home signal, the short right arm controlling the entrance to the up yard is cleared. Gradual

release of the brake with both needles up to 21 inches and we get the now usual tug from the rear, regulator cracked and power is applied for the final chapter. I look back from my side as the tail follows snake like via the crossover and into the large Exmouth Junction freight marshalling yard. Our charge on going to Torrington is booked to depart at 6am arriving at 11.10am. During this five hour journey it is booked to shunt at seven individual freight yards. From commencement at London's Nine Elms to termination our freight would have covered 224 miles. I can but reflect that the vast bulk of heavy goods were moved by rail. Now 50 years on the economy and population of these remote areas have greatly increased. The unobtrusive rail network has long since gone, surrendered to the environmentally poisonous unchallenged diesel transporters.

Released from the yard we join the queue of engines on the disposal pits at Exmouth Junction motive power depot. My impression is that it is on par with Salisbury Depot, about 50 times larger then Yeovil Town. My mate applies the engine brake, opens the cylinder steam release cocks and with a look that could be interpreted as, going to face the firing squad, climbs off the loco and is away to verbally explain our Honiton Bank dilemma to the running foreman. He will when we get back to Yeovil attach his written report to the daily work ticket. The fire is cleaned by the time of his return, while I complete the disposal he sits over his side jotting down the sequence of events. We then make our way for my introduction to the cavernous enginemen's mess room, which was to provide so many episodes of pranks and frolics and serious discussion over the following eight years.

After our meal break, we ride on a light engine to Exeter Central and then 'As passengers' to Yeovil via the 6.30am Exeter to Waterloo.

Back on our home pastures, quips such as "Have a good trip" and "Smithy will have "yer" guts ver garters" abound. I did not enjoy it, but would learn that it was par for the course. However I did receive a boost, as I heard my mate retort that shortage of steam was not a factor. My driver was eventually absolved of any liability as when the loading was checked it was found to have been erroneously calculated.

My introduction to passenger work on the Exeter route followed. Salisbury duty number 501 provided the S.R. workhorse for all classes of traffic, the 4-6-0 "S15". Signing on at 4.04pm we ride pass on the Yeovil branch to the Junction, relieve on the down at 4.25pm and work the 3.05pm stopping service ex- Salisbury to Exeter Central. We take water, I heave the coal forward and we are away on time at 4.31pm. My previous experience on the "S15", pseudonym 'Black un' has given me confidence. Harold gives the load as three (coaches) for 100 (tons). Full first valve on the regulator, and gradual adjustment of the reverser and we are well into them. I now realise that this is a different ball game than the "Stop the paper train" duty. Firing left handed I get into the swing. The box has a fair slope to the front. I trust I am reaching there. AWS (automatic warning system) bell rings, distant off, steam off, vacuum brake rubs, black smoke drifts back over tender and coaches, I pull down the ratchet operated fire hole door, drift turns light grey, injector on, pep pipe spraying tender. We are at Sutton Bingham. Right away, eight miles to Crewkerne, really belting along, can't believe the speed that this 4-6-0 with 5 ft.7in driving wheels has attained, as we get to Crewkerne bottom, 130 ¼ m.p. we develop tender vibration which has the coal frantically jumping forward, this occurred at the same spot each day as soon as the regulator was closed. Sometime later with driver Charlie Woolmington, he, with the initial tender shake, would turn with nonchalance, put a couple of rotations on the tender brake and "Bingo" the juddering would be arrested. Our Charl carried that irritable air of upper class importance, but what an engineman he was. The section time of 11 minutes for the eight miles, does at face value seem slack, but considering the sluggish pull away I consider it to be impressive.

The close uncle leading porter must somehow have kept tabs on me, as each run in at Crewkerne would have him giving me the thumbs up from the booking office entrance. Away up the 1in 80 bank passing the "uncle's" fathers crossing keepers cottage, through the tunnel, topping the incline and taking the falling gradient to Chard Junction, 7 ½ miles in 12 mins, reflects the handicap of the start on the incline from Crewkerne. Feeling at ease with shovel and use of the injectors, keeping my eye on the lubricator sight feeds as instructed I feel very much part of the team. I would soon learn however that it was a completely different cup of tea when firing to an engine that was not steaming well. I observe the guards right away from my mate's side. Following the gradients as previously described we call at Axminster and Seaton Junction. We take Honiton Bank in our stride and soon find ourselves ploughing through

"Snobs corner" Harold advises me to reduce the size of my fire as we have to perform engine requirements later.

Through the tunnel and down the bank we stop at Honiton, Sidmouth Junction, Whimple, Broad Clyst and Pinhoe, passing Exmouth Junction at 6.03pm. The Exmouth branch joins us from the driver's side. The AWS siren for Exeter 'A' Box two aspect coloured light distant is cancelled, through the 263 yard Blackboy Tunnel and St James Park Halt. Harold explains the significance of the three arm home signal. The middle arm is off, this leads us into the down local platform where we come to rest opposite the footbridge steps. "We detach here mate". I'm off platform side, back along the tender, drop down between buffers and platform, split the vacuum pipes, put ours on to the housing dummy, belt out "Ease up", coupling off and I emerge on the footplate from the opposite side to which I left, much to the amusement of my driver. The required subsidiary signal comes off and we move forward into the down carriage sidings. Looking from my side towards St David's Tunnel I am amazed at the steepness of the descending main line and pass comment to my mate. 1 in 37 is the gradient, explains Harold, and for good measure "Some heavy freight's have two or even three assisting bankers". I have a red tail lamp on the smoke box end. While waiting for the road I have to make an embarrassing admittance to the fact that I have miscalculated the size of my fire. Harold doesn't even bother to look, but simply shrugs his shoulders, as if to say, tough, that's your problem. I reckon he had a butchers when I was in between. Ground signal off and we are away tender first up the wrong road, which is the down through line.

CHAPTER 28

THE RUN- AWAY 'S.15'

The mind set shoots forward to 1963. It is my second coming with my old buddie from Pen Mill day's driver Frank Smith. We are on this same duty. The fog is as dense as I am ever to experience it. We are hardly moving searching for the coloured light prior to Blackboy Tunnel. The AWS siren sounds, I am over my mate's side two pairs of eyes probing. Suddenly "B****y hell" Frank yells, red light is there, problem is it is level with our footplate, reverser swung back, regulator open and we push back. At that moment "Sods law kicks in" and it turns green. Frank pushes up his large ejector handle and the needles rush up to 21 inches of vacuum. Quickly into fore gear, regulator pushed across and we're in the tunnel, although jet black the clearer air is welcome. I notice my mate, now in is 60s, he's extremely tense.

Clear of the tunnel the elements have not abated, we at greatly reduced speed creep through St James Halt, I stay and observe from my driver's side, the signals come through the "pea souper" when level with the smoke box. After which seems an age, we locate the platform, stop, back, detach as before, into the siding, ground signal off and we are away, again up the down through. Leaning over the side, I am able to distinguish perhaps a few yards to the fore of the tender, speed probably 15 mph –

suddenly a body with it's head turned towards the correct flow of traffic, in other words away from us – disappears from view in front of our tender. In sheer panic I shout - "STOP"- Frank looks across at me, and hesitates, I'm over his side and slamming down his big vacuum jet in a flash. He is stunned. I shout "We've just cut a bloke in two, Jesus Christ!". We stop. I jump off and belt towards the smoke box end. I did not know, but the Exmouth branch service was standing in the down platform. Its crew had heard a cry and was bending over the casualty as I arrived – Incredibly his limbs were intact, our tender had mowed him over, the entire length of our "S15" had passed over him as he lay prostrate in the four foot. His injury was a bruised spine, absolutely astonishing. Franks arrival was to herald my most amazing and lucky rescue act. The four of us suddenly heard an unmistakable exhaust beat. Frank had not opened the cylinder steam release cock's, the regulator had not been completely closed and had allowed steam into the cylinders, as the reverser was in full reverse gear, with the brake handle in release she was away from us. The four pair of eyes locked, we were open mouthed!

I was 28 years of age working full eight hour shifts and for good measure operating a window cleaning business. My fitness saved the day. I shot away on a race that I must not lose, jumping over track and sleepers the footplate steps was somehow gained, on board I did the necessary. Frank arrived, he was all but exhausted, he said something, but it was incoherent. Eventually we got on to Exmouth Junction dispersal pits where tension and panic took its toll. The fire had to be cleaned. Frank left to report the events to the depot foreman. I sat on my locker and tried to get a grip, but in truth by the time he returned I had not moved a muscle. Frank informed me that the foreman asked whether he wanted relief. I could not believe my ears and said, "didn't you request assistance for me?" "never thought of that" was the reply. As the route was set up, the outcome had the engine got away did not bare thinking about.

This down side of a character which in every other way was both friendly and warm came to the fore during this same period. To term the following freak is an under statement.

CHAPTER 29

BOX FULL OF FIRE AND THE BOILER INJECTORS WILL NOT FUNCTION!

We are on Exmouth Junction duty 551, the engine is a 7P/5F "West Country" class. Signing on duty at 5.33 pm we relieve our own men at 6pm and work the 5.34pm ex-Templecombe stopping service from Yeovil Junction to Exeter Central, light to Exmouth Junction and dispose. With a "West Country" and a load of four coaches this is a piece of cake. BUT not on this occasion, as the absurdity of our downfall would be one beyond compare. I'm having a ball. By now a veteran in the use of the steam operated, foot treadle controlled firebox door, I aim to quit firing at Seaton Junction, sit on my rear end and only have the boiler injectors to care for. However as early as Chard Junction I have problems. The regular injector is hesitant in picking up the flow from the tender and is therefore "blowing out" i.e. water not available. Machined into the footplate floor are two circular holes so as the injector action can be observed. I try the second injector, (termed the drivers injector) - OK. but soon, same malfunction. My concerns are expressed to Frank. "Frankly" he doesn't absorb the significance – but soon will. Trying the gently, gently approach the boiler contents is held at around ¾ of a glass, I have the fire box door open on the second nick, even so she adding to my worries as the safety valves keep lifting, shooting more of the diminishing commodity "water" to the Devonshire heavens. We top Honiton Bank and the reverse gradient reduces the contents to ½ a glass. Now even my "wish to be divorced from the situation driver" is stood up instead of sitting down. After Honiton we get a reprieve. Then both injectors pack up –"The ghost is out" no way can I get water into the boiler. She is blowing her brains out!

I implore Frank to come off at Sidmouth Junction, but for some cursed reason he will not face reality. I literally kick the boiler front in frustration and temper. The two miles into Whimple descend at 1 in 100 from m.p. 161¼. I recall being scared as we run into the platform with the boiler gauge glass reading "Empty" - I can hardly speak to my mate such is my concern and fury that he did not come off earlier. I belt along the platform as someone possessed and bellow our predicament to signalman and guard, back and drop down between tender and stock get rid of a little tension by shouting "EASE UP", coupling off, back on footplate. Moving forward towards Cranaford Gates our halt at the far end of the cross over points is as gentle as I have experienced with Frank, we both recognise that anything less may expose the boiler protection fusible lead plugs, reverse onto the up road, through the platform over points and into the yard.

During these movements the safety valves have been lifting. Now in the sidings and secured I prepare to drop the ample fire. Frank questions "you're not going to use the drop grate?" "Yes" I reply, "throw it out by hand" is that same inconsiderate reply. "If that is what you want you B***** do it, I've got a wife and two children at home" I retort. I knew that had I attempted the suicidal instructions to throw the fire out and the protection plugs in the underside of the boiler dropped I would have been scalded to death. "Get the staff, signalman, station master and all with water to douse the fire which I am going to drop as I reverse the engine". What a pantomime ensued. On went the drop grate rocking bar, back went the securing lugs – keeping the Ajax fire box door shut the drop grate is operated and the fire released as I reverse. My mate at long last realising the gravity of the situation has all hands to the pump in double quick time.

We had platelayers shovelling from track to yard, sleepers were ablaze, but were soon dealt with. After the centre of the fire had been discarded I hesitatingly inserted the clinker shovel and levered the residue through the drop grate. All done we made our way to Exmouth Junction on our own service, which was hauled by a relief engine. We then picked up the rear part of our duty. Outcome – Inspector Sam approached my driver with the explanation. On examination there was a host of waste cloth found in the tender which had blocked the water outlets. Evidently our "West Country" had just been serviced, during that time a card school which was been held in the tender had been interrupted, the likely lads scampered leaving their home comforts "seats" behind! Not one word in recognition of my participation was mentioned.

Returning to 501 duty and the admittance to having miscalculated the size of my fire. The coloured light approaching Blackboy Tunnel is controlled red to yellow by Exeter Central "A" box, yellow to green by Exmouth Junction. Our yellow takes us through the tunnel, on emergence the left arm of a three armed gantry is off with engine shed as opposed to goods prescribed in the box. There are two engine pit roads leading to an enormous coal hopper which has the capability of lifting loaded wagons to its vast height and discharging same into its cavernous depths. I was soon to cotton on to the fact that the points man would pull the road over so as unsuspecting, (who is he trying to kid) foreigners would go up (we had a four letter crude word for it) No. two siding, where the dust and small coal from each load would settle, the prime knobs would go straight down the hopper over one road. I would jump off the engine on the blind side from the point's man, race ahead and pull the point's lever over, we would then cruise up the knob side. This exploit would worry some Yeovil men to the degree of mouthing "You be going to get I reported". All agreed however that having decent coal available for making up the fire instead of bug dust would give us a head start.

On this introductory duty I was in a six and eight – state, having pulled the water column around for me, Harold climbs aboard and announces "be back later" and off he goes. The consequences of over firing would be a lesson I would never forget. Red hot fire had to be lifted out of the fire box before the clinker could be reached, I despaired at the number of times I had to use the coal pick to hammer the lip of the clinker shovel back into shape after the heat had made the metal soft. I took well over the allotted time to square up. The aftermath was that I was well and truly (sorry to use this so apt phrase) knackered. I was conscious of the fact that I had caused delay to the crews in line behind us. Not funny as some were waiting to sign off. Harold turns up with "Bet you won't do that again" blows off the brake, touches the whistle and we reverse to take coal, on to the turn table, usual procedure and we are onto our departure berth and screwed down. Washed off and in this monster mess room, locating a couple of berths would always prove to be difficult. The commotion,

no racket would be more descriptive, of 30 to 40 sets of West Country footplate men all buzzing in time was both deafening and electric. I push a line of personal drivers and fireman's boxes along the tightly joined tables to make way for our own, there was an almighty crash from the other end as one bit the dust, hush descended. A giant, who latter I was privileged to know as Jack Turton, stood, walked menacingly to our end, leaned over the table, lifted me up by my bib and brace overalls and demanded to know what I thought I was up to. Shook me rigid, until I looked along at the expectant faces and saw the twinkle which showed it was a set up. Jack for ever had an eye for me, and I for him for two opposite reasons. Years later on the Yeovil branch we had just taken water at the junction, in sped an up semi fast, they would hit the approach end of the platform at 50 mph with 12 on and stop unerringly on the "W" mark, a foot out and the tender could not be replenished. What expertise!) It was freezing and I was concentrating on getting as close as possible to the "devil" coal filled portable water column heater, suddenly a pair of giant arms embraced me, next I'm nearly sat on the red hot cylinder - Jack Turton. In fact he was a fun loving gentleman.

I would always be made welcome in that cabin, I reckon my reaction to that initial taunt put me in good stead.

CHAPTER 30

GRIME, SWEAT AND SLOG - BUT WHAT SATISFACTION

Thirst and exhaustion sated we are out on our "S15" preparing for the 9.25pm light engine off the depot. The procedure from trimming lamps to replenishing lubricator, making up the fire etc is as previously portrayed, with the trip to the stores for oil my longest jaunt yet, or it was before I located the engine sand furnace, trying to walk that distance with loaded sand shutes would have pulled one's shoulders out of socket, a four wheel trolley was provided, when available.

My driver's advice on making up the fire was appreciated. I had talked my wife into sewing elastic around the bottom of my overall trousers, with light weights added, army drill like, coal dust was prevented from getting into my boots. The fire made up to a satisfactory thickness. (I noticed Harold stealing a quick shuftie while I was getting the coal forward, but no comment was made) Lamps lit and placed to front and rear, I check that we have a storm sheet as our relief will have an hour sat on, as Harold puts it "an open ass engine" at Templecombe.

At 9.25pm we get the tip to reverse out of the loco yard. Picking up the yard shunters hand lamp we are guided back onto the 5.21pm ex-Plymouth Friary to Feltham freight, on contact we ease back onto the vacuum head, I couple up and connect the engine to vacuum head brake pipes, place the two lamp head code on the front end and rejoin the footplate. The fire has now burnt through. My instincts urge me insert the dart and press down thereby

opening the fire. I mention this, my mate sucking on a roll up says "why the hesitation?" "because it's already burnt through" answer "right". I content myself by putting a few rounds across the box. The guard arrives and confirms Harold's prediction "no of wagons equal to 59", a full load. Evidently should the load be under 59 it would be topped up with loaded ballast wagons. The service is termed Special Freight and is allotted a generous vacuum head. A twist on the blower and the boiler pressure shows just below 200lb per square inch, the tender is soaked, and the injector is turned off with the gauge glass showing an inch below the top nut. Spot on time at 9.45 we get the green from the yard foreman. Touch of whistle and the regulator is eased across as we gently take up the weight. As we progress towards the up main my driver informs me that as soon as he is assured that the train is complete, (this by virtue of the guard and I exchanging the tip) and we have the advance starter at green, he will give her the gun so as we can take advantage of the three mile descent through Pinhoe as the following 13 miles, apart from two short through station reprieves, are against the collar with gradients varying from 1 in 80 to 1 in 170. Looking back I spot the guards swinging lamp as his van rides the exit curve, "right the guard mate". I state as I acknowledge his signal "and the advance" is the reply.

The regulator is now eased open to ¾ of its travel with the reverser moved to probably 35%. The advice is to leave the fire until we hit the incline. I hear the AWS all clear bell for Pinhoe distant. The tender vibration has my high stacked coal shaking forward and overlapping onto the footplate, to me it's as if an orderly world has gone bananas. Coal dust is flying all over, I sit on my locker and hang on to the cab fittings keeping my feet clear of the bouncing loose knobs of coal. I catch my mate having a glance my way, I discern a smirk, he's actually enjoying the spectacle. Bell rings for Broad Clyst distant and chaos abates. After shovelling and scrapping coal from the footplate I start firing from under the tender firing plate. Steam pressure on the button, injector singing. If I had time for thought it would be "which comes first" shovel, firebox ratchet controlled door, injector, pep pipe, hand brush, coal pick or lubricator sight feeds, all of these so

Steam is not shut off as we take advantage of the brief descent of 1 in 100, pace however is arrested as we encounter the reverse gradient 1 in 100 to 1 in 80. With exhaust beats rapidly becoming distinctive I am back to my firing up mode, we get the bell for Honiton, through the station, engineered on a left curve we are, as they say, in to em, the curvature then reverses which adds drag to our tail.

Harold takes note that my focus is on the sand operating lever "She won't slip tonight mate, the rail is as dry as a bone". I catch sight of motor lights from the then, A30 London to the west trunk road. Topping the bank at the 153 mile post we are immediately into the tunnel. Emerging,

SALISBURY DUTY No. 500.
6F. (S.15 Class)

MONDAYS ONLY.
    Loco. Yard... ... ... 1.10 a.m. ||
    Salisbury ... ... 1.28 a.m. F

MONDAYS EXCEPTED.
    Loco. Yard ... ... 1.20 a.m. ||
    Salisbury ... ... 1.39 a.m. F

DAILY.
    (10.40 p.m. Nine Elms).
7.45 a.m. Exmouth Jc. ... ... 7.55 a.m. ||
7.58 a.m. Exmouth Jc. Loco. ... 3. 3 p.m. ||
3. 7 p.m. Exeter... ... ... 3.20 p.m. P
4.59 p.m. Yeovil Jc. ... ... 5.13 p.m. ||
5.18 p.m. Yeovil T. ... ... ——
    C—Shunting 5.25 p.m. to 5.35 p.m. } F.X.
    F—Shunting 5.35 p.m. to 6.30 p.m. }
    Yeovil T. ... ... 6.30 p.m. F
6.38 p.m. Yeovil Jc. ... ... 7.30 p.m. F
    (2.40 p.m. Exmouth Jc).
8. 0 p.m. Templecombe ... 8.15 p.m. ||
8.35 p.m. Yeovil Jc. ... ... 9.15 p.m. F
    (6.50 p.m. Axminster)
9.45 p.m. Templecombe ... 11.55 p.m. F
1. 5 a.m. Salisbury ... ... **||
    Loco. Yard ... ... ——

Salisbury Men.
(1) M.O.—Off No.   (Sunday) prepare.

(2) 1st set (M.O.) on duty 12.55 a.m. work to Yeovil Jc. change to No. 480 at 4.25 a.m. and work and relieved Salisbury 8.49 a.m.

Yeovil Men.
(3) M.X.—Off No. 503, prepare and work 1.20 a.m. etc., to Yeovil Jc. change to No. 512 at 4.25 a.m. and work and relieved in depot.

(4) Off No. 480 (M.O. ...
Yeovil Jc. 4.25 a...
change to No. 545

S15 class 4-6-0, 30845 passes Chard Junction with an east bound freight. 14.03.1961 - John Cornelius collection

essential items are in constant use. A rhythm is somehow achieved which shortly comes as second nature, above all the clatter and bedlam the footplate is kept reasonable swept, all is repeat, repeat and guess what, more of the same. Harold has to near shout to make himself heard "lubricator sight feeds O K?" I put the gauge glass lamp behind the sight feeds, "Yea OK mate".

I keep hearing the AWS bell, but as to where we are, in my language, I ain't got a clue. In fact our progress has taken us beyond Broad Clyst through Whimple, and tipped the incline at the 161 mile post. Sidmouth Junction distant coming up" expounds Harold, followed by "sit down and take a breather" I take the hint. Through the level crossing and station I am urged to come over his side, stood on the tender flap with hands gripping cab and tender supports we salute the signalman who is giving us the once over from his lofty perch and exchange insults via the whistle with a pair of our own men on another "S15" stood in the up siding heading the 1.55pm ex - Meldon Quarry to Woking stone train.

the emphasis is rescinded to one of retardation. Vacuum head application of a controlled nature is applied towards the next block post, Seaton Junction. I am called across the footplate to view the spectacle of our guards van, we are on a straight while the tail end is coming off a right hander. The guard has his brake well and truly screwed on, this gives the result of the van wheels appearing as "Fire work night Catherine wheels" which are about to set the van on fire. Harold comments "He's doing a good job" and explains that if the guard had not applied the brake and therefore allowed the load to push forward, the snatch when the brake was released and power applied would be such that a break away may well occur. I remember quite clearly that on all future trips down Honiton Bank with freight I would look back at that precise point.

Seaton Junction distant is off. The gradient temporally levels off as we run through. "Rebuild your fire mate" is the advice, which I do, also with the aid of the pricker the coal is pulled forward. After 13 miles of descent I observe my drivers keen attention to the exhaust and the density in which it flows back over the tender as the regulator is feathered. Our booked timing through Axminster is 10.42pm. Such was the adherence to schedules that on one occasion we were two minutes late passing this check point and yet regained this discrepancy to arrive at Yeovil Junction right time. My mate was approached for an explanation. Continuing through Chard Junction we have a slog up the bank to the 133.¼ mile post sited prior to Crewkerne Tunnel.

Must have been doing something right as steaming is no problem. Down the 1 in 80 Crewkerne Bank with the open fire hole door illuminating my home station as we pulsate through. I touch the whistle and raise an arm to the signalman. Harold looks and grins as he recognises the significance. I would later develop the habit of holding the whistle wire just off its face, the vibrating cab is enough to set off a series of "pop" whistles. Later this practise had to cease. My father in laws home was sited adjoining the down yard. He requested that I give him a blow. "Any time of the night son, like to know you be about" I duly as explained obliged. That was until the Station Master made a written complaint. The dates and times were given. It was not rocket science for the culprit to be exposed.

We race along from the bottom of the bank, the remaining nine miles is easy going with an adverse blip of 1 in 120 topping out at the 126¼ mile post at "Pendomer". I make sure my relief has no reason to moan, the fire is made up and as much coal as possible is pulled forward.

I am riveted in observance of my mates braking technique. Judging the weight of load and power of brake application which enables a full load semi - fitted freight to be brought to a halt on the 'W' mark, calls for a skill that has been honed by years of experience and application.
The huge contrasts in gradient meant that a differing attitude had to be applied to each unique approach. The approach to Yeovil Junction is on a falling gradient of 1 in 200 to 1 in 150. Initial brake application would be applied from perhaps a mile out so as a possible stop at the home signal would be catered for. Then when the home stop signal is seen to be off, the vacuum brake handle is eased upwards on its pivot resulting in a slight release of the brake. The 12 car platform is gained with the equal of 59 loaded wagons under the complete control of these master craftsmen.

Our relief is at hand with the driver, water column chain at the ready rearing to pull the arm towards the tender. I have scurried over the tender coals and am in position to accept the offered link and place the flexible tube into the tender. With a "cheers mate" the shut off valve is fully opened. My opposite number is now shovelling forward for all he is worth, as I pass him I remark that the fire is well up under the brick arch. He is much senior to me, and counters in good vein "It had better be nipper".

(Off the engine and we cross onto the bay platform and 548 duty engine to be ferried to the Town depot and home. On the run in I mention that we had not been checked by signals. I was assured that it was normal practice.)

It must have been a good 20 years after these events. My wife and I had occasion to halt our car in the Somerset village of Martock. Suddenly there is a shout "Colin Robins" and there was Ray Groves stood in a trench, still working

as hard as he was when shovelling that coal forward at Yeovil Junction, what a wonderful surprise, but the thought did occur, why on earth did he and many other terrific motive power men not take the opportunity when made redundant to occupy vacancies at other Southern depots and thus retain their footplate status?

The just described diagram No 501on at 4.04pm and 551 at 5.33pm would allow me ample periods of man hours in pursuance of my part time outside interests, which in our naivety led us to conjure a belief that we would be rich at 30. Most fireman jumped at the chance to gobble up my more sociable office hour turns of duty.

Each steam man was a law to himself and worked his charge accordingly. Jack Ostler, a near neighbour was a renowned hard hitter. Working a heavy freight or stone train with our Jack would see him get out his piece of chalk and with the assistance of the flare lamp mark the 30% and 40% cut off points on the brass sector plate of the screw reverser.

Jack's fireman could not believe his luck at me proposing that we change turns. Working the engine to his driver's specification had the fireman, sorry, 'Robot', shifting huge amounts of coal in comparison with the economic proficiency of the technically minded, who would time a similar load using fine adjustments to the cut off of steam entering the cylinders. My window cleaning buddy who was much my senior knew all about Jack's heavy hand. His probable thinking was that he would have to make up for an exhausted Colin. He therefore conjured up the suggestion that I take my own chalk and re - adjust Jack's intentions. I took up this idea, so when Jackie boy was in preparation mode going about his oiling, I would remove his "back break" etchings and make my own more tolerant strokes on 25 and 30% cut off. Must have changed duties with driver Ostler's mate for five years at least, not once did he tumble. Even so belting down through Pinhoe with the "S15s" regulator fully open, would have me with feet well off the footplate sheltering on my side box seat. The bounce would have my mountain of shovelled forward coal tumbling and shaking over from the tender. I used to urge one to catch Jack a glancing blow to the back of the leg, but his aggressive vein was never rewarded by a strike of like nature. I did however find solace in the following.

His stance was to stand upright, left hand on the screw reverser wheel, right arm crooked with thumb hooked into the overall brace with the ever present Woodbine stuck between first and second finger. It seemed that he abhorred niceties as the regulator had two positions, opened and shut. Seldom did he remove his gaze from the eye glass, when firing up I would often give a little flick with the shovel, the dust would be sucked by the footplate created vacuum to be attached to the space presented by Jack's upper back and neck. On the run in I would draw off a bucket of hot water from the pep pipe and give my face and neck an unmasking, Jack would be too involved with braking to indulge – consequence was that when we got into the mess room and Jack removed his hat, the circle created above the hat band was pure white while all above shirt collar was as black as the ace of spades.

Can't bl***y understand it he would curse when he confronted the mirror above the sink. Needless to say the mess room layabouts would split their sides. Good old Jack, he would buy 60 Woodbines each day from our local grocer in Eastland Road, Mrs. Whetam. He presented a tough exterior, but I can vouch that he had a heart of gold.

CHAPTER 31

A DRIVER, A TECHNICIAN AND GENTLEMAN

Admiration and respect was apportioned by all the staff at Yeovil Depot to driver Sid Bicknell. He was meticulous in all aspects of his trade. His demeanour was such that there was never a sign of complaint from men when Sid would reduce the meal break by undertaking a task on the footplate that the majority of his colleagues would not fulfil in their entire careers.

On the duty I have just described he would arrange via the running foreman at Salisbury that a particular "S.15" be allocated to this diagram for the week. With the admitted assistance of his good lady he would renew every single oiling point trimming on the engine. Such was this mans dedication that I for one found myself hooked.

The lubricator, which as I have explained was entrusted to the fireman, (four drops per minute through the two sight feeds) was purged of lubricating oil by holding the bucket underneath it, whilst tapping the drain cocks open with a spanner. It was then washed out with a mixture of boiling water and paraffin. True to his word by Wednesday the old girl was running as sweet as a nut. One duty saw us in the down sidings at Exeter Central. I climbed on board a "West Country" and Sid shouldered his lunch, sorry, tool box up for me to lift onto the footplate, he let me take the weight, how I hung on without letting it fall back onto Sid's head I shall never know. At 10 ½ stone the scales of fate tipped my way.

Drafted into the Great War he attained the rank of Staff Sergeant. That man was relegated to the Yeovil branch after a prostate cancer operation. Then with the "M7" push and pull operated Westinghouse air system working as it was intended, via the driver at the dummy end exercising control by opening and closing the engine regulator. This in its self was a work of art, hence all other drivers booked that duty would pull out the connecting pin and trust the fireman to adjust the regulator. This would badly back fire when Inspector Smith 'Big Sam' was about.

All firemen had their share of "M7" Drummond tank duties through relieving when annual leave, rest days or sickness occurred. Apart from Sid I can not remember another driver having the courage to work the push pull in the correct format. An occasion did arise when Sam presented himself on the platform. Panic ensued. The engine regulator coupled via the securing pin to the Westinghouse air pump system was put in place. Mr Smith elected to ride with the fireman, the right away was given, the driver in the leading 'dummy' end eases his control lever open, air pressure in turn moves the on the footplate attachments, which was

S15 4-6-0 E827 coming out of the west end of Honiton tunnel. 04.08.1928
- H.C. Casserley collection

intended to gently open the regulator. That was when all hell broke loose, the regulator went across its full travel, this resulted in a terrific wheel spin which if the air pressure release valve had not been operated would have emptied the firebox and wrecked the rail head with little progress towards Yeovil Junction. There was no alternative but to carry on in the unauthorized manner. No doubt the driver had a serious dressing down, but I suspect that a blind eye was turned.

CHAPTER 32

IN DISGUISE - WE HAVE 'SCRUMP' ON THE CHEAP!

I reiterate – the footplate experience was demanding, hazardous and at times exhilarating. It also provoked episodes of unexpected hilarity I volunteer the three following narratives. They involve the West Country beverage – Cider, alias "Scrumpy".

The diagram involved is Exmouth Junction duty 551. My driver is big, seemingly tough, but as gentle as a tabby, Bert Lambier. We are at Exmouth Junction depot having completed the first part of the roster. We now relieve 508 duty and prepare an "S15" for the 9.30pm light engine to Sidmouth Junction. The 11 miles is routinely covered. We follow through the station

2-6-2T being prepared for a railtour to Taunton by Yeovil fireman Dave Cook, Colin Robins and Norman Culverwell. 18.02.1964 - Authors collection

and come to a halt over the controlling ground signal for the up sidings. It clears and we reverse and attach to the 1.55pm ex - Meldon Quarry to Woking ballast train which consists of "the for ever usual" ten vacuum fitted 'full load' stone hoppers plus brake van.

We have a wait of 27 minutes prior to our start time of 10.20pm. Brake test completed the guard comes up for a chat. I give the fire the usual livener and as the boiler pressure gauge responds I have the cushion of boiler contents to replenish so as to keep the old girl quiet. We exchange the courtesy one long one short on the whistle with our own men as they flay by on the 9.45pm freight ex-Exmouth Junction. On the button the exit signal comes off. Bert eases the regulator over and we take the strain with this short, compact but ponderous load. The gradient drops away. Bert gives her the gun, but very soon we are into the hard slog up to Honiton station and over the summit into the tunnel. We are booked into the up local platform at Seaton Junction to facilitate the passing on the up fast of the 5.23pm ex - Torrington to London Nine/Elms freight at 11.23pm. The beating the firebox has taken up the bank has the boiler pressure gauge around on the red. We allow the safety valves to blast away down the bank and make up the deficit in the boiler whilst stood at Seaton Junction.

This particular night was warm and clammy to the extent that my mate seemed to be continually mopping his ample jowl. We brake to a halt, the brightness from the open fire box door enlightens my Driver's ear to ear grin. "What have ee got up yer sleeve Bert?"- "why don't you take this bottle and pop across to the Station Hotel and fill her up we Scrump". Requiring no second bidding, I shoot across the station approach like a bat out of hell. All heads in the bar swivel as one at my arrival. It is way pass closing

time. A broad Devonshire brogue questions "What bee on manoeuvres?" I instantly recall my khaki forage cap and black face. Instincts inform me that they have me marked down as a Marine Commando on exercise. Deciding to go along with it I reply "Yeh there are a few of us strung out along the railway bridge-any chance Land lord?" Voice from the bar, "Vill in up var in, I'll pay, and vill up another bottle as well" Bert could not believe our luck as I was too honest to charge him.

Cider nearly always gives the recipient extraordinary vigour. So much so that on attaining Yeovil Junction and relief I could not have engineered another shovel full into that firebox. 'Hic'.

Bert was, as they say, pretty big around the middle. He would boast of devouring a plate full of spuds and fried onions before making his way to work on early, and I mean any time after midnight turns. What a constitution!.

Another cider turn was Salisbury duty 479. Either a "U" class or a 76 "Standard" was provided. On at 1.10pm pass to Yeovil Junction and work a shunting freight to Axminster and return. This entailed shunting Crewkerne yard. I had only to cut through the down yard boundary hedge to be at my bride's family home. All drivers I had on this turn were made aware of the fact that father-in-law always had a barrel of scrump on tap. On the promise that I did not return empty handed there was encouragement given for me to spend an hour in their splendid company. I would return with a flagon of best "Dowlish Wake" Somerset cider which would hardly put a dent in the weekly delivery.

I give you a preamble to the most ludicrous but utterly truthful episodes of my railway career. Again the lure of cider takes centre stage.

CHAPTER 33

PEDIGREE BULL ON THE LOOSE IN TEMPLECOMBE BOOKING FOYER AND YARD!

The engine working is Yeovil duty No 513 allocated a 2-6-0 3P/4F "U" class engine. This engine departed Yeovil at 6.30am, had journeyed to Salisbury, Bournemouth, Salisbury and back to Templecombe.

My Driver was Albert, alias "Boxer" Chainey, the depot giant. We booked on at 9.15pm and travelled pass to Templecombe where we relieved 513 duty at 10.15. There must have been a recognised "fiddle" in operation, as with Boxer you were expected (no one would argue) to accompany him to the local watering hole which stands at the bottom of the station approach, you returned at about 11pm. Driver and mate would then board the vacant engine. The fireman's confidence would receive an unwanted boost as he was told "You can handle the shunting, do you good", followed by a departing dig "don't make any mistakes mind". And he would retrace his path to the pub. The shunting staff was fully aware of this rule breaking addiction.

Off the fireman, come driver would go with rafts of wagons in tow up the long shunting neck. Shunt moves were dictated via a sequence of signals operated by flicking the top yard main light switch. If memory serves me correct, one flick ~ pull up, two~ stop and three flicks ~ you let the shunt trickle back on the steam brake. The shunter's would cut off the shunt by means of dropping the brakes on the rear wagon of the detachment batch, the resultant buffer up would allow the shunting pole to easily part the coupling. The brake would then be lifted which would allow the shunt to peel away under the control of the under shunter come brakeman. Surely the method explained was within the rules (Who's kidding who?) as there were two traffic inspectors residing in the village.

Boxer would eventually turn up with a flagon of cider for his fireman, and then when "grub time" was signalled and we adjourned to the shunter's cabin he would knock back the best part of that.

I have set the scene! The events of "Laurel and Hardy" proportions are yet to unfold.

Booked on the same duty - same driver – same Inn, my thoughts of "here we go again" are

demolished as a decidedly agitated familiar station foreman bursts into the packed bar. His portrayal of panic is such that all are instantly hushed. Regaining a vestige of control he appears to look directly at boxer Chainey and bellows out "Albert Chainey in here?" "You're looking at him" retorts a not amused boxer. "What's gone wrong Bert?" "Bloody pedigree bull's escaped and is half way down the road, give us a hand Albert". At this the audience is divided between those that want to run to the rear exit and those that wish to witness the show that is about to take centre stage on the station approach.

"Right Bert, come on Robins" instructs Boxer. I do as commanded. Sure enough in the half light as we three make our way up the station road there is Billy Boy with his head buried into the left road side bank having a good munch. To the right is the semi - detached railway cottages. I have taken the precaution of positioning myself on the cottage side of a garden gate. Albert is beside Billy's head urging a "Steady Boy" and asking for a rope. Situation seems to be under control. Suddenly the slight ease in tension is blown asunder as an idiot runs out of the down side booking hall with lamp in hand shouting "stop the bull". The bull jerks, turns and works up a trot towards the light. We follow. The light makes a speedier entry into the booking hall then it had on appearance from it. Billy follows crashing through the swing double doors. My cowardice has evaporated, replaced by the dire necessity to witness the next act.

We are tight behind and into the white tiled booking hall.

Templecombe upper yard - showing S15 4-6-0 on a reception road and 0-6-0 Pannier on top yard shunting duties - Gerald Siviour collection

To the left, interrupted in their quest to purchase a ticket is a young couple. The look of sheer petrifaction on that young girl's face having heard the fracas, looked around and witnessed a scene of such stupefying dimensions that must have left her doubting her sanity. I did not see her partner's expression as he was endeavouring to push his head into the booking office via the ticket issuing aperture.

TEMPLECOMBE (1950)

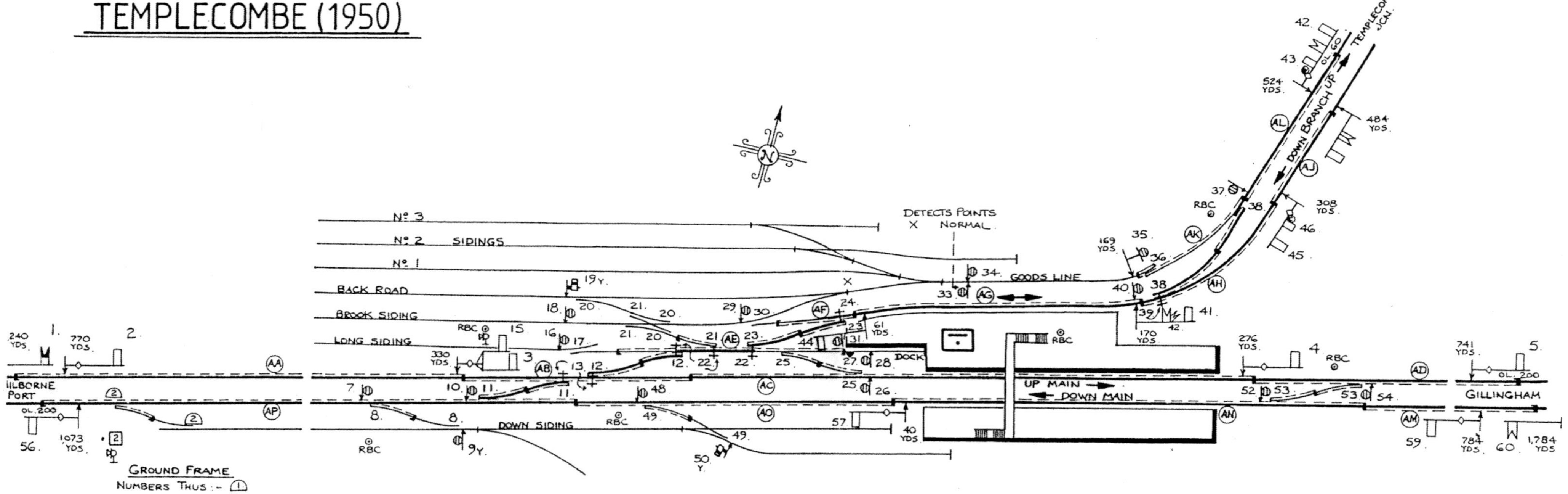

GROUND FRAME
NUMBERS THUS :- ☐
ELEC. REL ☐
G ☐

S.R. TYPE 13 BOX, 31' × 12' ELEVATED 9' (OVERALL LENGTH
INCLUDING RELAY ROOMS 54')
OPENED 15-05-1938 - REPLACED OLD BOX.
WESTINGHOUSE A2 FRAME, 4" CENTRES.
S.R. 3-POSITION CLOSED BLOCK ON MAIN LINES.
PREECE 1-WIRE BLOCK TO TEMPLECOMBE JCN.
CLOSING SWITCH - NIL.
ILLUMINATED DIAGRAM.

DETECTS POINTS
X NORMAL.

BOX OPEN CONTINUOUSLY

SPARE : 14 : 32 : 47 : 51 : 55 : 58 .

POINTS 30 LOCKS H.P. "X" NORMAL + REVERSE .

N° 3
N° 2 SIDINGS
N° 1
BACK ROAD
BROOK SIDING
LONG SIDING
DOWN SIDING

34 - GOODS LINE
UP MAIN
DOWN MAIN

TEMPLECOMBE JCN.
DOWN BRANCH UP
GILLINGHAM

BOX OPEN CONTINUOUSLY

(1968)

STATION CLOSED 07-03-1966 .
ALL CONNECTIONS EXCEPT N° 11 POINTS, FPL 13 WEST, AND
DISCS 10 + 26 TAKEN OUT OF USE 26-10-1966 .
10, 11, 13, + 26 ABOLISHED 12-02-1967 .
NEW SINGLE LINE LAYOUT INTO USE 02-04-1967 (BELOW) AND
LEVER FRAME REDUCED TO 1G LEVERS.

SHERBORNE
DOWN UP
DOWN MAIN
AB
DOWN SIDING
GILLINGHAM
BC
BB

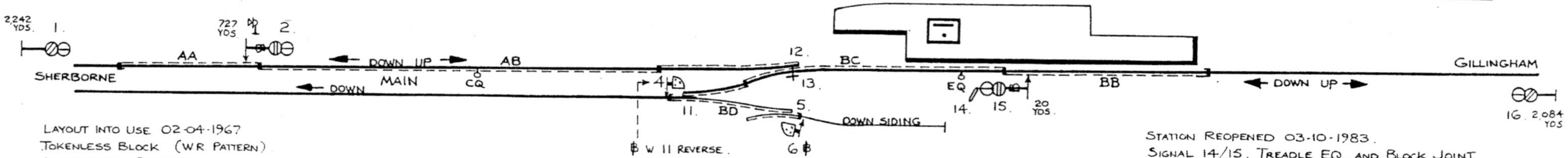

LAYOUT INTO USE 02-04-1967 .
TOKENLESS BLOCK (WR PATTERN)
ILLUMINATED DIAGRAM.

SWITCH LEVER - 10
SPARE : 3 : 7 : 8 . 9

STATION REOPENED 03-10-1983 .
SIGNAL 14/15, TREADLE EQ. AND BLOCK JOINT
OFF BC/BB TRACKS REPOSITION 44 YDS NEARER
SHERBORNE. 06-01-1988 .

Templecombe from the west, where Billy boy took Albert Chainey & Colin Robins for a walk - H.C. Casserley collection

Through the swing doors and on to the down platform goes Billy Boy with posse in close pursuit, we swing to the left. The down starter on the end of the platform is ON but we plough by into the down yard. He keeps going, trotting between the carriage and wagon sidings through a pair of stop blocks and onto the tenanted allotments. It is mid summer and incredible there is a railwayman still on his strip, he could not help but hear the raucous approach. I can see him now. At the bulls advance he lifts both arms, one holding a rake, in the surrender position, moving back as if under hypnosis he topples into a stream!

Boxer is giving advice that the Quarry must be nearing exhaustion, I'm thinking aren't we all. The bull turns, out flanks the pack and re enters the yard to re trace his steps towards the horse box he had made his escape from, during the attempt to water him. (This was in accordance with laid down instructions.) No one had informed Templecombe that the animal was loose. The horse box doors were swung down and out the blighter cantered.) I decide to peel away from the following pack and find safety by following between an adjoining deserted siding. Suddenly I cannot believe my eyes. The terror had cut through a vacant wagon space and was coming back towards ME! I was just about to desert my line of confrontation by diving beneath a pair of wagon buffers into the safety of another siding when I hear a voice even more threatening. Boxer yelling from between two wagons "hold your ground Robins". This was the most chilling order I was ever to receive. I had my small torch at hand and foolishly shone it at the bull. He rushed me – Jumping to the right I manage to evade his horns. His girth however knocks me over as he rushed by. Somehow Boxer had picked up a solid wagon plank, swung it with all his enormous strength and caught Billy fair and square across the eyes breaking the plank in two. With a loud grunt and exhalation of air this merry-go-round was brought to a shuddering halt. With ropes conducting him he was led from whence he came and tied for everyone's safety

to the securing metal rings in the horse box. Having no idea where the quarry would lead the attending pack, traffic control had put a block on both main lines.

This episode made the media from which we learnt that the pedigree sire was away on an overseas posting fulfilling stud duties. We can only conjecture whether his offspring developed a tendency to squint.

I would change turns for this duty with the extra monetary rewards for night work and the opportunity to pursue other activities during the day as the attraction.

Albert "Boxer" Chainey was a character and a half. Did his Army 1939/1945 Service in the Railway Engineers, married an Italian lady and devoted a lifetime to farming and railways.

An additional morsel to the volume I could write on Albert relates to a Yeovil branch trip. We depart Yeovil Junction. The night is pitch black. The signalman at "A" box is leaning out of his sliding window rotating his arms windmill fashion and gesticulating towards our front end. "Albert, I've left a red on the front" I say. Albert "Good we'll make him look a ****, come over here". I find myself in control. Albert climbs along the framing of the "M7" tank and reverses the red on the front. We run into the Town station. Foreman Watford is waiting for us. His expression turns from triumph into bewilderment as he saw the correct head code approaching.

Another quick gem – I get a cursing for bringing in an engine for disposing with an over the top fire. The roasting is well deserved. Boxer and his passed fireman mate are delayed their regular excursion to the Alexander Hotel. Next night I make a conviction decision and bring in a fire that they have difficulty in saving - ah well, you can't win 'em all.

2-6-0 U class stands alongside 4-6-0 S15 class at Templecombe. circa 1963 - Richard Duckworth collection

CHAPTER 34

RUN - BY AT MY HOME TOWN OF CREWKERNE

My home town of Crewkerne springs to the fore when run - bys are under discussion. Frank Smith and I are rostered on Exmouth Junction duty 550. We sign on at 1.10pm. Light engine to Yeovil Junction and attach to the 12.40pm ex-Salisbury and work to Exeter Central stopping at all stations, arriving at 3.33pm. The "West Country" element made the down trip a piece of cake. We then transferred to 546 duty which would be berthed with its empty coaching stock in the up sidings, with a "S15" class on the front.

The 2.20pm ex-Ilfracombe with a "West Country" on the front would then come belting up the 1 in 37 incline from St David's. This service then formed the 4.30pm ex-Exeter Central to Waterloo. It departs from the up local. The ground signal comes off and the shunter gives us the tip to proceed in its wake. The guard would as per usual give us the damages "load", "four for 120 tons driver". Contented? Not really. At this stage in my career I would have cherished the opportunity of handling the vacuum brake, if only from the distant signal into the platform at one chosen station. With Frank however, no chance. At right time we are away for what we surmised would be our usual mundane stop all stations foray, but as for so many trips from a front end prospectus one never had a clue what was lurking around the corner, sorry, around the bend.

The nine stops to Chard Junction were unmemorable run of the mill kit. This admittedly can breed complacency. Could that have been the culprit for the following?

We were booked eight minutes at Chard Junction, ample time to set back from the platform onto four Wilts United Dairy's milk tanks which would be stood open in the up siding. Each tank when loaded contained 3,000 gallons of milk and weighed in at a substantial 27 tons 8 cwt. Attachment made according to script, even had time for the usual banter with the operating grades. The guard gives us the revised load which has nearly doubled the tonnage. Out onto the platform we get the right away.

My mate as expected had to wind the reverser over to 40% cut off, the regulator was across my side well into the second valve. The response of the "S15" to the caning she took on the six miles of rising gradient to Crewkerne summit spoke volumes for this superb mixed traffic workhorse.

The section of eight miles was allotted 18 minutes, which when one considers the standing start, gradient and load involved, was not in any way generous. As per usual I tug the whistle wire as Hewish Crossing box hove into view. My mate's dad is on duty and will recognise the significance. Frank shuts off as we lip the summit at the 133 ¼ mile post. With black smoke belching directly from firebox over the train, passengers that have not lifted the leather control strap and snapped the window shut will soon be lifting smuts from their attire.

The brake is feathered as we enter the tunnel. For some unknown reason I have my beady eye on Frank as we emerge. His expression of complacency abruptly changes to one of astonishment, a second of hesitation and the vacuum brake handle is slammed down to the full application position. I shout "What's wrong?" "No bloody brake" is the alarming answer!

Sure enough, although I could detect a resistance to the forward momentum, there seemed as if there was a force pushing us from the rear. A reflex action has me diving for the tender hand brake which I screw down with all the energy I can muster. For a stopping train our speed passing through the level crossing is suggesting that there will be a surprise in store for my home town of Crewkerne, as we pass through. I disengage brain and shout across

Colin Robins shunting the yard at Crewkerne on Yeovil engine 2-6-0 U class 31792
- Authors collection

4-6-2 Battle of Britain class 34084 253 Squadron calls at Crewkerne after heavy snow, with an Exeter - Yeovil stopping train. 07.01.1963 - John Cornelius collection

the footplate "Thank **** the gates were open". This unthinking remark did not offer any favours to my mate's loss of control. We could do no more apart from, and I was to do this many times during the following 35 years, curl our toes down.

The brake on engine and train was gripping but not with sufficient ferocity to assist our appointment with my home town station of Crewkerne.

The platform staff, all diligently awaiting our habitual arrival, is with disbelief confronted with a conveyance of runaway proportions. Around the severe right hand approach we hurtle. Frank with despair emitting and brake handle fully applied – myself – confident after hanging on to the whistle wire that all within a wide radius are aware that all is not as it should be, have a sensation of detached from responsibility inquisitiveness – "how?".

The engine comes to a stand straddling the still remaining east of the station foot crossing. I jump down onto the cess and make way to the guard. All windows are down and packed with an incredulous array of heads demanding a reply to the question in local dialect "Wass gone wrong?" We reach the attachment point between coaching stock and milk tanks where the speculated obvious makes way for reality. The cause of the debacle springs to light as a glaring fundamental error. The vacuum pipes between rear coach and tanks were not connected. The accumulated solid rear weight of near 110 tons had been swingers. It was obvious that we had not had the compulsory brake test.

Brake pipes united, continuity brake test carried out. Authority obtained for the propelling movement into the platform. Our guard relaying the hand signal from the box beckons us back into the platform.

My driver an exceedingly proud and private individual kept his cards close to his chest so I was not party to the meted discipline. That knuckles were severely rapped there was no doubt.

The incident taught me a never to be forgotten lesson, whenever I was involved in either attachments or detachments those two so important words "Brake Test" would forever come to the fore.

CHAPTER 35

MY 18 HOURS ON DUTY

A "once" in the history of the Waterloo to Exeter main line occurred on the 1st of October 1960. A record rainfall resulted in the collapse between Seaton Junction and Honiton Tunnel of a large section of embankment which resulted in the blockage of both up and down main lines.

Running on time the 1.15am ex-Waterloo down paper train sped through Seaton Junction. On the approaching up road the 4.04am ex - Exmouth Junction freight booked to pass Honiton Box at 4.43am was also on time. An incredible scenario was about to unfold. There was no advanced warning that this impenetrable mass of bank had collapsed.

One can only envisage the scene on the "Merchant Navy" footplate. Honiton Bank, the last hurdle to mount. The regulator was probable levered via the drivers shoulder to horizontal, maximum. Pointer in the sector plate dropped over to 40, perhaps even 50% cut off – why not give her the works, once through the tunnel and over the bank we're home and dry. Then they really were in it, solid mud, yards high. We footplate men deemed it a miracle that such a severe check did not smash the crew against the boiler front, but unscathed they were. The up freight ploughed likewise into the west side of the disintegration.

The sequence of events that permeated through the footplate grades was that the two firemen trudging over the mud and debris with the intention of protecting the opposite running road, in accordance with the rule book, met. However the press version had it that the up freight was detained at Honiton.

I was to foot this particular stage when signing on spare at 2pm that same day. My driver one "Nobby" Clarke and I had been looking forward to a shift playing cards. No such luck, the land slide scuppered that. A Yeovil 2-6-0 "U" class was prepared for us and we were away light engine to the Junction. Attachment made, brake test etc, Guard in position and we were away to Seaton junction with 30 to 40 low sided engineers wagons in tow. On arrival we detach our charge on the down local, run round, and attach to the guards van and receive instructions. Permanent way staff had been drafted in from all over, and the majority loaded themselves onto our empties, we now under hand signals propel up the bank. These low wagons were to be filled by hand shovel from ground level. As one by one the wagons were filled so we pushed forward.

We had the storm sheet up, I lifted the firebox baffle plate out, turned around with the fire hole door closed on its lips and filled with white hot fire, we were as comfortable as bugs in a rug. The guard, one Harold Purse, had joined us. By 10pm we had without thought devoured our grub. Off the down road there were a few bungalows, I suggested that their privacy be invaded, Harold in his broad Devonshire brogue "You ant got the neck to do that av'e?" Nobby "Ee Av". With can in hand I knock the rear door. Apologising for the disturbance, I explain our predicament with such sensitivity that I am urged to gather a little something from inside their rear fence in a while. A cardboard box containing baked beans, soup, cakes and rounds of B & B was presented, what a feast, fair do's we left a monetary thank you in the emptied bean tin.

At 4am much against my drivers wishes I explained to the officer in charge that we had been on duty 14 hours, and that I was concerned that my wife would have no knowledge as to my whereabouts. "Mobile's had not been dreamed of". It transpired that our situation had been overlooked. Our relief duly arrived. 18 hours on duty was ridiculous.

A sequel – Many moons later the same 'Nobby' had been elevated to Motive power supervisor at Salisbury, he was popular in many ways but took satisfaction in disciplining footplate crew who had completed their duty but had left the depot prior to their signing off time. A practice countenanced by all depots. I was in their mess room hearing all the gossip regarding my long ago mate when in he walked with a haughty "What ho Robins". "Hey Nobby" I rejoin "just telling the lads about our record 18 hours on duty up Honiton bank and how you went bananas when I requested relief". We did remain the best of mates.

2-4-0WT 30586/85 paused at Yeovil en-route to Eastleigh. 22.06.1962
- John Day collection

CHAPTER 36

YEOVIL CREW - WORK TO BARNSTAPLE

More then a week had elapsed before the main line was given the all clear. During this period the North Devon freight traffic was routed from Yeovil Junction across the branch via Langport to Taunton and thence on Western Region metals to Barnstaple.

I must have been spare the following week as my diary has me booked with driver A. Hardwick for three consecutive special duties to Barnstaple. The motive power provided was the trusty 2-6-0 'U' class, of the breed stabled at Yeovil. The full loads were marshalled at Templecombe. The engine was exceptionally well prepared for us with the tender trimmed to perfection. No doubt as the special notice workings portrayed a very long day indeed, the shed master had whispered in someone's ear.

Tender first to the junction we ease back onto our special freight. The number of wagons gives the impression that we are in for a lighter then expected trip. The numerical classification afforded to the 2-6-0 is three, allowing a maximum of 41 loaded wagons for the severe gradients from Crewkerne to Honiton. However the guard giving us the load shoots our expectations down in flames. The load was calculated on the full loading allowed for the gradients from Taunton to our destination of Barnstaple and they were to be the most severe I was ever to encounter.

The trip across the branch from Yeovil to Curry Rivel Junction was the usual procession of changing single section staffs with the load insubstantial for the section giving no problem. We are routed down the main via Athelney and into our county town. A Western pilotman is provided from Taunton. The bag is pulled around and while the tender is topped up I get the coal forward while my mate enlightens our conductor to the controls of, to him, this strange beast. The Taunton man does the driving.

We come off the Great Western main and onto the Barnstaple branch. Throughout the lengthy, to us, expedition, we get a well in advance professional appraisal of the on coming extreme gradients. A guide to the difficulties the regular footplate grades encountered was the fact that after we had been detached from our freight at Barnstaple our engine was taken to the coal stage for a much required top up, such was the volume of coal we had consumed. Those three days were to be my sole experience over the route, yet I vividly recall our pilot man parading the top of a single line distant which we viewed through a short tunnel from the base of an obviously steep incline. The signal was positioned on the reverse slope which I remember was as rigidly demanding in brake control as was the incline for opposing reasons.

After the deserved meal break we three return to the "U" class to find a relief crew had turned our engine on the triangle and taken water as well as the mentioned visit to the coal stage. We are light engine to Yeovil. Arthur oils around while we await a pathway. I realise the reverse trip is going to be a doddle, but the thought of the number of times I will have to change the single line authority does not excite me one iota.

Before jumping ship at Taunton the pilot man confides that his previous doubts regards the suitability of the Yeovil "U" class to lift such a load over the Barnstaple branch gradients had been wrong, as after handling one his opinion was that it was on par with the best of Western engines of similar power ratio.

The three days on this duty gave me a boost, which at the time must have been important, but now seems undoubtedly insignificant. Departing Taunton my mate handed the reins of driver over to me. OK, I realise it was only a light engine, but the gesture must have been greatly appreciated. In all that slip at Honiton did my back pocket no harm at all.

Arthur Hardwick was another character and a half. Trouble was from the firemans perspective, there was never the slightest indication when his mischievous mode would kick in. The following gave me more then 'goose pimples'. We were booked as passengers to Exmouth Junction in order to work a light engine bound for Eastleigh Works as far as Yeovil. First sight of our charge caused much child like amusement.

It was minute, even in comparison with Yeovil's "M7" tanks. The 2-4-0 "Well tank" was built by Beattie in 1874 for the LSWR and was one of three allocated to Wadebridge. They were numbered 30585, 30586 and 30587.

Arthur was portly and his first crack was that he would have to work it on his own as there wasn't room on the footplate for me. After preparation I found that the elf like bunker would have to be topped up, this was accomplished by one of the coaling staff from an open wagon. Boiler gauge glass up to the top nut with tanks over spilling and we make our way. The 48 miles to Yeovil Junction was not going to be accomplished in a hurry.

It seemed that any speed approaching 20mph would send the old girl into instability, akin to a speed wobble. We get the distant signals in our favour as far as Sidmouth Junction where we relax in the up siding as a booked service takes preference. The section clears and off we toddle. I was leaning over the side in a sort of day dream. I look across the tiny footplate and immediately I'm startled witless. I was in sole charge – panic – first thoughts are the obvious – he's fallen off – out, it never mattered which, Arthur was absent. I slam the brake handle down. I am very frightened. Suddenly I register a tapping. Going back to my side intending to look along the framings via the small face size circular window, I find it full of Arthur Hardwick's beaming features. He had some how pulled himself along the framings, negotiated the smoke box and up my side to eyeball me. I suppose I should have shown annoyance, but the relief of seeing him relaxed my extreme tension.

We were together again riding pass in the guards van from Templecombe to Yeovil. I was prepared for a little kip, 'Shut-eye,' no way, not with Hardwick about. There was two Exeter based guards on board. One in his official capacity and the other like us riding spare. Arthur belts my leg with his as if to say 'Watch this'.

We notice that when the brake has to be screwed on they seemed to take turns at it. A few choice wind ups from the master stirrer craftily insinuating that it looked as if the spare guard thought the brake wasn't been applied correctly, by the time we got to Yeovil Junction they were nearly having a punch up. He was such a comedian that each time I saw him I wanted to laugh. The Beeching cuts had him transferring to Reading and sundry electric depots, but he could not settle. What a lovely man. He sadly passed away just a few years after leaving Yeovil.

CHAPTER 37

PAINFUL MEMORY OF CITY BREED CLASS 'H15' N0. 30335

The diagrams worked from Yeovil Town were split over the old Southern section between the extremities of Salisbury and Exeter. I preferred the Exeter work as it was the more challenging. On one occasion however a duty to Salisbury presented me with a difficult and painful test.

Salisbury duty No. 503 was the provider. Harold Ham and I booked on at 7.55pm. Pass to the Junction and relieved a N15 4-6-0 "King Arthur" class at 8.20pm. The engine diagram did not allow a sufficient time for engine requirements prior to departing Exmouth Junction at 3.3pm. The work load then included stone, passenger, freight and the 6.7pm mixed passenger, milk and parcels ex - Axminster.

This "Arthur" was labelled as the depot's roughest square up. Off the Junction at 8.23pm our triple roll allows added station time. This additional minute or two is a bonus for us fireman as we are able to breath, sorry, belt via the heavy dart, blower and anything else on hand, life into a fire that had all but given up the ghost.

First port of call is Sherborne, where I get the boiler pressure around on the (200lb per sq. inch) red mark in preparation for the 1 in 80 incline. Right away and I soon have to sacrifice the boiler level in order to maintain sufficient steam pressure. We turn the top and I take advantage at the closure of the regulator by twisting the blower on full pelt. I now turn on the injector. Respite at Milborne Port and we are away. Breasting the incline my mate gets a grip of the brake for the 1 in 100 descent into Templecombe. The water level in the boiler gauge glass is low which will allow us ample space in the boiler to keep her quiet during the 45 minutes we are put away in the up yard.

I vividly recall this duty and the small luxury it afforded. Our arrival often coincided with the late running 6pm semi fast service from Waterloo. The times we managed to stop along side the griddle restaurant was incredible. I lean over from the footplate and bang on the kitchen window, cook lets it down. "Any chance mate?" I enquire. On every occasion this bold request extracted a grease proof bag of mouth watering chips spiced with lashings of salt and vinegar. I am sure that the novelty of the situation coupled with my obvious expectancy gave the cook reciprocal pleasure. They were equal to any rich mans caviar. Our hands were never washed but the fingers were spotless after the meal.

Under the guidance and signals of the platform foreman and guard we propel back into the up yard.

Adjustments to our load are spelt out as our guard hands up the damages. Guard in his van and we have the brake test. Up yard to up main exit signal off, a green from the guard and we move out onto the up road. On the platform we get the right away on time at 9.32pm. Starter and advance off we quickly pick up speed, the descent is at 1 in 80. After a mile

URIE 4-6-0 H15 departs Salisbury with a Southampton - Andover train . Circa 1947
- Phillip Brown collection

H15 class 4-6-0 (City breed) at the coal stage Eastleigh MPD. 24.08.1955
- Michael G. Harvey collection

the gradient levels off, then rises from 1 in 90 to 1 in 100 to the east of Gillingham Tunnel. My mate now allows the "Arthur" to have its head as we belt down the reverse gradient, then, with expert use of the vacuum brake the mixed passenger and parcel stock is brought into Gillingham without a hint of a jolt.

Away right time at 9.53pm we are into the four mile, 1 in 114 to 1 in 80 gradients to Semley where our status as a passenger train terminates. The same term could also be applied to our steaming capabilities for we would as always on this duty, using polite fireman's language "Be down the pan" Stirring life into the decidedly old girl via every firing appliance at hand would attain a vestige of response. We must not linger, in fact, I can never recall a driver reversing his gaze from a "hypnotised" along the platform mode, to the, in my mind, more practical observation of the steam pressure and boiler contents gauges. I am sure some were nervous of taking fright.

At 10.12pm we Yeovil men are in for a rare thrill, namely the opportunity of 17 miles to get up some real pace as we shoot through Tisbury, Dinton and to a lesser extent Wilton. We are now running into Salisbury, looking over my side at the motive power depot I miss a fixture. For a considerable period of time a Dugald Drummond 4-6-0 class H15, No 30335 had found, which we fireman prayed would be a permanent resting ground, namely behind the depot departure ground frame points box. I shout this news to Harold. He retorts that with any luck it's gone to scrap.

Arrival in the up through at Salisbury is on time at 10.37pm. After detaching our engine and placing the correct head lamp code in position the signals clear for our move forward into the short middle road and then the tender first journey through the station and onto Salisbury motive power depot's disposal pits. I get on with my disposal duties. Harold is away to the running foreman's office and returns with the usual good news that our "N15" is for "Washout" which means all remnants of fire and ash has to be cleared from the firebox on to the mountain of clinker that stretched the length either side of Salisbury's two disposal pits, smoke box and ash pans were likewise treated. Most

drivers and all passed fireman would lend a hand, but not me mate Harold – no way.

Eventually I wash off in the communal bucket which I never saw emptied, the scum was 'creamed' off the top by hand. It was continually topped up from the king-sized iron kettle which irrespective of seasons had a permanent base on the cabin open fire.

It was great to relax and once again pay attention to the banter of this "A" classified depot. We now change over to Salisbury duty No 500. Harold brings back news of our allocated engine. I cannot believe my ears – 30335. Grasping the significance of my exclamation of astonishment the men around the table have a laugh at my expense.

The "H15" was known throughout the footplate grades as the "City Breed" but described in our fireman's terms as a B******. The firebox was 9ft 6ins in length and was dead flat, in layman's terms there was not a slope to the front, it was a long throw. In fact on my initial introduction I joked that I would need a plank and a wheel barrow to get it up the front. A redeeming feature was that you could fill the boiler up to the whistle with little danger of the old girl priming.

Destiny would have it that I would not battle with the elements on this occasion. Our charge was placed a couple of engine lengths inside the shed on No. 10 road. During the course of preparation I was on the framings, probably checking the sands. Harold was beneath me oiling the motions, we both had flare lamps. He looks up, sees an excuse which will avoid him having to climb onto the footplate - me. "Wind er over into fore gear mate" had I been any where else the following would have been averted.

No hesitation. Leaving the all important flare lamp, I double hand it along the length of the boiler safety rail, swing "Monkey" like around the cab frame onto the footplate. The interior of this cathedral sized shed was at this time unlit. The adage "Familiarity breeds contempt" now raises its head. All footplate equipment we could find blindfolded. Right hand knocks the screw reverser stabilising lever forward. Left hand on reverser wheel winding handle and I swing it clock wise with all my strength – only went half a turn – Harold had his solid built carrying box beneath. The full momentum was halted by my middle finger becoming jammed betwixt box and wheel, I well remember bellowing S***, several times!

What a mess. My driver went mental and raved at the shed turner and his mate as if they were responsible for the overall negligence of the shed been unlit. Fitter Bill Lambert (ex-Yeovil) was the on duty St Johns Ambulance first aid official. He accompanied me to Salisbury Hospital. The casualty emergency doctor remarked that my hand, oil and coal stained, was the dirtiest he had ever treated. His concern was that septicemia would set in via the crushed finger and missing nail. Injections and dressing etc applied, I was instructed to visit my GP first thing in the morning. I endured a throbbing ride back to Yeovil Junction hunched in the guards van of the 10.40pm ex - Nine Elms which formed our 1.39am freight ex- Salisbury West Yard. I ride into my depot with Harold and the Salisbury fireman on the 'ferry' light engine.

It must have been 5.30am before I got to bed, and up at 8am. I am first in queue at my doctors. He insists that he sign me on the sick. I insist, and win the day that he doesn't. Down at the depot I am told "sorry son we are not permitted to sign you on light duties" There was no short term sick pay at that time and I could "NOT" afford to stay at home. Overcoming my wife's advice to the contrary I sign on with finger swathed in gauze and bandage for my booked duty. I meet Harold in the signing - on lobby. His greeting was less then cordial. "Don't think I'm doing your work mind" I remember checking myself from retorting "haven't asked you to", but said mildly "OK mate".

As soon as we left Yeovil Junction I realised what a complete idiot I was. Every operation with the firing shovel had the blood coursing up that finger, I had to lever the finger back so as the weight would be shielded from it. There was no stroke of luck at Salisbury, again our engine was for wash out. I vividly recall that every other day the nurse at the surgery had the disagreeable task of redressing that finger.

CHAPTER 38

STUCK IN GILLINGHAM TUNNEL WITH A SICK PILOTMAN AND UNCONSCIOUS GUARD!

During the early 1960s the bed of the 720 yard Gillingham Tunnel was excavated to a depth that would allow the original footings to be underpinned. To facilitate this long term engineering project a block post was established thereby facilitating single line working. It was evident that the overall costs was exorbitant (all brought into the equation, as was the new signal boxes and colour light systems to substantiate the case to single line the route from Salisbury to Exeter just a few years hence.)

Do you detect bitterness? Correct!

I am booked to work Salisbury duty 471. My driver is Bill (for some obscure reason he was referred to as "Herbie" Shire.) Bill was large in stature and gleaned prestige from his part time position as special constable, although at times his slight pompous air would result in muffled titters. Personally I was always "chuffed" to have him as my driver. On at 1.50am we prepare a "King Arthur" 4-6-0 class, then 2.50am light engine from the depot to the Junction, the "N15" was then turned on the down side table. (The turn table remains in excellent condition via the expertise of the local preservation society) Back over the crossovers we stand in the up bay platform.

On the arrival of the 4.40pm freight ex - Wadebridge, the train engine would be cut off and run light into the depot. The bay starter would come off, we would go up over the controlling ground signal, upon its clearance it would back onto the vacuum head. I would attach. Brake test completed and load of train ticket in the hands of my driver. Time allowed for the

guard to rejoin his van. (The easing of tension on release of the van brake was often discernible.) The time book departure was 3.40am, after which, with the starter off, the regulator would be cautiously eased open, couplings now taunt, the "Arthur", with a weight of equal to 48 loaded wagons was, "given the gun". My mate would catch the advanced starter as I exchange lamp signals with the guard. We are soon hammering towards Sherborne, the regulator is eased but with the sighting of the distant at green Bill gives her the full works (2nd valve) with reverser on 30% cut off. With a clean fire Sherborne Bank with its 1in 80 gradient did not present a problem. I let the boiler gauge glass level drop as we pass through Milborne Port and drop down into Templecombe. We reverse into the up yard for a wait of 25 mins. The spare capacity in the boiler now pays dividends as I top her up allowing all a quiet respite.

4-6-0 S15 Crewed by driver Don Wilcocks and fireman Colin Robins, emerging from a single line working in Gillingham tunnel . circa 1959 - Authors collection

4-6-2 WC/BB 34091 Weymouth heads a van train towards Salisbury through Semley station - Richard Duckworth collection

The load is adjusted to equal 53. The pilot man with his regulation red armlet positioned above the left elbow introduces himself. We are the last train to travel from Templecombe through the single line working at Gillingham Tunnel, hence his presence, he will then stay at the Gillingham end and ride back to Templecombe on the last train travelling in that down direction. All went according to plan except for the fact that the pilot man took the liberty of commandeering my seat. We strictly adhere to the mandatory speed of 15 mph over the cross over onto the "wrong' down road prior to Gillingham Tunnel, 'as the man in charge is aboard'. The situation off the up road is ablaze with arc lights illuminating engineering machinery, concrete blending requirements and messing facilities. Big Bill takes exception to the pilot suggesting that he should give ample warning of our approach and counters with a couple of choice expletives as he tests the rigidity of the whistle wire for good measure. The mirth of this incident still gives me convulsions.

However, happenings were about to take a distinct change of direction.

Our exhaust beat on entry was unhesitant, strong and singular as we make determined headway, we were now probably half way through the tunnel, and I was over Bill's side peering down at the labourers in the depth of the up road excavation. Suddenly in an instant all order was belted into touch as our exhaust goes ballistic and driving wheels loose all semblance of adhesion, a fleeting memory shot of those men below us cowering in understandable fright stays with me. Bill pulls the regulator shut. I shoot across the footplate and yank the sands lever back to the open position, but remember giving myself a sever reprimand as without doubt I should have been over my own side with my hand on said operating lever in order to hopefully arrest such an eventuality.

Now we really had problems for as soon as the steam was shut off, up went the safety valves. I whack the injector on. Bill gently-gentle eases the regulator across, two beats and "zzzzzzz" the wheels take off again. The injector being on is not making one iota of difference, she's still blowing her brains out. Up goes the exhaust as does the solid steam from our boiler safety valves, the roof of the tunnel takes the brunt of the assault and discards both to curl around the driving cab and invade the footplate. Driver and mate have issued clothes to their mouths while our panic stricken pilotman with eyes like organ stops has only a handkerchief. The situation was claustrophobic and alarming as the heat from steam and exhaust fumes was cutting the ceiling of available air down to knee level. Bill is coaxing her to keep her feet, I'm jerking the sand lever between the open and shut positions. Bill shouts "push the shovel against the downside wall I don't bloody know whether I'm going forward or backwards". I do, and shout likewise "

C***** we're slipping backwards" Bill bellows another "not to be repeated" expletive. Followed by "To hell with this I'm going to let the ****** drop back". The pilotmans authority is one of overall control. My driver however was not for "pussy footing", as far as Special Constable Bill Shire was concerned, he was the kingpin. Our friend was physically sick and would have been pushed to tell us what the time was. His presence on the footplate however was as if we had an official order to ease back.

Bill informs the man in charge what he is going to do. I must be recovering as I remember having tears of mirth as I digest this "Cart before the horse" scenario. My mate remarks that it is weird that there is a lack of resistance from the rear as with great caution and warning pulls on the whistle wire we drop back out of the tunnel. Clear air had never been more welcome!

Off I go with instructions on where the train has to be split. The throwaway remarks re resistance rears its head, all wagon couplings are strung out, so much so that if a coupling was prized off, the rear of the train would undoubtedly run away. I recap, the guard was in his van when we left Templecombe, so why has his brake not been applied?

I reach the van, not a sound, which I'm thinking he probably is "sound asleep". Up the steps onto the veranda I ease the door open – there he is, dead to the world. I remember thinking "How the hell did he sleep through this" I give him a rude awakening. His first words "We soon got up east yard"- Salisbury. I'm afraid I lost my cool and yelled "for your information me old mate we've just propelled back out of Gillingham Tunnel" and for good measure "the pilotman on board is not amused." Never seen a bloke come to so quickly. He knew that if it came to light that he was asleep he would have been in for more then the high jump. He was a character, rumoured to have taken a bail of straw down west from Salisbury to make a bob or two.

Now transformed into a more then willing helper I had him, after the van brake had been screwed on, accompanying me back to the cut off point. As I sprinted back to the engine, he swung a green light for Bill to ease back so as the wagons could be split.

With the pilotman on the engine there was no need for the guards pink wrong line order form "A"

I am sure that both senior men on the engine read the situation, but not a word was said.

I assure driver and pilotman that our guard was dropping brakes on the front wagons of the rear portion and placing three detonators ten yards apart at the prescribed 100 yards to the fore. Bill, for the benefit of the man in charge, "did you remember to write down the number of the rear wagon?" "course I did" is the haughty reply as I show him the indelible scratching on the forearm.

All satisfied that the regulations contained in the British Railways issued 1950 Rule Book have been applied, my mate does his best to wake up the slumbering country side with a piercing pull on the whistle wire. Now with half a load we pull away and make a mockery of our previous failed assault. Through the tunnel we revert via the cross over from the single down line onto the correct up road.

I take the opportunity to make up the depth of the fire as we run down the bank into Gillingham. The home signal is cleared after our approach has been drastically curtailed.

Our caretaker drops off on the platform to confer and update the situation. I note that the Salisbury men on 503 duty working the 1.50am milk from Basingstoke had advanced from our booked change over point at Tisbury and were standing in the down platform. We get the tip and are signalled to propel into the up siding. Engine cut off and out into the up line. I put a white head lamp onto the tender. The pilotman must be a glutton for punishment as surprise, surprise he elects to ride back with us tender first to pick up the rear end. I was all for changing over with the Salisbury men but the suggestion quiet rightly made little progress. Thankfully it is a mild morning, so after giving the tender the works with the pep pipe the chance of getting dust in the eyes is taken and we are off tender - first to rescue our tail. Firebox door wide open, we three are warmed to the rear and buffeted to the fore. Into the tunnel the sudden blaze of fierce lighting from an open tender aspect is startling and brought comment on the enormous expenditure of this engineering project. Should either of us proffer the idea that in a short number of years the main would be single lined the other two would have suggested that he consult a psychiatrist.

Bill is issuing a series of warning "pop" whistles and I'm peering over the side trying to spot a couple of likely lads from my wife's home village who are, as they would phrase it "making a bomb", working 12 hour nights. We rumble along at 15mph. The cacophony of echo's resounding from heavy engineering plant and pneumatic drills within the confines of this tunnel is truly deafening. I remember the scene with clarity. Legislation re Health and Safety at work is for the distant future. There was no regard for the protection of one's hearing or sight.

It was a relief to emerge from mayhem into a natural environment. I'm standing on the tender firing plate trying to sight the guards hand lamp, but the brightness of the tunnel approach lights illuminating engineering paraphernalia make it impossible, then three shots (detonators) vibrate through the countryside and simultaneously I see his green lamp been waved from side to side guiding us back. We touch and Bill eases back until he senses resistance. I follow the pilotman off the footplate and remove the head lamp from the tender, seeing the guard and his nibs having a few words I duck under the buffers and throw on the coupling. I later saw the guard and he acknowledged the fact that I did not let on that he was having a kip that morning. I asked him for a dozen eggs in return, he agreed but his source must have turned broody (stopped laying). Green light from the van. Bill takes up the slack, I exchange signals with the rear end, the pilotman takes up position behind my driver as we make our third sortie into the western portals of Gillingham Tunnel. Bill gives her the works. With much of my previous efforts with the sanding lever still stuck to the running rail there is adhesion a "plenty". The ferocious barking of our exhaust echoes throughout the tunnel, the response from the workers in the bowels of the dug out up road is one of awe. I cannot make out why Bill is making an attempt to create a cavity in the overhead brick work. Out into the open and as before we cross over onto the up road. I am firing up aiming to give my relief a good start from Gillingham.

The pilotman suggests that we change over with the

Salisbury men who are stood on the down platform. For some reason Bill does not regard the pilotman as his flavour of the month, as he replies "I was going to do that in any case" – Ah well. The usual "Mickey taking ensues" during change over with cracks from our Sarum mates such as, "Short of steam then Yeovil?" The motive power provided is an "N" class 2-6-0. We are running a good hour late, but as we are booked in Templecombe Yard for a period from 6.02 until 7.25am the control envisage that a sharp departure from Gillingham will have us prepared to depart from Templecombe at the correct time of 7.25am. Upon hearing this and before anyone has the quickness of mind to object, I'm off the footplate tea can in hand and up the signal box steps like the proverbial scalded cat. Kettle is boiling, 'Great', top up the tea can and back down the steps before the conveyor of the news "The signalman" has got off the engine. Bills comment – "well done nipper".

The load of the train has been conveyed via the Salisbury driver. The man in charge of the single line working gives his authority, the road is cleared (starter and advance signals off) and Big Bill realising that any attempt to make overtime has been stymied shows that he is not for hanging about by flaying the "King Arthur" away from the blocks. Waste of time trying to pour our tea so I hang the can on the boiler gauge glass shut off cock. My Salisbury opposite number Pete Sampson, alias 'Sambo' has blacked out the fire under the door. I lift the heavy dart from the tender, push it into the under the door mass and lever down, this lifts the near burnt through fire and redistributes it forward, result – exhaust from the chimney is now jet black. Bill bellows across "moved something there nipper". I let the boiler water contents drop until we breast the 1 in 100 incline where Bill shuts off and reduces our speed to the semi permanent restriction through the tunnel.

My strategy works a treat as with injector on, blower off its face and firehole door cracked we move through in a completely opposite vein to our previous thunderous passage.

As predicted we make up for lost time by departing Templecombe right time at 7.25. After running around our train at Yeovil Junction we are in Yeovil Town and have completed our allocated carriage shunting duties by 8.45am. Into the depot we dispose of the engine and sign off. It had indeed been an incredible eight hours encompassing challenges, excitement and danger, plus in retrospect the humorous situation involving the Salisbury guard.

CHAPTER 39

MY DECEPTION - BUT THE DRIVER HAS THE LAST LAUGH

The ethos of the footplate fraternity was to feast on moments of mirth, which at times occurred by accident. One such light hearted situation occurred when booked with my regular driver Harold Ham.

We have worked the 10.40pm ex - Nine Elms freight from Salisbury. Having arrived in Templecombe up yard for re - marshalling, we come to a stand opposite the shunters cabin. I screw on the "S15"s tender brake and prepare to make the tea. Harold in buoyant mood announces that he has (as he put it) nicked some Oxo cubes so as we can have a change. His words as I exit the footplate was "just top her up with water Col" "cheers mate" and I'm off like a rocket with tea can in hand hastily picking my way between the loose shunts as they rattle past. I get into the cabin, making sure the can is hot and clean I half fill it from yet another giant iron kettle, swing it around and tip the boiling water into the filthy sink. My look into the sink extracts an involuntary "B****", my mates Oxo cubes were floating about with bits of soap and other debris, scooping up the residue as best I could it is put back into the can. Quandary - should I come clean with Harold or take a chance and hope for the best. Topping up the can I decide on the latter.

Back on board my innocent driver has his cup at hand "fill it up then" he encourages, followed up with "you alright fancy your gone quiet?" I'm thinking "here we go" as two tea can tops of oxo (plus) are filled. I wait with baited breath for some comment, there is none. I go through the motions, but none pass my lips. Apart from a few belches we see the turn out. That night I sign on to find there is a passed man in place of Harold. With apprehension I ask the night chargeman what my mate's problem is. "Hammer's gone sick with stomach cramp, probably ate too much rhubarb" is the educated reply.

Our partnership resumed the next day. There seemed a reluctance to "open up" on his personal problem. Had Harold sniffed out my ploy? If he had, an opportunity for retribution was soon to emerge.

We are on 514 duty shunting in the up yard at Templecombe. During the previous few days I had endured a stomach virus, ignoring my wife Joy's common sense advice to take a day off I had soldiered on. Now about to work the 5.20am freight ex - Templecombe to Yeovil Junction with one of our own "U" class engines, I have problems. Topping the 1 in 100 bank out of Templecombe we descend and rattle along the near level section through Milborne Port, then down Sherborne Bank and through the station. This is by far my most uncomfortable ride, and all for the wrong reasons. I am facing away from my drivers position, even though he must have seen that all was far from well, he said nought.

The situation (please suppress that chuckle) further deteriorates. My hopes prayers and much else is dependent on the signalman at Yeovil Junction "A" Box pulling off his down home signal. I am leaning over my side encouraging co-operation but all to no avail, as much to my frustration both the local and main home pegs stay obstinately horizontal. Reaching the extremity of endurance as we come to a halt I tell Harold I have to get off. He suggests the bank beside a couple of line - side cottages. Had I expected sympathy the opposite was shown as my mate had a grin on his countenance as wide as the Cheshire cat. With much humiliation I make it – then a severe and cruel twist of fate. I hear a most dreaded and distinct 'clang', look up, 'NO!' the home signal is off, and to rub it in, I hear my mate blowing off the engine brake, "Lifting his vacuum pressure" was I in a state! (I urge you not to envisage the scene) panic compounds my personal

problem as realisation takes hold that the couplings are extended. Apart from mouthing a useless "the swine" there is no time for conjecture, I'm up and lurching along the cess. Harold's observance from the footplate is rewarded by a truly pantomime like scene.

Pulling myself aboard I choke on my natural instincts and keep quite, as indeed he had. We get relieved and I find relief at the junction… Phew!

CHAPTER 40

MY PAIRING WITH AN UNCOMPROMISING MATE

The majority of footplate staff at the "A" classified depots of Salisbury and Exmouth Junction and ourselves at Yeovil Town had little reason to consider there was any threat to our collective futures. However from the middle to late 1950s a breeze of uncertainty commenced to ruffle that confidence and in 1958 certain areas of the Western Region was handed over to the Southern, this included Yeovil Pen Mill. It was not rocket science to conclude that the two depots would amalgamate which duly happened in January 1959. Some of our respected senior passed men concluding there was little future at Yeovil sought pastures new. My first driver George Vickory was among that number.

Through retirements and the filling of vacancies caused by the aforementioned the expected redundancies were avoided.

In 1959 at the age of 24 I was placed in the spare link, this was the depots second in the seniority stakes. Promotion through the structure at Yeovil did not have the financial award afforded to the "A" classified sheds of Salisbury and Exmouth Junction, where substantial monetary awards were gleaned via mileage bonus payments. All London Waterloo via Salisbury to Exeter fast services was diagrammed to be worked by those depots, whilst tiny in comparison Yeovil, geographically situated betwixt was left with the scratchings of short freights and stopping passenger services. The local union reps in the time honoured way placed the duties with sociable start times in the senior links, but to be honest apart from the fact I was privileged to work with a vastly experienced body of men there was little in it. I took the position vacated by a most popular fireman. Maurice Ball had reluctantly handed in his notice.

He shared with me the dubious distinction of having part time employment. The driver involved was one Walt P. His pedigree throughout the depot was that of a moaner and this had been born out, as nagging about Maurice's part time pursuit of chimney sweeping had pushed him over the top.

My first few weeks with Walt were a revelation. He was excellent from a fireman's perspective, whether we had an "S15", "N15" our own "U" or a "West Country" class, the steam or screw operated reverser was in constant use, pulling her back to 15% cut off at each opportunity. His nick name "Powder Puff" however was justified for at the first sign of dust his handkerchief would appear which would be used to "Powder Puff" his face. Injector on, and prudent spray (none on Walt's shoes) would ensue. An additional feature of Walt was that his shiny top hat would never fall over his eyes as for a small man he had an enormous pair of ears. I was continually asked "How are you getting on with powder puff Robins?" "As good as gold" was the riposte. I was told by senior men that if I did something that he did not agree with I would be nagged to "Somerset phrase" kingdom come.

4-6-0 N15 King Arthur class No.746 passes Yeovil Junction with the up Atlantic Coast Express. 21.05.1935 - H.C. Casserley collection

Along came Yeovil duty 512. We signed on at 10.50am to prepare a 4P/3F "U" class 2-6-0. As per usual all was laid on for Walt. Feeder, oiling can topped up and polished. He must have been satisfied as his ears did not waggle. Oiling and brake tests etc completed he head's to the cabin for a wash off. It was Thursday, pay day, we collected our "pennies" from the attached to the driver's cabin upstairs office. I was now to commit a cardinal crime. Clean fire made up under the doors, footplate washed down and boiler front shined up, I took all the necessary safety precautions, touched the whistle, opened the regulator, and moved forward to the water column, topped up, hand brake on etc, off and up the office stairs. 31791 had made more then the desired steam pressure and "disaster" she lifted her boiler safety valves. I sprinted across and was on the footplate in a trice, water valve opened, live steam handle pulled down and the injector was singing, as Tommy Cooper would say "Just like that", the disturbance was quelled.

Walt came on board. His scowl told me that the depot's prophets had been proved correct. Our cordiality had been shot down in flames. Grumble and moan was the order of the day, and endless day's after. All had expressed the opinion that Walt was the reason Maurice had jacked in his "since school days" only occupation. I resolved that this would not be my fate and that two can play at that game. For the following 18 months I did not utter a word to my driver in a sociable vein. Observations and signals that were sighted from my side of the footplate would be relayed across the cab in a loud and clear voice. Signals from guards and assorted traffic grades were transmitted in the time honoured way. When there was need for the pep pipe, it would be "mind your feet". Walt would have his P.N. (Personal Needs) break in the guard's room at Exeter Central and I would be in the Shunters cabin. I have always been a gregarious type so the period was not pleasant. Our footplate responsibility's and team work was not in any way jeopardised. The bonus was that his moans were accompanied by the fireman singing the "Top of the Pops". He shortly switched off, I have vivid recollections of those times and I can vouch that not once did he complain regards my firing.

CHAPTER 41

BACK WITH 'FRANKIE' BOY

I move forward to 1961 and into the top link where the vacancy to be filled reunites me with my initial driver at Yeovil Pen Mill, Frank Smith. Many of the happenings that were to befall me during this, my final pairing as a fireman have been given prominence in differing contexts on previous pages.

That the breeze of uncertainty had gathered in velocity there was no doubt. Across the spectrum of grades there was concern re their future tenure. I would listen to serious discussions conducted in various mess rooms. There was the certainty that our railway system was to be modernised which to the orators meant "goodbye" steam. We younger breed endeavoured to be unaffected but deep down there was a sadness that the status quo was in doubt.

No. 1 link consisted of 12 sets of men, the earliest signing on time was 1.45am and the latest booked on at 9.13pm. Apart from the office hour starts of 10.45am, 11.17am, 11.55am and 1.10pm the other eight duties were of an unsociable nature. The term "top gang" did not allow any concession to men bordering on retirement.

My Trade Union diary for the period records that train men worked 11, 8-hour turns per fortnight which allowed one day off, termed "Rest Day". There were three rates of pay for fireman namely 1st, 2nd and 3rd year, which was the top rate, paid at the princely remuneration of 190 shillings, in present day English £9.50. Frank after 48 years service was on the top drivers rate of 229 shillings (£11.45)

If I ever felt sorry for a driver I did for Frank on Exmouth Junction duty 549. We signed on at 5.25am and prepared a 4-6-0 "West Country" class. This particular freezing morning our engine was as usual positioned over a pit road. It was blowing a gale and raining. I left him in the cabin having a chin wag, made my way down the coal road and got on the footplate. Noting there was good fire up one side of the firebox I popped over the stores and collected our ration of oil. Back on board and adopting my practised routine I laid out my mate's oiling can, (referred to as feeder) and lit his paraffin fed flare lamp. Didn't we fireman look after those revered craftsmen, hallelujah!

We have around 120lb pressure of steam registered on the boiler pressure gauge, enough to kick the generator into life at the first time of asking. This I take as a sign that we have a "Goodun" (Slang for top performer). Usually one had to get on the deck, open the dynamo/generator housing and chance losing the tip of one's finger by turning the blades with the securing clip. Pinning the firebox door operation handle down I attempted to warm the cab area for Frank's arrival. Did my well meant intentions intoxicate my driver into a sense of invulnerability?

I can delay the dreaded task no longer. On the floor I gather the adapted ladder, with rubber pads to arrest the tendency of sliding along the sleek framing of the Bulleid pacific's, place it into position for filling the sand boxes, of which there are two either side of the engine, they are positioned 6ft apart and 10 feet above the running rail over the driving wheels. It is lashing down. With a forlorn hope that the sand boxes will be full I climb the ladder. Pull back the sliding trap protection plate, hand in, ******, can only feel emptiness. Around to the sand furnace, fill two scoops and labour on the return journey. Back on the drivers side of the framings I lift the topped up and heavy sand carrier onto my right shoulder, up the rickety rackety ladder I go, I'm just about to fit the slender end of the scoop into the sand box receptacle when to my left and towards the smokebox end at ground level I perceive an apparition. Frank with flare lamp in left hand, feeder in right, is rounding the buffer beam. "NO, NO, NO" I bellow, the wind is against my not inconsiderable vocals. I drop the chute as certainty informs my senses that he is going underneath (there are no oiling points under original Bulleid light pacific's). Jumping to the floor I belt to the fore just in time to witness my old mate, realising too late his mistake, going momentum assisted, down the steps. The inspection pit is three to four foot deep, and this one was up to the rails in smokebox ash covered water. In utter astonishment I shout, "B***** me Frank, what the hell are you up to" to this day I regret that aggression. He is already starting to shiver as he emerges up the steps. We had prepared countless "West Country's" and this was his first and only trip down under. "I be going up the cabin mate" was his parting comment as he squelched away with water coursing out of his trousers. Having filled the sand boxes I ran up to the cabin, peering through the window, Frank had his trousers off and was wiping ash from his tummy. He must have rung out his trousers and long grey (was white) under pants. I go in "Your going home mate?" I ask, "I'll be alright as soon as these Bloody rags be dry" is the staggering reply. Followed by, "do the oiling for us Col". The driver's mess room fire was topped up with best Welsh coal, and as he had his "soiled dressings" hung so close to the heat, I mistook the clouds of steam for smoke.

I have little time to waste as this engine has to go through to Ilfracombe it is coaled after the fire is made up. Sands filled and back on the footplate I withdraw the long clinker shovel from the tender channel, insert it into the firebox and spread the fire over the bars. After making sure the coalmen are aware, I touch the whistle, create the brake, ease the steam reverser into reverse, touch of regulator and we move back and stop for coal. There is a hinged steel door with three securing clip's in the centre of the enclosed tender. Knocking the clips up with the coal pick the weight of tender coal swings the door open and allows the contents to cascade onto the cab floor, this is handled or shovelled into the firebox. No skill or finesse, just brute force labour, providing you had a good base and the damper's (air vents) were open the fire would soon burn through. Should there be insufficient fuel on the footplate floor, no problem, for if the tender door was not shut the first tub of coal delivered courtesy of the steam crane would come tumbling onto the footplate whether you wanted it or not.

Fire well made up, tender coaled and trimmed, cab washed down and spruced up, I drop our Bulleid back through the coaling road and stop for water. True to his word my mate emerges, pulls himself onto the footplate and takes up his position as if walking into the office. He takes my remark that he could have popped home and got his missus to put the iron over his trousers with a pinch of salt. He did however come out with a cracker "take more then a drop of water to stop me doing my turn" I was gob smacked, drop of water indeed. They were with out a doubt a tough breed.

Off the depot at 6.30am we are booked carriage shunting until 7.20 after which we have a break. I race across to the mess room for a can of tea. The shed turner and his mate plus other Yeovil men gave their opinion that my mate at his age

4-6-0 S15 departs Sidmouth Junction on a stopping passenger train to Exeter Central - crewed by driver F. Smith and fireman Colin Robins - Authors collection

was taking a chance with his health by carrying on with his duty after such a soaking from freezing water. I suggested that they go over to the engine and put their concerns to Frank. Needless to say there were no takers.

I am peeved that Frank after asking me to do the oiling is performing the task. Back on board and after knocking back a couple of cups of tea he admits that apart from the seat of his pants feeling peculiar he was 'fighting fit'. Getting the tip from the carriage shunter we pull down to Yeovil Town middle platform. The load is the usual three coach's equal to 100 tons, a picnic for a "West Country". Starter off, our guard gives us the green flag. At the right time of 7.50am Frank opens the regulator. Whether the rail is wet or dry my mate makes a right b**** up of pulling away. The Bulleid pacific's are equipped with a steam chest pressure gauge. The Southern men would lift the regulator watch the pressure gauge needle rise, check that rise in pressure and providing there was adhesion to the rail, in other words the driving wheels did not spin, would show their professionalism by gently nursing the regulator handle to stay constant at that point.

Not me old mate Frankie boy, there was a right hander "bend" and an adverse gradient leaving the Town. I can see him now, sat on his tip up side seat with both hands on the base of the near vertical regulator pulling it towards him, the all important steam chest pressure gauge would be obstinately ignored. That pressure gauge needle would rise needlessly in excess to that required on a slippery rail face. Up would go the wheels, I would pull the, mounted on the boiler front, steam sands control lever open, Frank pushes the regulator forward to the closed position and just as quickly open it again, result, more spin. Many a time I would shout in frustration "here we go again". Eventually gaining adhesion we would, when the rail was wet, arrive at the junction, (footplate expression) "down the pan" for time.

Down Devon Belle passes Exmouth Junction MPD. 08.07.1947 - H.C. Casserley collection

Off Yeovil Junction at 7.58 the duty had us stopping at all stations with an arrival time of 9.29 at Exeter Central where we were relieved by Exmouth Junction men, who in turn would stop all stations to Ilfracombe arriving at 12 mid day. A total of 30 stations would be served since departing Yeovil Town.

We would conclude our duty by relieving the 8.55am ex - Ilfracombe at Exeter Central, departing at 11.12, again stopping all platforms to Yeovil Junction where we would detach and go light engine into the depot.

35023 with up Devon Belle passing Exmouth Junction. 08.07.1948 - H.C. Casserley collection

CHAPTER 42

MY MELANCHOLY HOME DEPOT

Time marches on and we are into 1963 the year that would herald uncertainty regarding all our futures, the like of which one could not imagine. For the last two years it was evident that changes to our historic working practices were taking place, the majority of us in the lower echelons however had opted to ignore the obvious. Now we were to witness the modern breed of cross country services in the guise of diesel multiple units taking over the Weymouth to Bristol route. Steam was also in retreat as the Western diesel hydraulic "Hymek" progressively took its place over that same sector.

We felt isolated from these alterations as all duties operated from Yeovil shed and indeed the Salisbury to Exeter main line were the preserve of steam.

Then an announcement that was to seal our fate. British Railways Board decided on a change of boundaries. All former Western branch lines and to our utter dismay all Southern region lines west of Salisbury were to be taken over by the Western Region. This made it obvious that the Paddington to Exeter St David's route to the West Country would take precedence over our route, which was eventually down graded.

We collectively were "gutted". Optimism which somehow had been maintained was torpedoed over night. We were now under no illusion. I well remember senior drivers, expressing their concern for young colleagues who had based their family's future on the permanence of which ever depot.

Any lingering ray of optimism was administered the coup de grace at the end of March with the publication of the dreaded "Beeching" report which heralded the closure of so many stations and branch lines.

The structure of the timetables continued through the year, but the inevitability of down - grading and closure was fast approaching. Minds had to concentrate on the future. My wife, bless her, was all for giving it a crack and moving to a Southern Region depot. This option was made possible by an agreement thrashed out by our trade union and management which entitled all southern footplate grades a boundary move, if they so wished, which would transfer them to a Southern Region depot of their choice when a vacancy so occurred.

This so generous scheme was given the cold shoulder by many of my colleagues as they considered it was so good that there must be a catch in it. We as a family had no such misgivings. There was no alternative. The railway was my only trade and after moving all those tons of clinker and coal I considered that a decision to take redundancy would be one that I would deeply regret.

Salisbury was the bordering southern depot but my seniority would only allow a fireman's vacancy to be contemplated. However, scrutinizing the southern motive power vacancy list I was surprised to find that driver's positions were available to me in pure "juice" electric areas.

Armed with the additional free travel passes Joy and I had ample time to, as they say, run an eye over juice depot localities. The majority of the eligible areas however were in the Home Counties, this decided us to delay our decision. Perhaps it was our country "Bumpkin" apprehensions of the big city which made us hesitate.

Then a shaft of inspiration, which would ultimately secure our future. My revered friend and first driver George Vickory was now a driver at Portsmouth. I decided to put pen to paper. The answer was both encouraging and exciting. George assured us that the Portsmouth area was most attractive and that the quality of work and routes emanating from Portsmouth's mixed traction depot would be without a doubt, "just up my street".

Analysis of the Southern region all line vacancy lists I was "knocked out" to find that although my seniority date was low I may with good fortune be able to attain a driver's position at Portsmouth.

Having made the decision was a relief, but to bring the ambition to fruition I would have to pass my professions ultimate test, the examination to become an engine driver.

For seven years I had regularly attended our local 'Mutual Improvement Class' but even so I found myself apprehensive at the thought of facing motive power inspector Mr. Sam Smith. No doubt it was the weight of responsibility and the notion of me jeopardising our future should I fail.

I felt confident in my knowledge of the British Railways Rule Book 1950 edition which contained 240 rules and their accompanying clauses. However, the part of the examination which made me anxious was the questions I would have to field on the complexities of the steam engine with its myriad of side rods, cranks, pistons, eccentrics, differing valve gear, etc, and how to remedy the inherent faults and failures.

In order to overcome my concerns I decided to abandon my natural instinct for playing pranks and making light of sombre situations. Senior men recognised with disbelief that there was a serious side to young Robins and very soon a variety of well worn enginemen's and fireman's examination guide books was made available to me. The aforementioned senior driver Sid Bicknell invited me to his home, his ability and patience as mentor gave me a confidence which I honestly thought was beyond me. I was without doubt privileged to have been a close associate of such MEN.

Unfortunately my remaining year on "Home Territory" is remembered for all the wrong reasons. My immediate colleagues and those at adjoining depots were under no illusions. There was to be no reprieve for the previously announced reduction in service. Connecting branch lines were to close, and we at Yeovil had, to put it crudely, no more hope then a snowball in hell! Despondency among my once irrepressible work mates was a bitter pill to swallow.

Now into 1964, and the pinned on the notice board, anticipated "Southern Region" vacancy list. There is the usual host of drivers and fireman's positions to be filled and among them there are four drivers vacancies at Fratton mixed traction depot. The seniority date of the highest ranking eligible home depot applicant was given as junior to me. I distinctly remember punching the air in relief, and then feeling self conscious at howing delight in the air of gloom. I am no weirdo, but the majority of those men who after deep deliberation had decided to stay put, and therefore except redundancy were as close as family to me. I submitted my application for a driver's position during

Retirement presentation to driver Bert Laimbeer. (L to R) Station inspector, John Gillham, Den Norris, Mr E. Shapley, Reford Clarke, Albert Chainey, Bert Laimbeer, George Eason, Trevor Hayward and Gordon Woolmington - J. Gillham collection

February.

Now for the end game, waiting, did I have patience – no way. I was like a cat on the proverbial hot tin roof, would I - wouldn't I get the desired transfer?

CHAPTER 43

MY AMAZING BRUSH WITH FATE

Just to break the monotony, during this period I was involved with an incredible escape from the clutches of the grand reaper.

The regular pairing of driver Frank Smith and fireman Robins signed on Exmouth Junction duty No 551 at 12.40. Frank was up the driver's cabin immersed in probable a game of crib. I was on the coal road performing engine requirements. The engine was a "W C" class 7P/5F. We were taking coal and I was on the floor shovel in hand cleaning out the side ash pan. To my right was the steam crane, its driver was charged with lifting filled tubs from each side of the coal wagons and depositing the full loads into the tender of our engine. Had some sixth sense warned me of an impending danger I would naturally have looked up, that would have been curtains. The crane driver had dropped an empty tub to the far side of the wagon, attempted to move the jib of the crane to the opposite side of the opened door wagon in order to collect another full tub, in so doing he had given the steam crane too much regulator.

There was a stunning and resounding crash. I well remember a stupefying sensation. Completely dazed I looked about to find the jib hook swinging away from the side of the West Country, there was, what I could only describe as a ringing sensation in my head, my shiny topped hat was on the floor with its green British Railways badge badly dented, incidentally it is in front of me as I write.

George Cox the driver was in such a state of shock that he had to be assisted off the crane. Through tears of tension, the poor man told me later that after slamming his foot down on the jib brake he was transfixed by the heavy connecting hook as it swung on course towards the engine framing and my bent figure. "Colin" he said, "when it made violent contact with the side of the engine and took your hat off, there was no doubt in my mind that I had killed you" and he broke down again.

Strange to relate, that after the initial shock I got on with the engine requirements. It was not until I was in the cabin having a wash off that my close shave had an affect, suddenly my hands went into an uncontrollable shake which lasted for a good ten minutes. True to pattern I did not take the advice of one of the many St John's ambulance trained sage's "you wanna go home me Son". The thought of having to go sick and therefore have a reduced pay packet soon brought me back to normal.

CHAPTER 44

PREPARING FOR MY DRIVER'S EXAMINATION

The time was ticking by and the concern and frustration of having had so little practical driving experience was causing me anxiety. Frank was at ease for me to move our particular engine in depots and yards but as for letting me have a go when we were out on the main – no way. I felt badly let down by my drivers attitude for although he was undoubtedly in charge it was an unwritten law that one's regular mate would do all in his power to assist his fireman in his endeavours to successfully pass the drivers examination.

I had assisted Frank in every way possible during our footplate partnership, chasing the run away engine at Exeter Central and saving the West Country's boiler at Whimple plus the fact that each time we had a rebuilt Bulleid pacific to prepare I had without hesitation gone underneath into the pit with full feeder 'Oil can' in one hand, flare lamp in the other, pulled myself up behind the inside big end, and oiled the main bearing and the eccentric strap such was my concern for my mate at his age performing those more suited to the gyrations of a contortionists duties.

Such was my desperation to handle the vacuum brake, that prior to leaving Exeter Central with a Sunday stopping service I put to Frank that if I applied the injector, partially opened the firebox door and gave the blower a twist, could I brake the train into the first stop at Pinhoe? There was no reply in the affirmative, nevertheless I thought he would oblige. As suggested at the given time, I stood expectantly behind him. He never moved. That was akin to a body blow to me. I am sorry to say that the partnership from this incident was never the same. I tried to be my usual breezy self but that rebuff smarted.

Saturday 28th March 1964 is entrenched in the memory stakes, walking past the old cleaners and coalman's cabin on my way to our signing on point I receive the greeting "On 'yer' way then Col" from a passing mate. The seldom experienced twin emotion of elation and apprehension hit me. In the notice case was the Southern Region vacancy result sheet. The four successful applicants for the driver's positions at Portsmouth's Fratton shed were from areas other then the home depot. Surprise, surprise, many thanks to the deception which senior staff bestowed on me at Crewkerne, yours truly was the junior applicant.

As the notice observed my appointment was subject to passing the driver's examination. The following week had me exhibiting an untapped streak in my nature, impatience. I put it down to anxiety. Every day I was vaulting the office stairs requesting information regards my driver examination date and the time scale of my transfer should I be successful. The office staff was, with justification, not amused.

I relate this edgy period to our domestic situation. Months previous as we made the decision to move away from home territory there came an opportunity to purchase our poorly maintained rented terraced house. We grabbed it.

I threw the window cleaning ladders into touch and had from there on devoted all my spare time and separately banked part time nest egg into transforming the property into a saleable asset. I now reckoned on another five to six weeks to complete the project, hence my apprehensive and therefore tense state.

To reiterate, the area west of Salisbury was now Western Region territory, even so no one expected the undisguised inter regional bitterness to throw up the following analogy. The redoubtable and respected Mr Sam Smith had for many years examined Southern Region men on their suitability to be engine drivers. It was now deemed that the examination had to be overseen by two motive power inspectors at separate locations. My practical driving appraisable was to be conducted at Exeter by Sam on the 7th of April, followed by a journey to Plymouth on the 16th where I was to be tested on my knowledge of the rules and regulations appertaining to a train driver.

Lady luck was to play me a fortunate hand as prior to my appointment with motive power inspector Sam, my mate "Frankie" was booked a week off duty, so for each of those, to me vital days, a passed to drive fireman (passed man) was rostered his duty. The word had got around that I never had the chance to, as they say, have a go over the driver's side with Frank. Those wonderful friends did all they possibly could to give my confidence a boost, not only did they insist that I did all the driving but having passed Sam their selves they impressed on me the likely practical questions I would be quizzed on.

The Locomotive Engineman's & Fireman's Examination Guide revised by S. Smith was a must for many incumbent and the majority of those wishing to be successful, all questions were based on those compact 119 pages. I was put through my paces on e.g. relative positions of side rods, cranks, pistons, valves and eccentrics, how to locate broken steam ports, differing valve gears and action to be applied so as failures could be rectified. Interrogations on the subject of the boiler and its steam connections alone were open to a possible 64 questions. We also dealt with my knowledge on the workings of the vacuum and steam brake. The consensus was that my improvement class attendances topped up with accepted invitations to knowledgeable driver's homes would see me succeed. I went home after each shift full of gratitude but with a head like a bucket.

I have that well worn book in front of me, and looking back through the contents I realise it must have been some sort of miracle that this layman in the field of engineering absorbed such details.

Along came the first of the two days that would make or break my railway ambition. In actual fact all candidates were given three chances, I believe there was a lapse of three months between examinations, but no one contemplated the ignominy of failure.

I was booked on duty to ride as passenger on the previously described Exmouth Junction 549 duty which commences with the 7.50am from Yeovil Town to Exeter, where I would meet the much revered Inspector for the theory side of my examination. This would be followed by my practical appraisal which would involve driving the 11.12am passenger, which was within the framework of Exmouth Junction 551 duty, to Yeovil Junction.

Arriving for duty all kitted out in freshly ironed bib and brace, I was chuffed to discover the footplate crew booked to work the Exeter stopper were (at least to my age group) the affable previously described driver Jerrard and my most close mate, fireman Ken Fay, who now by virtue of that fortuitous introduction was a family member. True to the well established pattern as soon as I got on the "West Country" footplate, Jerry was suggesting amid guffaws of laughter that the best thing he could do was to get in the front coach with his Daily Herald and let Ken and I get on with it. "Cheers Jerry that is just what my doctor ordered." I reply. With the proviso that he is at the controls when we run into Exeter, the most cheerful of characters took his leave.

Bill Poole stands at the top stage of Hewish gates signal box - M. Clements collection

Away right time with the derisory load of three coaches on a greasy rail, my concentration was glued on the steam chest pressure gauge, as the needle denoting the pressure reached a point I thought sufficient I adjusted the regulator accordingly. Ken did not have to use the steam sands. We did not slip! That minute show of ability gave my confidence the desired boost.

To share this "First time" experience with a guy who was as close to me as a brother was a bonus beyond compare. Nine years of observations, boiler control and swinging the shovel had ingrained in me a thorough knowledge of the gradients over the Salisbury to Exeter route. The confidence gained from the previous week's experience in handling the vacuum ejector dispelled my uncertainties. I now seemed at ease judging gradients on the approach to stopping points. This allowed me to arrest the speed of approach by gradual but decisive brake application until the load was fully under control. The trick then was to feather the brake, i.e. apply the ejector handle with slight variation of application and release whilst moving towards the objective which would hopefully be attained with the train pipe needle actually rising, train brake coming off. The perfect stop is described by two words - NO JOLT!

The novelty of that day brought about by so many factors made it one of my most treasured.

I had been in the mess room absorbing the senior driver's comments on the abilities of respective fireman (they were indeed a critical group) often when leaving their company fellow fireman would ask "Who's going through the hoop in there this time" Ken's firing abilities was under examination. I was all ears. The consensus was, in local dialect "the boy's on the small side but I'll tell ee what ee's a good un" Now from my exalted position of unofficial driver I was able to judge how accurate the jurymen verdict was. OK this is a light load, but even so his firing technique was smooth and flawless combining the swing of the shovel with the placement of the right foot on the firebox door operation treadle, his left foot pivoting on the heel. What a shame that as with so many other terrific motive power men the trauma of the coming closures and redundancies would see him abandoning a position he relished.

The distant signal for the penultimate 11th stop, Pinhoe, all too soon came into view. True to the arrangement our driver regained the footplate and urged me to "take her in Col" (drive the train into Exeter,) but with the motive power top brass likely to meet us I reluctantly declined.

Running into the city Ken did his best to further boost my spirits by remarking in typical loco men's jargon "You made a bloody good job of that Robins"

Had the journey down been spent sat idle on the cushions I would no doubt have been fretful concerning this all important interview, but now with the previous "In charge" handling of the "West Country's" regulator, steam operated reverser, vacuum brake and reading the gradients and stopping distances with, at least in my opinion, proficiency, I felt confident and assured.

CHAPTER 45

I TAKE MY DRIVER'S PRACTICAL EXAM

Mr. Smith was on the platform as we ran in - as he conducted me to his down side office the tone of his conversation was both considerate and warm. The feared harsh exterior disciplinarian had seemingly mellowed. I remember feeling so much at ease that the harrowing 90 minute question session on the workings of the steam engine and its, as previously illustrated, inherent faults and failures was actually enjoyed.

As we made our way to the up platform Mr Smith told me a little of the internal politics that had relieved him of his responsibility to fully assess his own region's men on their capabilities to drive. The restructuring of the regional boundaries which resulted in the ceding of the Southern area west of Salisbury to the Western Region had caused unnecessary bitterness. Mr Smith was in the twilight of his career. He was respected for his expertise and technical knowledge. Had revised 'The Locomotive Engineman's & Fireman's Examination Guide'. It was humbug that the Western Region hierarchy had saw fit to humiliate a man of such proven quality.

receives the bag and inserts it into the tender. The time is 11.07am we are booked away at 11.12am. As the Exmouth Junction men take their leave the driver remarks "All the best youngin" fireman "You'll be all right mate". As my best mate heaves the coal forward Mr Smith explains his brief. He is there to judge me on my competence to be a Driver, "You are the person in command of this service, you have the section timings, have confidence in your ability and you will enjoy the experience".

"Water coming up drive" bellows my mate. His remark 'drive' awakes my humorous vein, as I cut the water supply I catch his eye, his relaxed grin of confidence immediately rubs off on me. Water column in place and secured by chain and we are on the footplate.

Our guard gives me the load. The usual stopping all stations load of four coaches equal to 120 tons. Feeling confident and responsible I lift the large brake handle to the running position and open the small ejector, the needles either side of the gauge slowly lift to 21 inches, I now close the small ejector, both needles remain stationary. His nibs stood on the tender plate directly behind me will note my test for leaks. The guard now drops his van brake, the vacuum re-creates, brake test completed.

All was perfection. The firebox door was open to the second notch exhibiting burnt through coal. Boiler pressure needle just below the red line, the water level in the boiler gauge glass is bubbling ½ an inch below the top nut. A typically vibrant, straining at the leash, "West Country" front end scene. My mate is sitting side saddle and looking to the front. Trying to impress I lift my newly purchased 7s 6d Ingersole pocket watch, coming up to 11.12am. The starter with its

4-4-2T class 0415 and coach stands at Lyme Regis before next of duty - John Day collection

Arriving at the up platform relief point we meet up with my mate's from the down service. Ken had to turn his back to cover his amusement as Sam invited driver Jerrard to ride back on the cushions. Jerry later remarked that "If I had known that I was going to spend the duty in the train I would have taken the day off". The 8.55 ex - Ilfracombe announces its approach as it blasts out of the 1 in 37 gradient tunnel. As if in slow motion the diagrammed "West Country" profile lifts into view as it lips the incline summit. Up the platform and coming to a rest on the "W" mark for taking water, I grab the water column chain and swing the arm around, Ken has vaulted up the rear mounted ladder,

adjacent local to through signal arm is off. Operating the steam reverser control lever, the pointer in the sector plate is placed in full 70% fore gear.

Looking back gives me a clear view of our guard, he waggles his green flag. Large ejector is raised, brake needle instantly shoots up to 21 inches, right fist drops to clench the bottom of the regulator. I lift the long handle, in an instant display of front end steam (the initial exhaust beat frees residue water from the cylinders) the release cocks are closed. Thanks to recent rehearsals I feel at ease pivoting my position to enable the safe departure along the platform to be witnessed. My examiner has adopted a position to my rear where he is able to observe my every move.

Everything goes like clockwork, the needle in the steam chest pressure gauge rises to 120 lb per sq. inch. I tap the regulator with the flat of my hand so as that pressure stays constant. Turning out from the up local onto the up through I unlock the steam reverser control handle and with a series of ratchet like movements the pointer in the sector plate is positioned at the 35% cut off point. All the sticks (signals) are in our favour as with such a light load we forsake the clutter of Exeter Central's point's and cross over's. Up the short 1in100 gradient through St James Park Halt I bring the cut off back to 25% and lift the regulator, we have a green in the three aspect signal sited just prior to the 263 yd Black Boy Tunnel. Prior to entry I stretch to the cab roof and yank the whistle cord. The exclusive "West Country" tone reverberates. This warning will be similarly marked at mid section and exit. Glow via the generator cuts the blackness. Thrusting into daylight I note that the required middle arm of the three armed gantry sited on the lip of the bank is as forecast off. Now well into our stride with the enormous motive power depot looming ever larger to our left, I check that the three minutes time allowed from start to passing Exmouth Junction has been met.

We are now on a falling gradient. I ease the regulator to the closed position. My mate has his injector singing away, now in a simultaneous movement he adjusts the firebox door to the first notch and eases the blower off its face thereby lifting the drift of smoke. The distant signal for our first stop, Pinhoe is off. Using the large ejector as previously described our speed is arrested, now under control my confidence receives the required fillip as we come to that perfect 'no jolt' stop. We depart Pinhoe. The 1 in 100 gradient levels out and then rises through our following stops at Broad Clyst, Whimple and Sidmouth Junction where we are booked one minute station time. The section to Honiton falls for a short period and rises for three miles at the familiar 1 in 100.

Very seldom does a passenger service get checked by a distant signal and making good speed up the bank we get the AWS which denotes that Honiton's twin aspect colour light distant is at green. Having observed the braking techniques of so many experienced drivers and their judgement of speed and load on approach I instinctively know where to close the regulator. The severity of the gradient immediately arrest's the speed. We are along side the so familiar level gradient up siding which cuts a curious angle to our harsh incline approach before I begin to drop the brake handle. Making much of my vaunted one day only position I proffer a nonchalant left hand gesture to the familiar signalman observing us from the lofty perch of his signal box at the top of the yard. With the weight of the train under control I lift the large ejector handle, the train pipe needle rises allowing partial release of the brakes. Along the level station gradient I am able to choose the exact point to bring my charge to a halt. The initial inhibitions of

The crew of Adams Radial Tank with Exmouth Junction locomotive inspector Sam Smith. Every footplateman from Salisbury to Exeter was answerable to Inspector Smith - feared by some but respected by most - M. Clements collection

my practical exam have left the footplate. Sam is across having a chat with Ken establishing the correctness of his perceptions that our ties were closer then footplate partners. Getting the right away, what I would have given to have been able to really lift the regulator and drop the needle in the sector plate over to 60% cut off, that urge of course was a non starter. I did however allow myself the thrill of a faster then need be exhilaration up the 1 in 90 incline which rubbed shoulders with the (then) A30 London to Exeter trunk road. This indiscretion did not get rebuked as Sam knew this was to be my first and last official occasion driving a train over the same route that I had plied my trade for so many years as a fireman. Cresting the bank and into Honiton Tunnel I adjust the cut off to 15% and all but close the regulator, touching the whistle at intervals, we hurtle out of the tunnel at 80 mph. Now shut off, with speed increasing I bring down the brake handle and hold the train pipe at 17 inches thus controlling our descent. Seaton Junction distant is off, and as we take the gradual left curve, I check that the left signal on the two arm home gantry (up main to up local) is off. Dropping the train pipe further we reduce our speed to the near pedestrian 15 mph so as we take the points at that required speed. I now give her a burst of regulator, shut off, get a final grip and come to a halt, again with brake pipe rising. I look at the pocket watch and see that we are a minute early. Black mark Robins – but not a word was said.

Right away from Seaton Junction at 11.57am we are shortly on a rising gradient which encompasses Axminster (change for Lyme Regis) and Chard Junction (change for the Western branch to Chard and Taunton). I particularly remember the section Chard Junction to the block post at Hewish Gates. (`Please note the gradient chart) I knew that wonderful guy, my uncle George and the father-in law of my close friend sat over there on the fireman's seat, would be on duty at Hewish Gates. Of course I wanted in some way to mark this occasion. I decided to put the cards on the table. So over the sheer footplate bedlam of a

vibrant 86 ton "West Country" engine I managed to obtain Inspector Smith's approval to give a double barrelled whistle awakening to the man who encouraged me to become a railwayman. I can see Uncle George as clear in my mind as I write this as I did that day. He had the box side window fully open and was looking so happy with arm held aloft in greeting. Date - Tuesday 7th April 1964.

Shut off well prior to Crewkerne Tunnel. Level crossing distant positioned just prior to entry is off, customary through the tunnel pulls on the whistle wire. I bring down the Driver's brake control handle and keep it steady, as we pass my home town's distant and cross that so familiar narrow road I am conscious of the fact that I will NOT come this way again. Melancholy away, we come around the right hander under complete control and make my Crewkerne the perfect stop.

The allowance of 11 minutes for the nine mile run in to Yeovil Junction is more then generous. The engine allocated to this duty departed light engine ex - Exmouth Junction at 4.35am and has been in service to Ilfracombe and back to Exeter where we took over the reins. Ken has run his fire down, Now at the Junction with tail lamp in hand he is in between, I have destroyed the brake, Ken splits the vacuum and reconnects the engine vacuum pipe to its dummy, I hear the sought after bellow "Ease Up Mate". Brake made, touch of regulator, ease back, and my best mate has the coupling off and is back on the footplate in a flash. Jerry now rejoins us. Starter, up local to up branch is off, into fore gear, I lift the regulator. and our light engine departs the junction for the one and a half mile trip into the town depot, I with the aura of a person who has done it all before.

After relief Mr. Smith has me on a recognition and explanatory examination of all visible working parts of our "West Country" class engine and for good measure one of the "U" class engines is likewise assessed. Beside me

```
NINE ELMS DUTY No. 23.
          5 P. (V. Class)
    —      Nine Elms ...  ...  ... 6.50 a.m. ||
7. 6 a.m.  Waterloo ...  ...  ... 7.20 a.m. P
10. 3 a.m. Salisbury ...  ...  ...10.10 a.m. E
   **      West Sidings  ...  ...10.17 a.m. ||
10.16 a.m. Loco. Yard...  ...  ...12.26 p.m. ||
   **      Down Bay  ...  ...  ...12.40 p.m. E
   **      Salisbury  ..   ...  ...12.46 p.m. P
1.59 p.m.  Yeovil Jc. (Turn) ...  2.18 p.m. ||
2.23 p.m.  Yeovil Loco.  ...  ... 4.15 p.m. ||
4.20 p.m.  Yeovil Town  ...  ...    —
        C—Shunting 4.20 p.m. to 5.30 p.m.
   **      Yeovil Town  ...  ... 5.35 p.m. M
11.36 p.m. Clapham Jc.  ...  ...  ** ||
   **      Nine Elms ...  ...  ...    —

Salisbury Men..
(1)  1st set on duty 12.1 p.m., work and relieved
     Yeovil Jc. 2.0 p.m., relieve No. 497 at 2.15
     p.m. and work and relieved in depot.

(2)  Off No. 479, relieve at Yeovil Jc. 2.0 p.m.,
     work to depot, complete requirements for
     No. 478. 3.40 p.m.||, work and relieved
     Salisbury 6.10 p.m.

Yeovil Men.
(3)  No. 1 P. and D. men, relieve in depot,
     perform requirements, work 4.15 p.m.||
     and relieved 4.45 p.m.

Salisbury Men.
(4)  Off No. 501, relieve 4.45 p.m. and work
     and relieved Salisbury 8.38 p.m.

(For Rosters East of Salisbury see London
District Diagrams).
```

4-4-0 class 'V' 30909 St Pauls at Yeovil Town MPD awaiting next duty. Circa May 1959 - John Fox collection

as I write is my 1960 Locomotive Engineers & Fireman's Examination Guide. Priced at three shillings and sixpence. (17½p). 120 compact pages appertaining to every aspect of Southern Steam and its inherent faults & failures. The well fingered pages remind me that it was my constant companion prior to the ultimate appraisal.

Mr Smith shook my hand in congratulations at passing the practical part of the driver's review, but as his authority to complete my exam had been usurped I would have

to travel to Plymouth for the Western Region to test my knowledge on the rules.

With the practical section of the driver's exam in my back pocket I resolved that the rules appraisal would take a like course.

Until my visit to Plymouth on the 16th April my black 'British Railways' rule book was my constant companion.

CHAPTER 46

DEJECTION AS I PASS TO BECOME A DRIVER BUT FAIL MY MEDICAL

This so unnecessary Plymouth venture had me on duty at 6.55am, routed via Taunton I was to sign off in Yeovil at 7.20pm

On meeting my Western Region inquisitor I sensed an air of disdain as he referred to Mr Smith. I was certain that his uncalled for remark was vindictive and calculated to raise my hackles. If that was the case it completely backfired. Apprehensions out of the window replaced with a determination not to let Sam and my mates down.

Hewish gates 4-6-0 N15 King Arthur class, 456 Sir Galahad - H.C. Casserley collection

Hostilities commenced with the old chestnut Rule 55 titled "detention of trains on running lines" and it's myriad of clauses and exceptions. Then we were jostling with the 56 separate driver headings in the rule book. One named "drivers to reduce or regulate speed" related to 11 separate rules. Single line working with "tablet or staff and ticket". "Single line working over a double track". The four – Pink, Green, White and Yellow coloured wrong line order forms and their use.

Questions then centred on the protection of trains and other running lines should there be a derailment or other such emergency etc. Lastly I was asked to explain the method and rules appertaining to trains been worked under the jurisdiction of a pilotman. I wished to explain my Gillingham Tunnel trauma come farce, but as he had shown no sign of cordiality I did not feel at ease in breaking the status quo. Not even

4-6-2 Merchant navy class, 35022 Holland-America line. Driver Colin Robins takes charge at Fareham. 1965 - Authors collection

a smile as I was told that I had passed. Ah well!

I was now heading for what I thought would be a foregone conclusion – My medical, which would conclude my ambition to become a qualified train driver. Into the medical centre I marched with a tank full of confidence. I walk out in utter dejection. The medical officer had found that my body contained a higher amount of sugar then was permissible for me to become an engine driver.

One can imagine my state of mind on the return journey. All our ambitions had seemingly been blown out of the water. I have inserted in my diary the one word "dejected" it does not justify my state of mind at that time.

Brush type 4, 47513 "Thames" at Guildford, driver Robins stands in the doorway. 19.01.1983 - Authors Collection

CHAPTER 47

ELATION - I AM A QUALIFIED ENGINE DRIVER!

The following day I was booked on duty at 10am in a spare capacity. On arrival I was ushered in to the depot masters office to be informed that already that morning the Western and Southern Medical Departments had got their act together and in the most professional and urgent of manners had liaised with Yeovil's main Hospital. It had been agreed that I have blood tests on three consecutive days so as my glucose level could be assessed.

What a miracle of an achievement. It was excellent news for me that the absurdly poor relations between the two motive power departments did not in anyway influence the medical areas.

I was to be booked on the Yeovil Town to the Junction Branch so as these arrangements could be utilised. It was without a doubt "fingers crossed" time for the family Robins.

The Robins family at Weston-S-Mare one week before their move to Fareham in May 1964 (L to R) Colin, Joy, Lorraine and David - Authors collection

On Tuesday 21st of April 1964 at the age of 29 I received clearance from Plymouth which would enable me to report for duty as an engine driver at Fratton "Portsmouth" mixed traction depot.

It was with heavy heart that I bade farewell to not only a host of close friends but to a way of life and togetherness that I recall with much nostalgia to this very day.

PS Within a short period the 'Robins' family nest was to be reallocated at Fareham in Hampshire

I was introduced to a motive power way of life that was a

complete reversal to the disciplined "everything has to be done by the book" regime.

Safety was not compromised, but often when booked spare it was the done thing to relieve fellow driver's so as they may, 'as they say' make their way home.

High jinks and partnership was the name of the game. BUT that dear friend is for another day.....

EPILOGUE

An ex - train driver colleague has invited me to describe his incredible front end experience which happened on the 27th January 1963 when he was 24 years of age.

The winter in question is recorded as one of the most severe. We front end men still refer to it as the "White Out". Signing on duty at Salisbury motive power depot I learn that a top link passed to drive fireman on the roster to work the 11am ex - Waterloo from Salisbury to Exeter had been up graded to fill a drivers vacancy, and that I would take his place.

This was a bonus indeed as not only was the service in question the prestigious "Atlantic Coast Express" but the mileage Salisbury to Exeter and return would entitle me to the monetary reward of an additional mileage bonus payment. My driver was the popular and irrepressible Walt Clissold.

Usual signing on procedure and we make our way to the relief point on the Salisbury down through platform. In ran "Merchant Navy" class No. 35017 "Belgian Marine" with the usual full load of 12 coaches. Tender filled and coal shovelled forward we are away at the booked time of 12.52pm. Our first stop is Sidmouth Junction.

There is little vocal contact, I get on with providing Walt with the required power – 35017 is steaming well – 18 miles out from Salisbury we top the incline at Semley. Regulator closed and we coast down the 1 in 80 bank. As we speed through Gillingham my Driver gradually lifts the regulator handle. We belt up the gradient and lip the summit. Power is eased back. As the steam assisted generator is off all is black as we rush Gillingham Tunnel. Suddenly there is an alarming "Bang" followed by a current of unexplained cold air. I feel as if a stinging grit like substance has invaded the footplate.

The scenario on emerging into day light was one of utter bedlam. My mate Walt is laid out across the footplate, he is holding a blood soaked cloth to the upper face. My instincts kick in. We are in a precarious situation travelling at speed. Walt is conscious and recognises my intention as we struggle from floor to my fireman's seat. He manages to steady himself there. An icicle had burst through the driver's window and entered his eye. The grit like substance was ice particles, further evidence was the portion of ice on the tender firing plate.

I was not a passed to drive fireman but realised there was no alternative but to take over the controls. I did however have a good knowledge of the gradients. By cautious use of the vacuum brake we come to a stand in Templecombe. The platform staff are in attendance and my driver is assisted from the engine and then via ambulance to the nearest hospital. An Eastleigh driver who was on board travelling to Exeter volunteered to drive the train to Yeovil Junction. As the drivers window was out this was achieved at greatly reduced speed. On arrival we stood on the down main. A relief engine and crew worked the "Atlantic Coast" to Exeter.

An interesting sequel to this event was that I travelled as a 'passenger' to Exeter where I picked up my return working with an Exeter driver. This man was so annoyed at the inconvenience, that he sated his temper by hammering the daylights out of the engine on the return Exeter to Waterloo semi fast.

My next pay packet did not contain the all important mileage bonus. I complained only to be told that as I did not complete the full mileage I certainly was not entitled to the bonus. I said THANK YOU very much. Some would say rough justice indeed.

Every one's friend Walt Clissold had lost the sight in one eye. It was the end of his driving career.

I was presented with a framed citation in recognition of my initiative on that day in January 1963.

George Redman – retired driver
– Fareham, Hampshire

B.R. 14300/801

BRITISH RAILWAYS
SOUTHERN REGION

Telephone:
WATerloo 5151
Ext. 2488/9

Telegrams:
SOWESTRAF LONDON SE1

JS/BH

LINE MANAGER
SOUTH WESTERN DIVISION
WATERLOO STATION
LONDON S.E.1

My:- MPS.54/394.W6   28th February, 1963.

Dear Sir,

It has been brought to my notice that whilst working the 11.0am Waterloo to Plymouth on the 27th January, 1963, your Driver met with an unfortunate accident, and you immediately took charge of the locomotive and brought it safely to a stand at Templecombe.

The prompt action taken by you on this occasion is much appreciated, and I would advise you that the circumstances are being recorded on your staff history.

Yours faithfully,

Mr. G. Redman,
Fireman,
Salisbury.

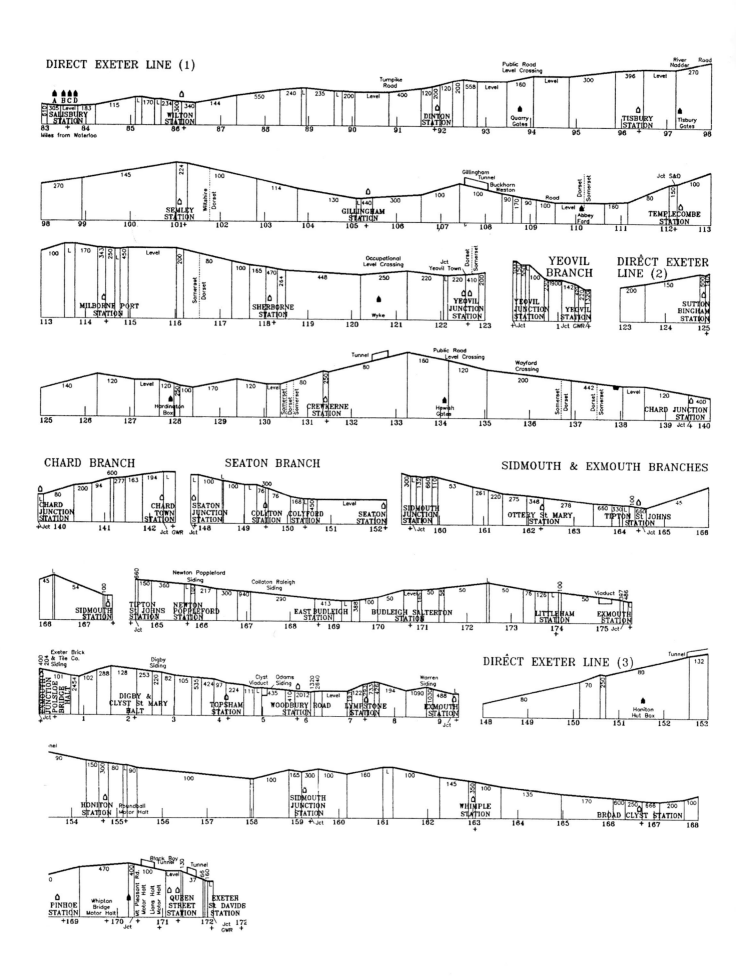

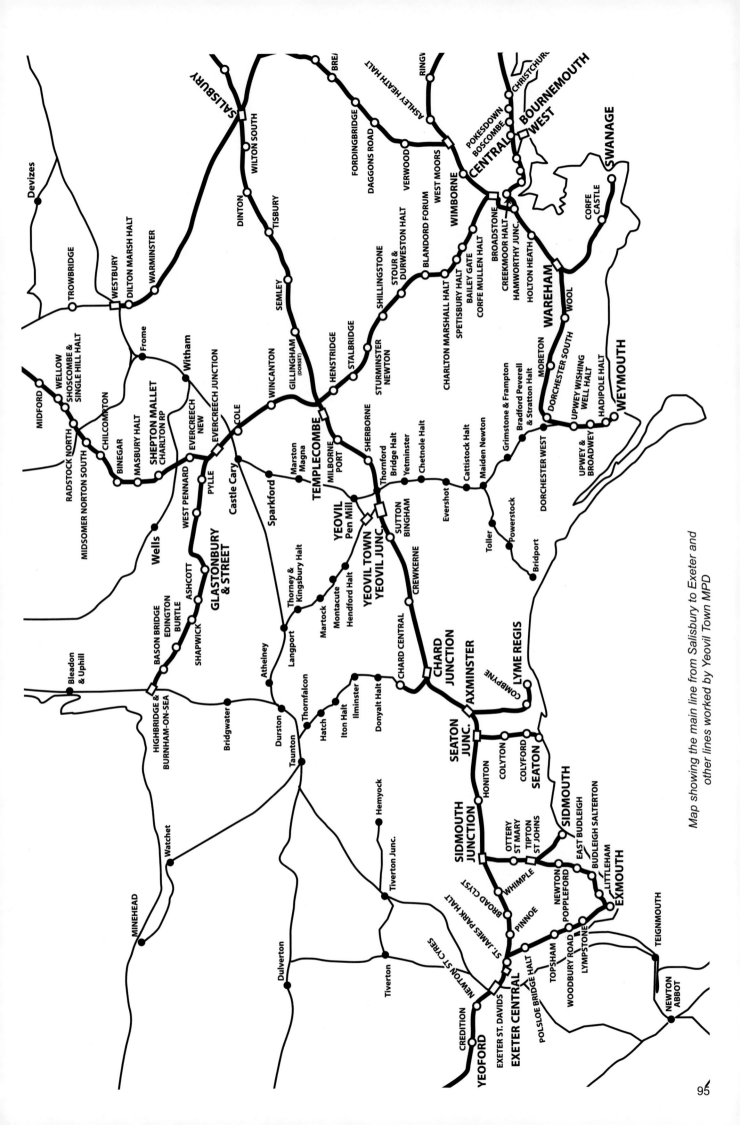

Map showing the main line from Salisbury to Exeter and other lines worked by Yeovil Town MPD

Acknowledgements

I have endeavoured to recapture the realities of footplate life. It certainly was no picnic. At the end of the day however we had a 'Togetherness' and 'Partnership' that was as solid as any in the land.

I devote this book to my family with a special credit to my wife Joy who coaxed me to stay the course.

I extend a vote of gratitude to George Redman for granting me permission to utilise his personal experience.

My wholehearted appreciations is expressed to the following railway connected friends, as without their funding of advice, literature and photos this admitted layman would have failed – 'Friends of the Railways Studies Collections' Newton Abbot – Stephen Fay, Nick Wiley, Gerald Jacobs, Mike Clement, Bernie Briggs, John Fox, John Day, John Cornelius, Richard Duckworth, Roger Marsh, Ken Drew, Reg Woolmington, Dave Hearn, Phillip Brown, Max Wilkinson and many others.

A sincere 'thank you' to my proof readers Michael Harvey and David Robins, you both have an abundance of patience!

A special 'Cheers' to David Brown who selected the excellent photography contained in the 47 chapters of the book. He also provided me with the head of steam required to get me to the 'Stop Blocks' on time.

In the field of DTP and professionalism I owe a debt of gratitude to Ms Rachel Brown of Brown Ink (www.brown-ink.co.uk) who produced the layout, design and promotion of the book.

Finally – appreciations to Mr Carl Joice of ASHFORD COLOUR PRESS LTD. The courteous advice proffered was so much appreciated.

Thank You All

Colin.